Paul moves out

Also by Michel Rabagliati:
PAUL IN THE COUNTRY (2000)
PAUL HAS A SUMMER JOB (2003)

Translation: Helge Dascher.
With thanks to Dag Dascher, Mark Lang, Caroline Rossier-Lang, and Marina Lesenko.

Hand-lettering: Dirk Rehm.
Production: Rebecca Rosen, Tom Devlin, Chris Oliveros.
Publisher: Chris Oliveros. Publicity: Peggy Burns.

Drawn & Quarterly
Post Office Box 48056
Montreal, Quebec
Canada H2V 4S8
www.drawnandquarterly.com

First hardcover edition: May 2005.
Printed in Singapore.
10 9 8 7 6 5 4 3 2 1

Library and Archives Canada Cataloguing in Publication
Rabagliati, Michel
    Paul Moves Out / Michel Rabagliati.
Translation of: *Paul en appartement*.
ISBN 1-896597-87-4
    I. Title.
PN6734.P38585R3213 2005   741.5'971   C2004-906908-X

The publisher gratefully acknowledges The Canada Council
for The Arts for its support of this edition.

Distributed in the USA and abroad by:
Farrar, Straus and Giroux
19 Union Square West
New York, NY 10003
Orders: 888.330.8477

Distributed in Canada by:
Raincoast Books
9050 Shaughnessy Street
Vancouver, BC V6P 6E5
Orders: 800.663.5714

Paul moves out

Michel Rabagliati

DRAWN & QUARTERLY BOOKS
MONTREAL

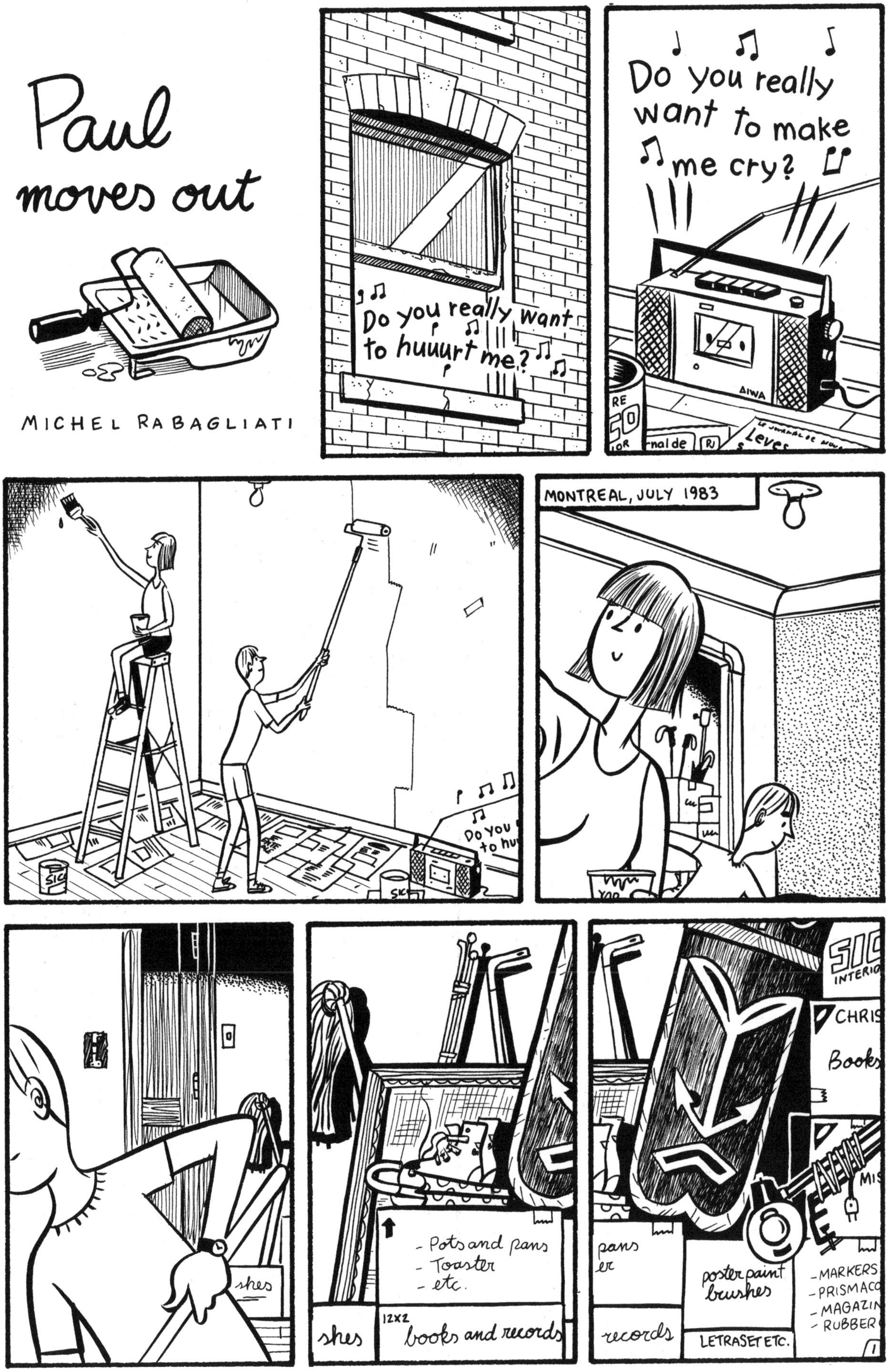

Paul moves out
MICHEL RABAGLIATI
Do you really want to huuurt me?
Do you really want to make me cry?
AIWA
MONTREAL, JULY 1983
- Pots and pans
- Toaster
- etc.
books and records
poster paint brushes
-MARKERS
-PRISMACO
-MAGAZIN
-RUBBER
LETRASET ETC.

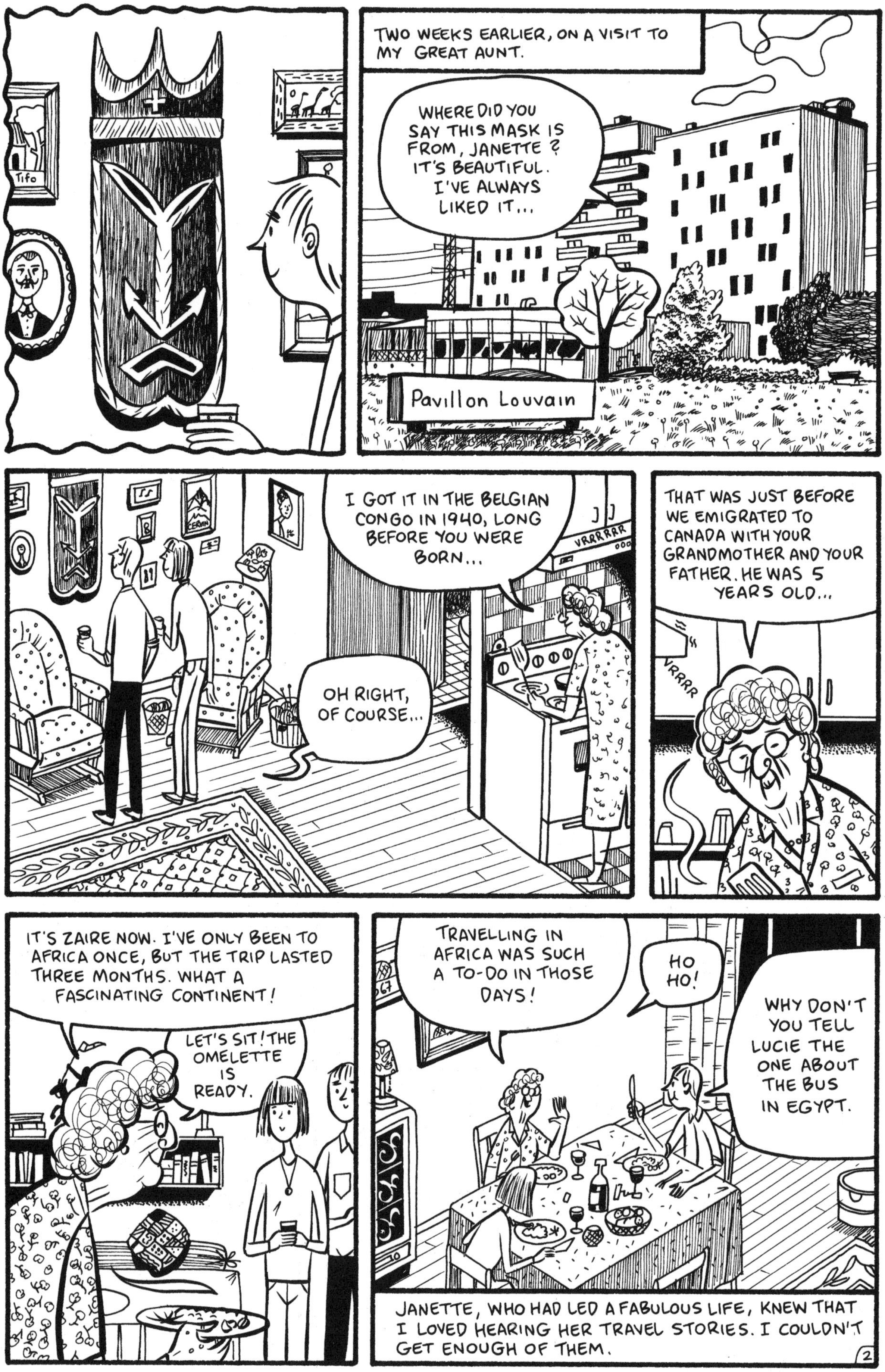
Tifo
TWO WEEKS EARLIER, ON A VISIT TO MY GREAT AUNT.
WHERE DID YOU SAY THIS MASK IS FROM, JANETTE ? IT'S BEAUTIFUL. I'VE ALWAYS LIKED IT...
Pavillon Louvain
I GOT IT IN THE BELGIAN CONGO IN 1940, LONG BEFORE YOU WERE BORN...
VRRRRRR
OH RIGHT, OF COURSE...
THAT WAS JUST BEFORE WE EMIGRATED TO CANADA WITH YOUR GRANDMOTHER AND YOUR FATHER. HE WAS 5 YEARS OLD...
VRRRR
IT'S ZAIRE NOW. I'VE ONLY BEEN TO AFRICA ONCE, BUT THE TRIP LASTED THREE MONTHS. WHAT A FASCINATING CONTINENT!
LET'S SIT! THE OMELETTE IS READY.
TRAVELLING IN AFRICA WAS SUCH A TO-DO IN THOSE DAYS!
HO HO!
WHY DON'T YOU TELL LUCIE THE ONE ABOUT THE BUS IN EGYPT.
JANETTE, WHO HAD LED A FABULOUS LIFE, KNEW THAT I LOVED HEARING HER TRAVEL STORIES. I COULDN'T GET ENOUGH OF THEM.
2

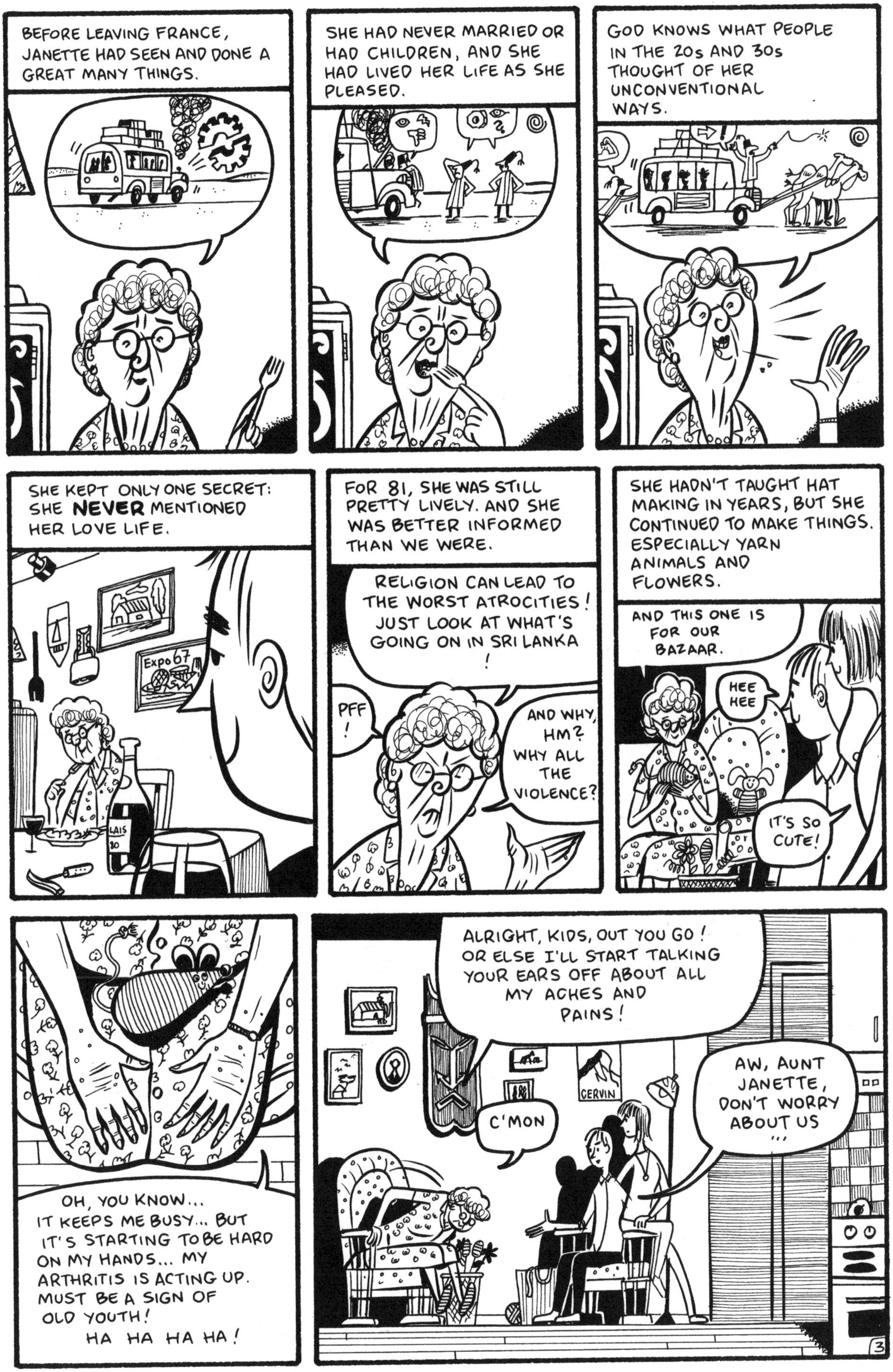
BEFORE LEAVING FRANCE, JANETTE HAD SEEN AND DONE A GREAT MANY THINGS.
SHE HAD NEVER MARRIED OR HAD CHILDREN, AND SHE HAD LIVED HER LIFE AS SHE PLEASED.
GOD KNOWS WHAT PEOPLE IN THE 20s AND 30s THOUGHT OF HER UNCONVENTIONAL WAYS.
SHE KEPT ONLY ONE SECRET: SHE NEVER MENTIONED HER LOVE LIFE.
Expo 67
FOR 81, SHE WAS STILL PRETTY LIVELY. AND SHE WAS BETTER INFORMED THAN WE WERE.
RELIGION CAN LEAD TO THE WORST ATROCITIES! JUST LOOK AT WHAT'S GOING ON IN SRI LANKA!
PFF!
AND WHY, HM? WHY ALL THE VIOLENCE?
SHE HADN'T TAUGHT HAT MAKING IN YEARS, BUT SHE CONTINUED TO MAKE THINGS. ESPECIALLY YARN ANIMALS AND FLOWERS.
AND THIS ONE IS FOR OUR BAZAAR.
HEE HEE
IT'S SO CUTE!
OH, YOU KNOW... IT KEEPS ME BUSY... BUT IT'S STARTING TO BE HARD ON MY HANDS... MY ARTHRITIS IS ACTING UP. MUST BE A SIGN OF OLD YOUTH! HA HA HA HA!
ALRIGHT, KIDS, OUT YOU GO! OR ELSE I'LL START TALKING YOUR EARS OFF ABOUT ALL MY ACHES AND PAINS!
CERVIN
C'MON
AW, AUNT JANETTE, DON'T WORRY ABOUT US...

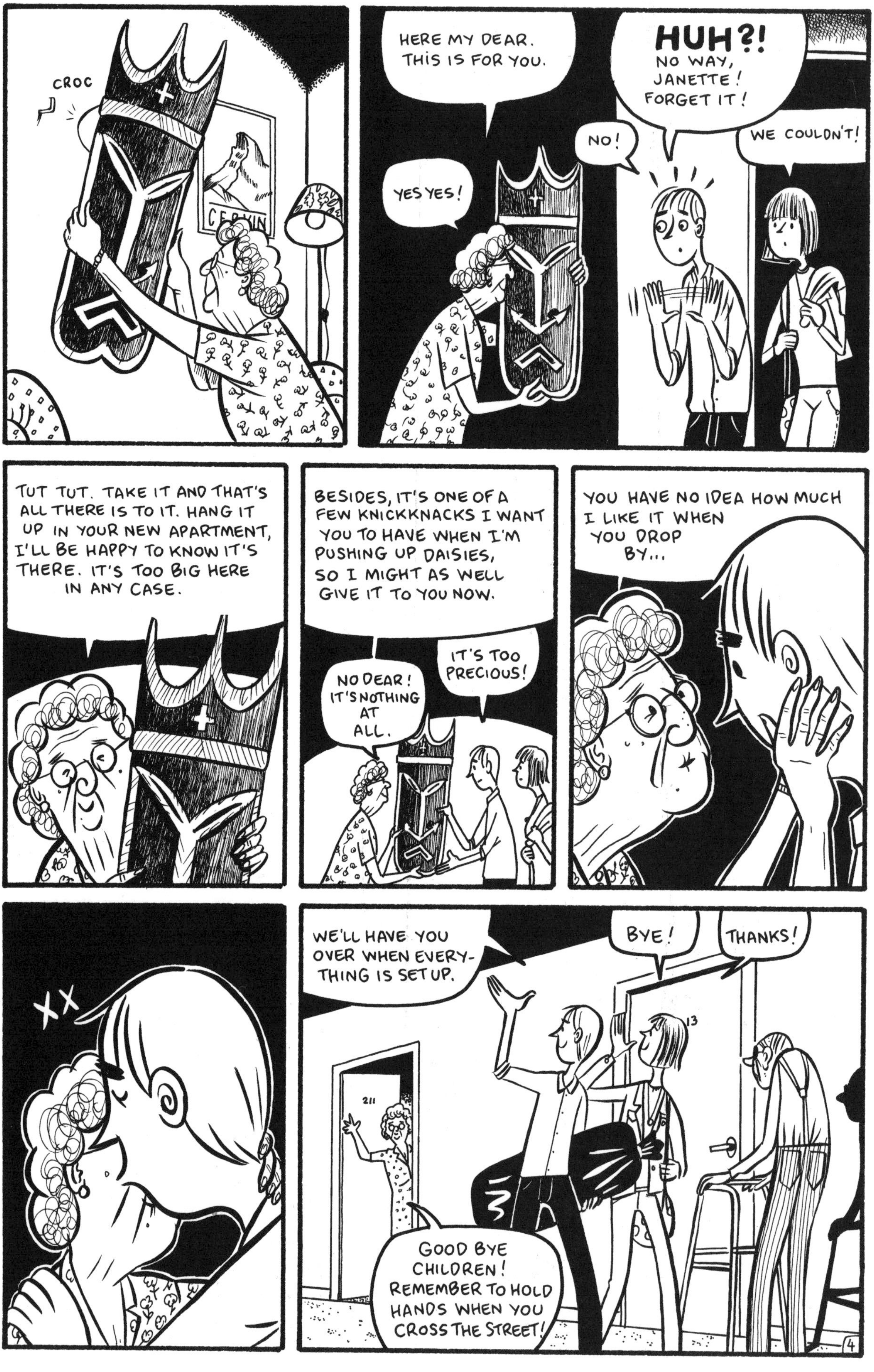

CROC
HERE MY DEAR. THIS IS FOR YOU.
YES YES!
NO!
HUH?! NO WAY, JANETTE! FORGET IT!
WE COULDN'T!
TUT TUT. TAKE IT AND THAT'S ALL THERE IS TO IT. HANG IT UP IN YOUR NEW APARTMENT, I'LL BE HAPPY TO KNOW IT'S THERE. IT'S TOO BIG HERE IN ANY CASE.
BESIDES, IT'S ONE OF A FEW KNICKKNACKS I WANT YOU TO HAVE WHEN I'M PUSHING UP DAISIES, SO I MIGHT AS WELL GIVE IT TO YOU NOW.
NO DEAR! IT'S NOTHING AT ALL.
IT'S TOO PRECIOUS!
YOU HAVE NO IDEA HOW MUCH I LIKE IT WHEN YOU DROP BY...
WE'LL HAVE YOU OVER WHEN EVERY-THING IS SET UP.
BYE!
THANKS!
211
13
GOOD BYE CHILDREN! REMEMBER TO HOLD HANDS WHEN YOU CROSS THE STREET!

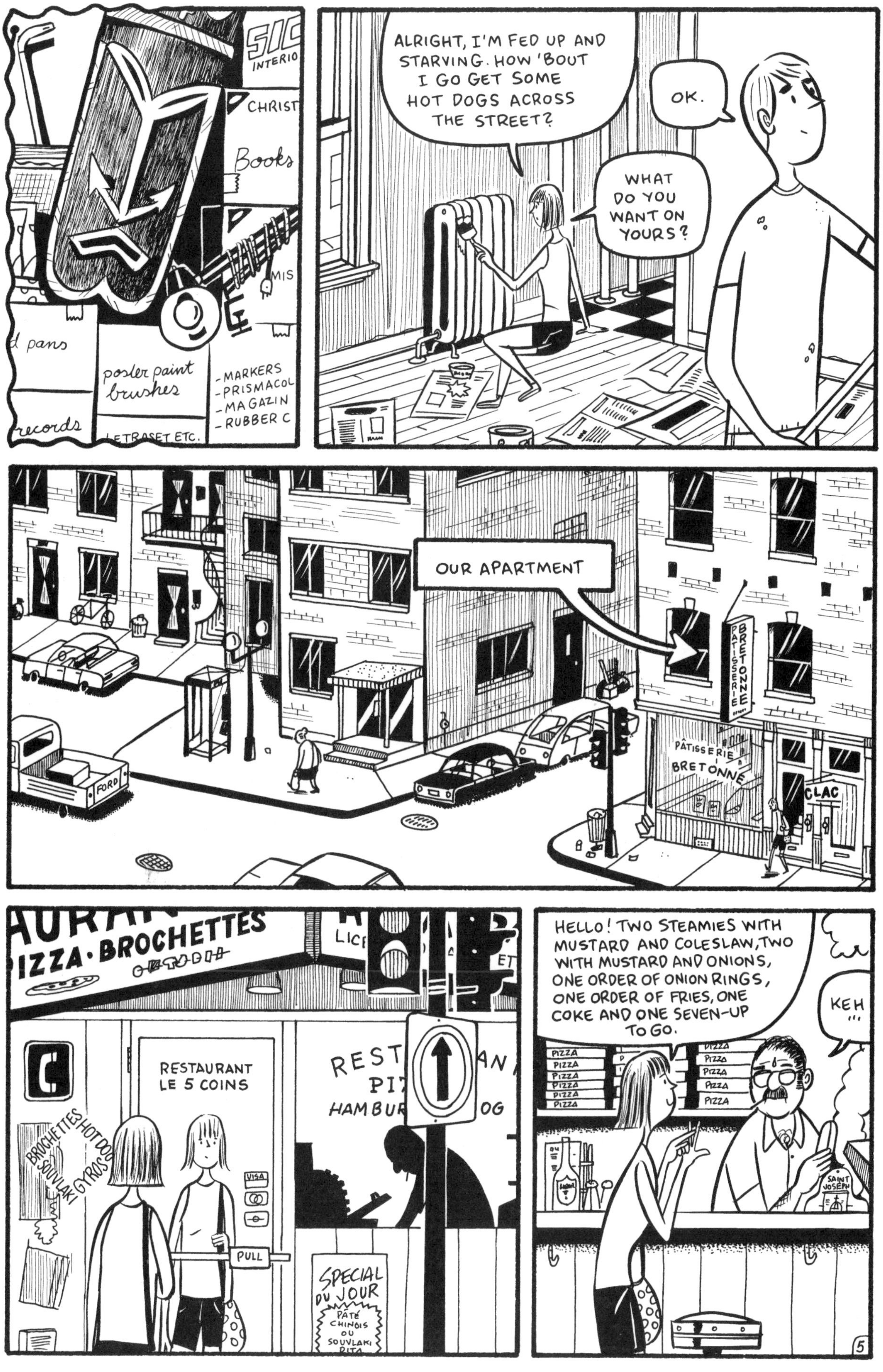
INTERIO
CHRIST
Books
MIS
d pans
poster paint brushes
-MARKERS
-PRISMACOL
-MAGAZIN
-RUBBER C
LETRASET ETC.
records
ALRIGHT, I'M FED UP AND STARVING. HOW 'BOUT I GO GET SOME HOT DOGS ACROSS THE STREET?
OK.
WHAT DO YOU WANT ON YOURS?
OUR APARTMENT
PÂTISSERIE BRETONNE
FORD
PÂTISSERIE BRETONNE
CLAC
PIZZA · BROCHETTES
RESTAURANT LE 5 COINS
BROCHETTES HOT DOG SOUVLAKI GYROS
PULL
HAMBUR
OG
SPECIAL DU JOUR
PÂTÉ CHINOIS OU SOUVLAKI PITA
HELLO! TWO STEAMIES WITH MUSTARD AND COLESLAW, TWO WITH MUSTARD AND ONIONS, ONE ORDER OF ONION RINGS, ONE ORDER OF FRIES, ONE COKE AND ONE SEVEN-UP TO GO.
KEH ...
PIZZA
SAINT JOSEPH

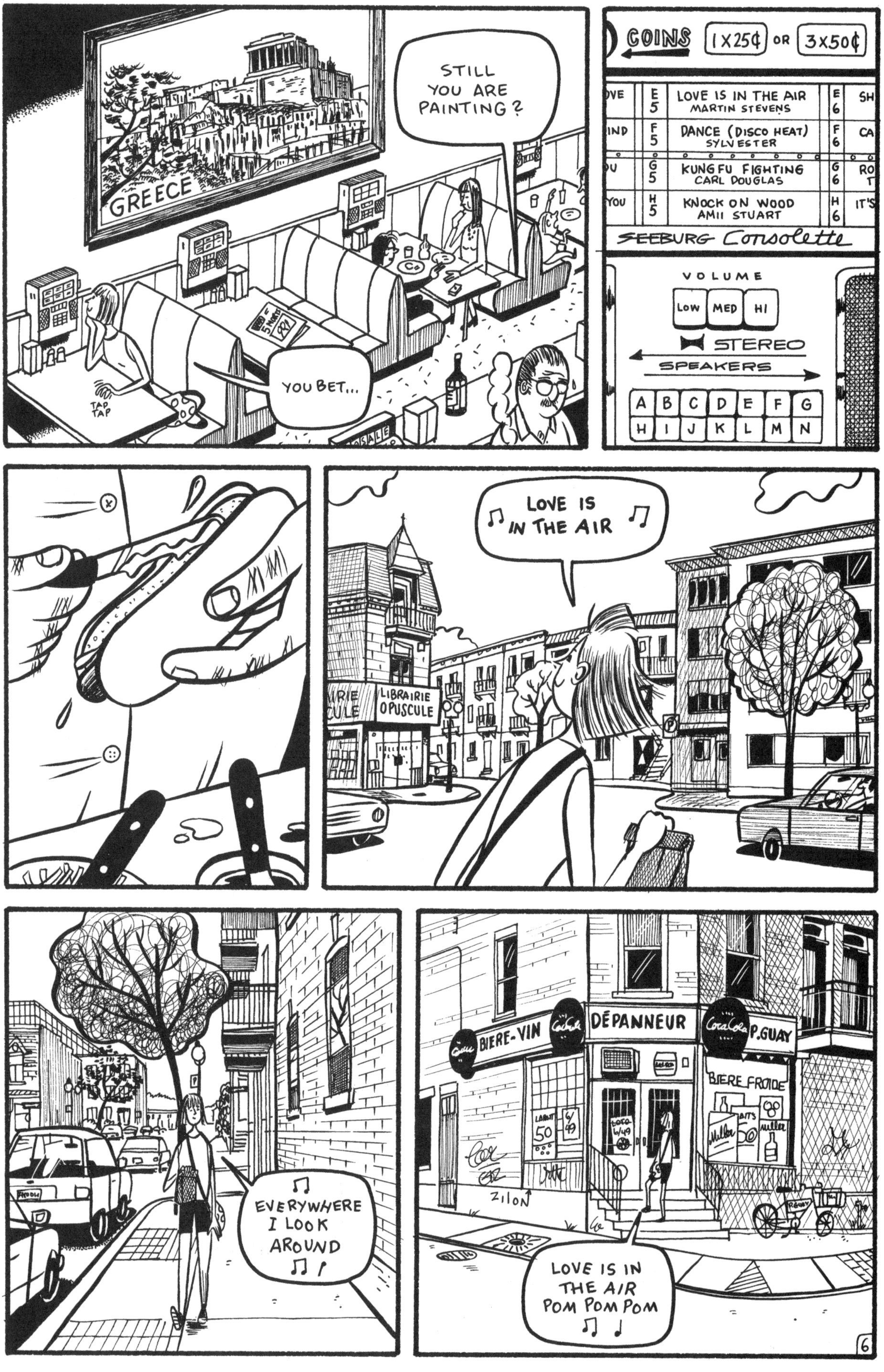
GREECE
STILL YOU ARE PAINTING?
YOU BET...
TAP TAP
COINS
1X25¢ OR 3X50¢
E5 LOVE IS IN THE AIR MARTIN STEVENS E6
F5 DANCE (DISCO HEAT) SYLVESTER F6
G5 KUNGFU FIGHTING CARL DOUGLAS G6
H5 KNOCK ON WOOD AMII STUART H6
SEEBURG Consolette
VOLUME
LOW MED HI
STEREO
SPEAKERS
A B C D E F G
H I J K L M N
LOVE IS IN THE AIR
LIBRAIRIE OPUSCULE
EVERYWHERE I LOOK AROUND
BIERE-VIN
DÉPANNEUR
P.GUAY
BIERE FROIDE
LOVE IS IN THE AIR POM POM POM

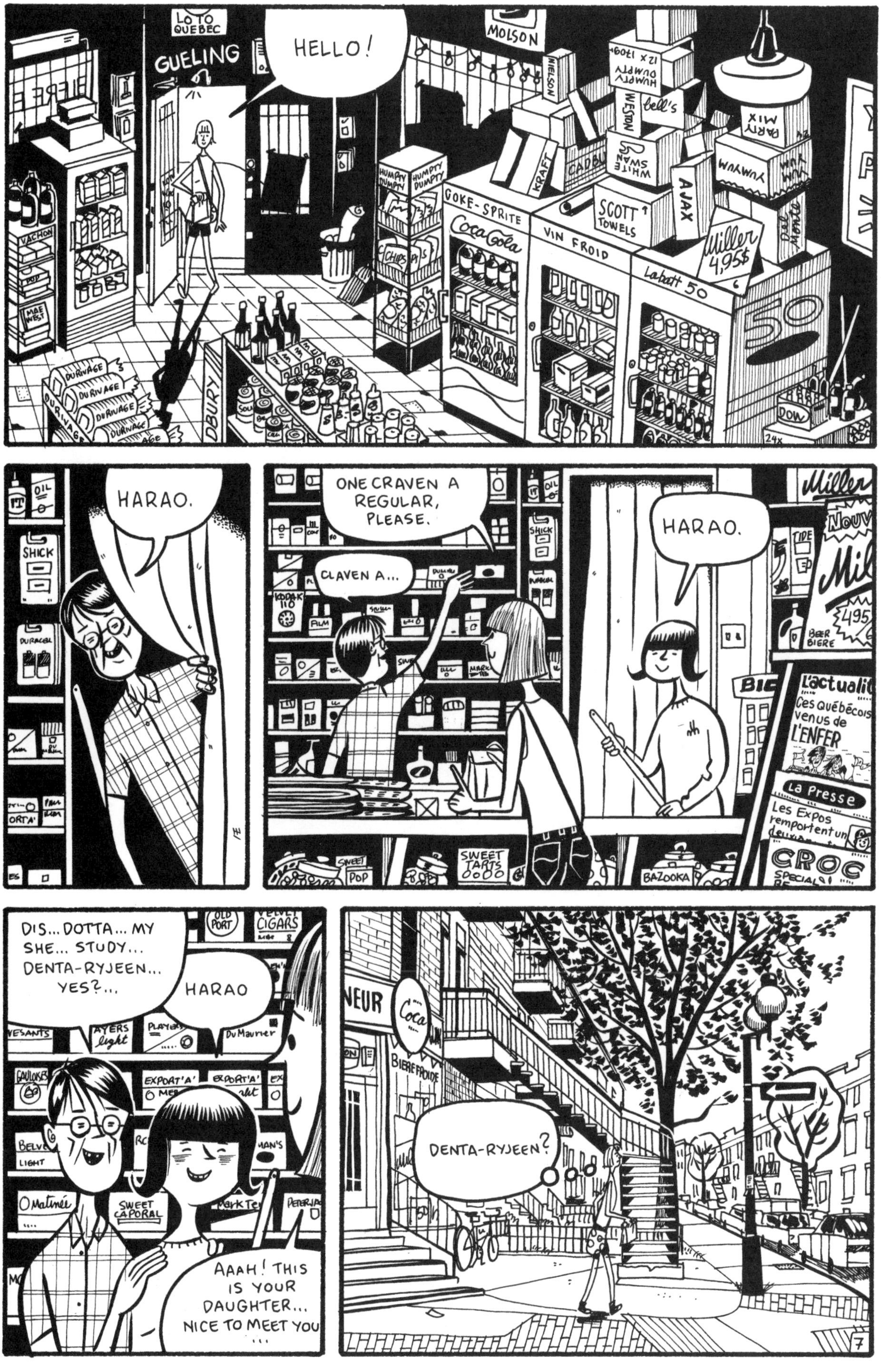
HELLO!
HARAO.
ONE CRAVEN A REGULAR, PLEASE.
CLAVEN A...
HARAO.
DIS... DOTTA... MY SHE... STUDY... DENTA-RYJEEN... YES?...
HARAO
AAAH! THIS IS YOUR DAUGHTER... NICE TO MEET YOU...
DENTA-RYJEEN?

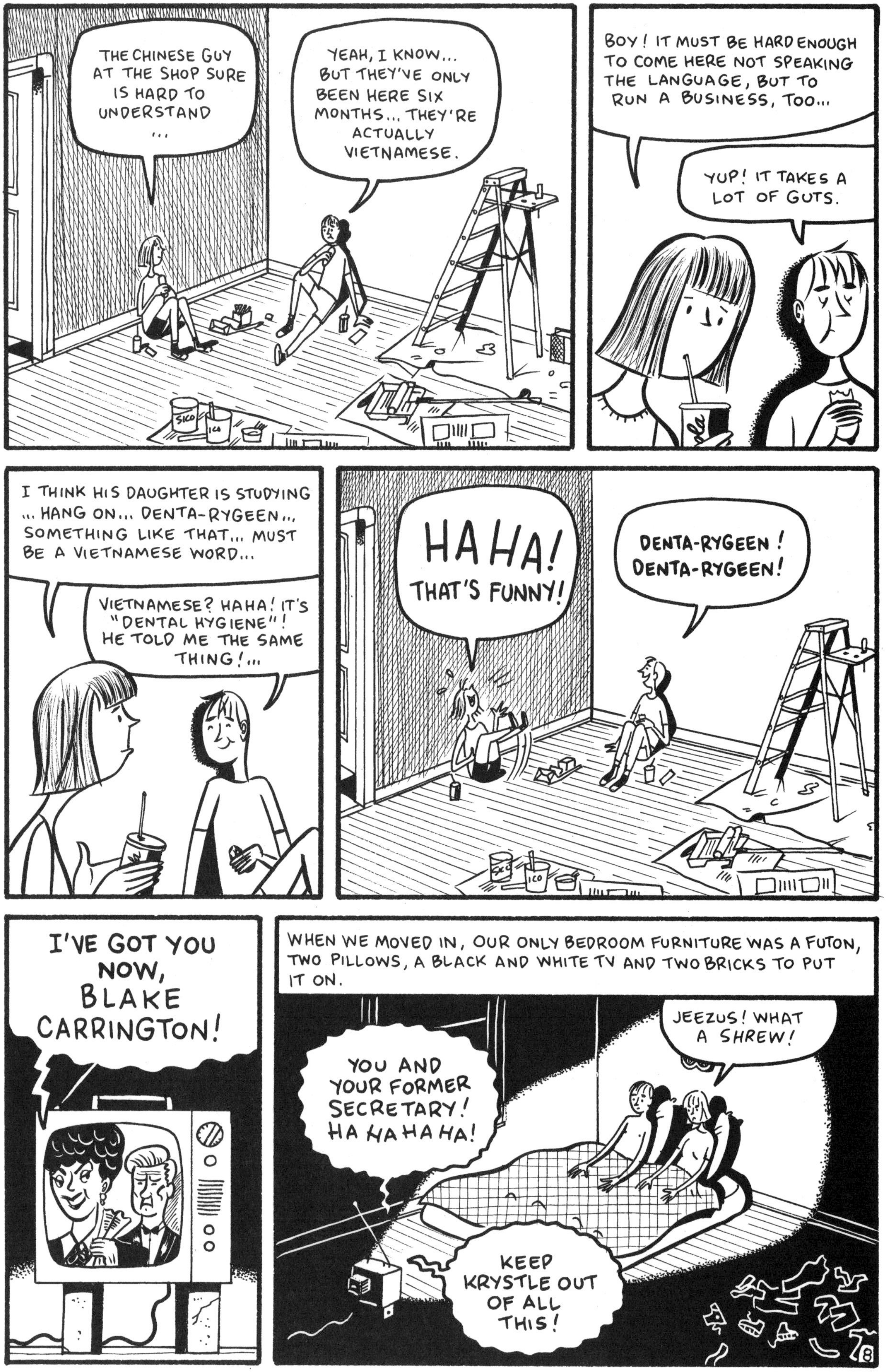

THE CHINESE GUY AT THE SHOP SURE IS HARD TO UNDERSTAND ...
YEAH, I KNOW... BUT THEY'VE ONLY BEEN HERE SIX MONTHS... THEY'RE ACTUALLY VIETNAMESE.
BOY! IT MUST BE HARD ENOUGH TO COME HERE NOT SPEAKING THE LANGUAGE, BUT TO RUN A BUSINESS, TOO...
YUP! IT TAKES A LOT OF GUTS.
I THINK HIS DAUGHTER IS STUDYING ... HANG ON... DENTA-RYGEEN... SOMETHING LIKE THAT... MUST BE A VIETNAMESE WORD...
VIETNAMESE? HAHA! IT'S "DENTAL HYGIENE"! HE TOLD ME THE SAME THING!...
HAHA! THAT'S FUNNY!
DENTA-RYGEEN! DENTA-RYGEEN!
I'VE GOT YOU NOW, BLAKE CARRINGTON!
WHEN WE MOVED IN, OUR ONLY BEDROOM FURNITURE WAS A FUTON, TWO PILLOWS, A BLACK AND WHITE TV AND TWO BRICKS TO PUT IT ON.
JEEZUS! WHAT A SHREW!
YOU AND YOUR FORMER SECRETARY! HA HAHAHA!
KEEP KRYSTLE OUT OF ALL THIS!

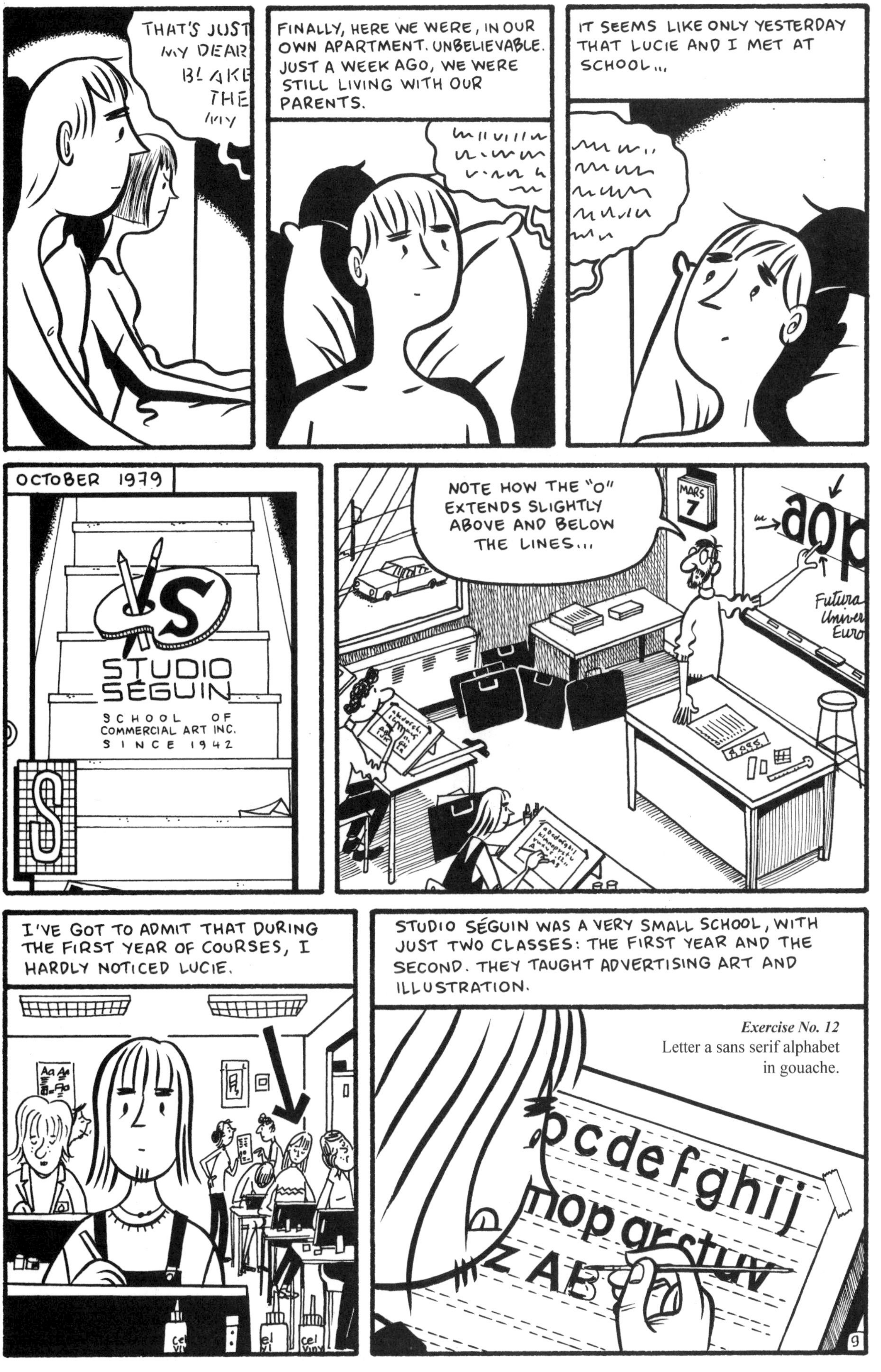
THAT'S JUST
MY DEAR
BLAKE
THE
MY
FINALLY, HERE WE WERE, IN OUR OWN APARTMENT. UNBELIEVABLE. JUST A WEEK AGO, WE WERE STILL LIVING WITH OUR PARENTS.
IT SEEMS LIKE ONLY YESTERDAY THAT LUCIE AND I MET AT SCHOOL...
OCTOBER 1979
STUDIO SÉGUIN
SCHOOL OF COMMERCIAL ART INC.
SINCE 1942
NOTE HOW THE "O" EXTENDS SLIGHTLY ABOVE AND BELOW THE LINES...
MARS 7
Futura
Univer
Euro
I'VE GOT TO ADMIT THAT DURING THE FIRST YEAR OF COURSES, I HARDLY NOTICED LUCIE.
STUDIO SÉGUIN WAS A VERY SMALL SCHOOL, WITH JUST TWO CLASSES: THE FIRST YEAR AND THE SECOND. THEY TAUGHT ADVERTISING ART AND ILLUSTRATION.
Exercise No. 12
Letter a sans serif alphabet in gouache.

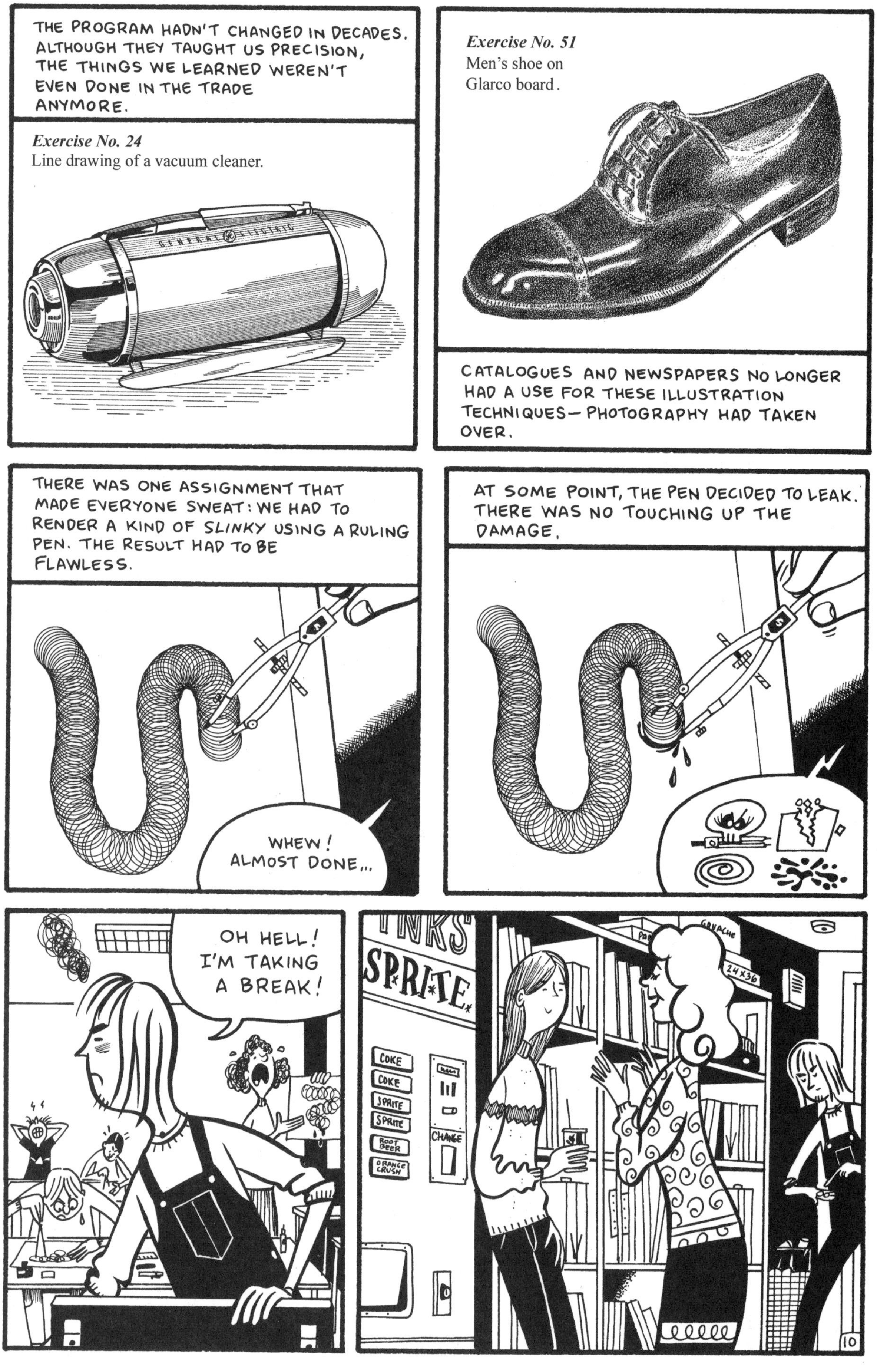
THE PROGRAM HADN'T CHANGED IN DECADES. ALTHOUGH THEY TAUGHT US PRECISION, THE THINGS WE LEARNED WEREN'T EVEN DONE IN THE TRADE ANYMORE.
Exercise No. 24
Line drawing of a vacuum cleaner.
GENERAL ELECTRIC
Exercise No. 51
Men's shoe on Glarco board.
CATALOGUES AND NEWSPAPERS NO LONGER HAD A USE FOR THESE ILLUSTRATION TECHNIQUES— PHOTOGRAPHY HAD TAKEN OVER.
THERE WAS ONE ASSIGNMENT THAT MADE EVERYONE SWEAT: WE HAD TO RENDER A KIND OF SLINKY USING A RULING PEN. THE RESULT HAD TO BE FLAWLESS.
WHEW! ALMOST DONE...
AT SOME POINT, THE PEN DECIDED TO LEAK. THERE WAS NO TOUCHING UP THE DAMAGE.
OH HELL! I'M TAKING A BREAK!
INKS
SPRITE
COKE
COKE
SPRITE
SPRITE
ROOT BEER
ORANGE CRUSH
CHANGE
GOUACHE
24X36
10

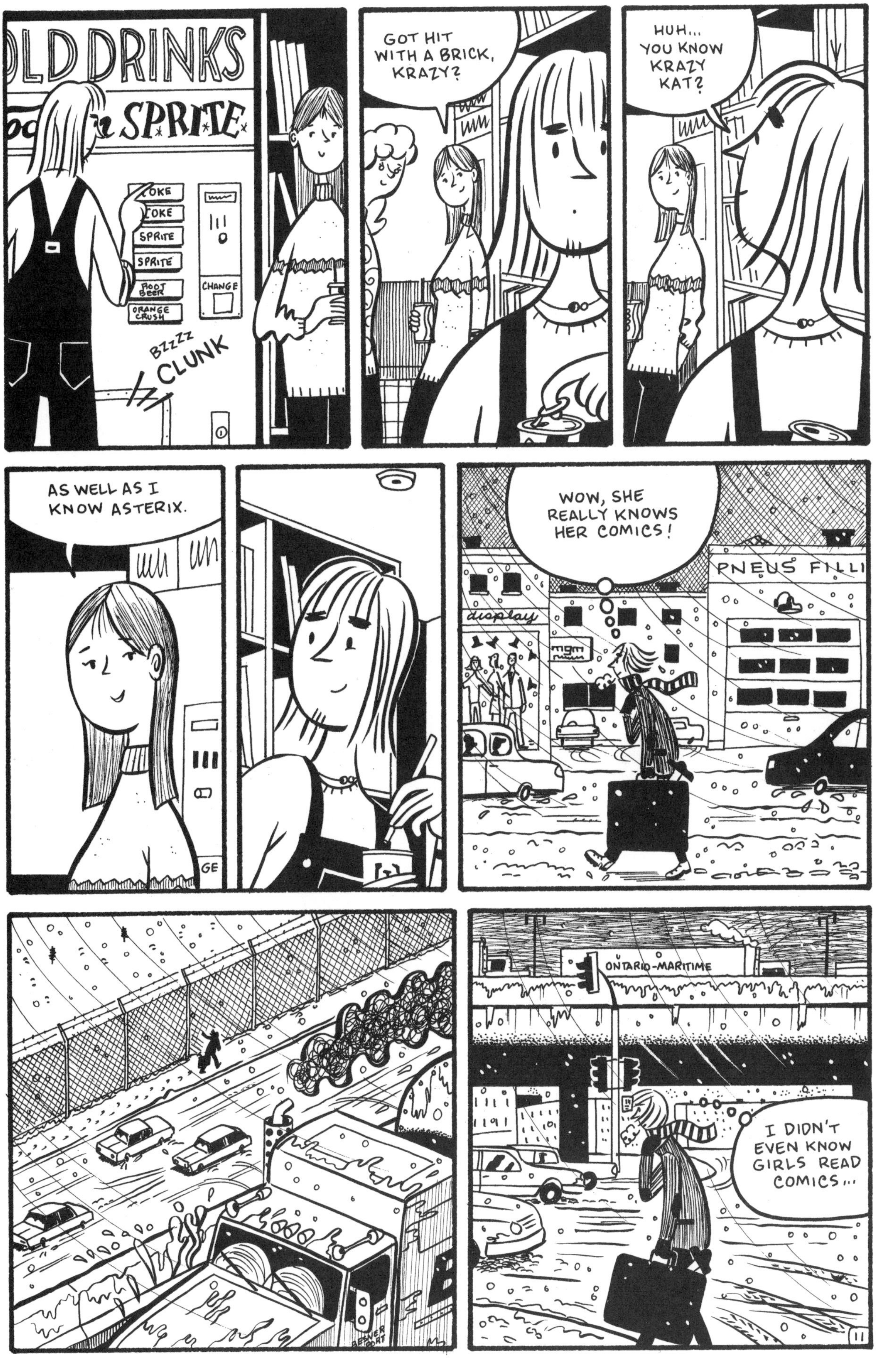
OLD DRINKS
SPRITE
OKE
OKE
SPRITE
SPRITE
ROOT BEER
ORANGE CRUSH
CHANGE
BZZZZ
CLUNK
GOT HIT WITH A BRICK, KRAZY?
HUH... YOU KNOW KRAZY KAT?
AS WELL AS I KNOW ASTERIX.
WOW, SHE REALLY KNOWS HER COMICS!
PNEUS FILLI
display
mgm
ONTARIO-MARITIME
I DIDN'T EVEN KNOW GIRLS READ COMICS...

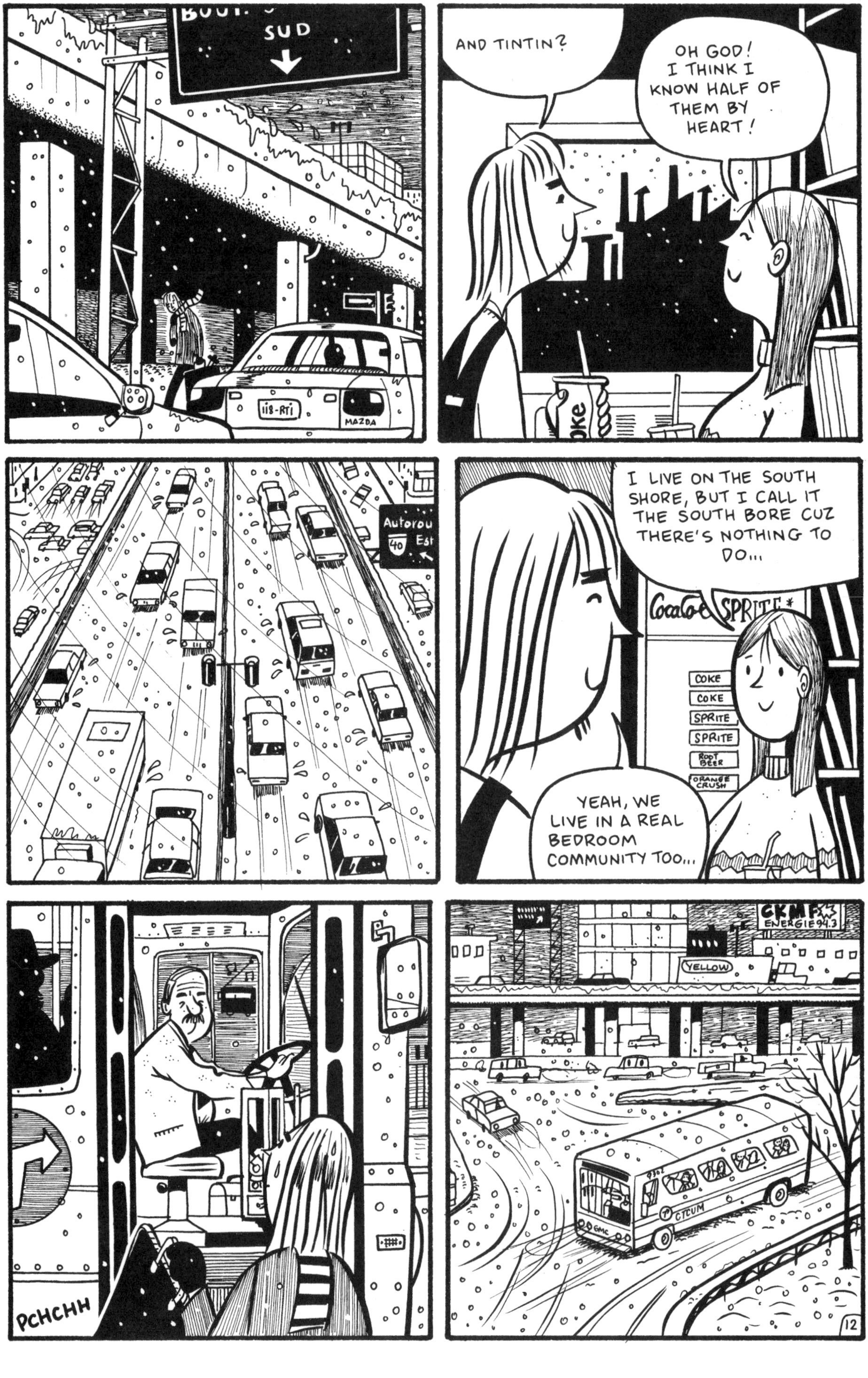
SUD
AND TINTIN?
OH GOD! I THINK I KNOW HALF OF THEM BY HEART!
I LIVE ON THE SOUTH SHORE, BUT I CALL IT THE SOUTH BORE CUZ THERE'S NOTHING TO DO...
YEAH, WE LIVE IN A REAL BEDROOM COMMUNITY TOO...
PCHCHH

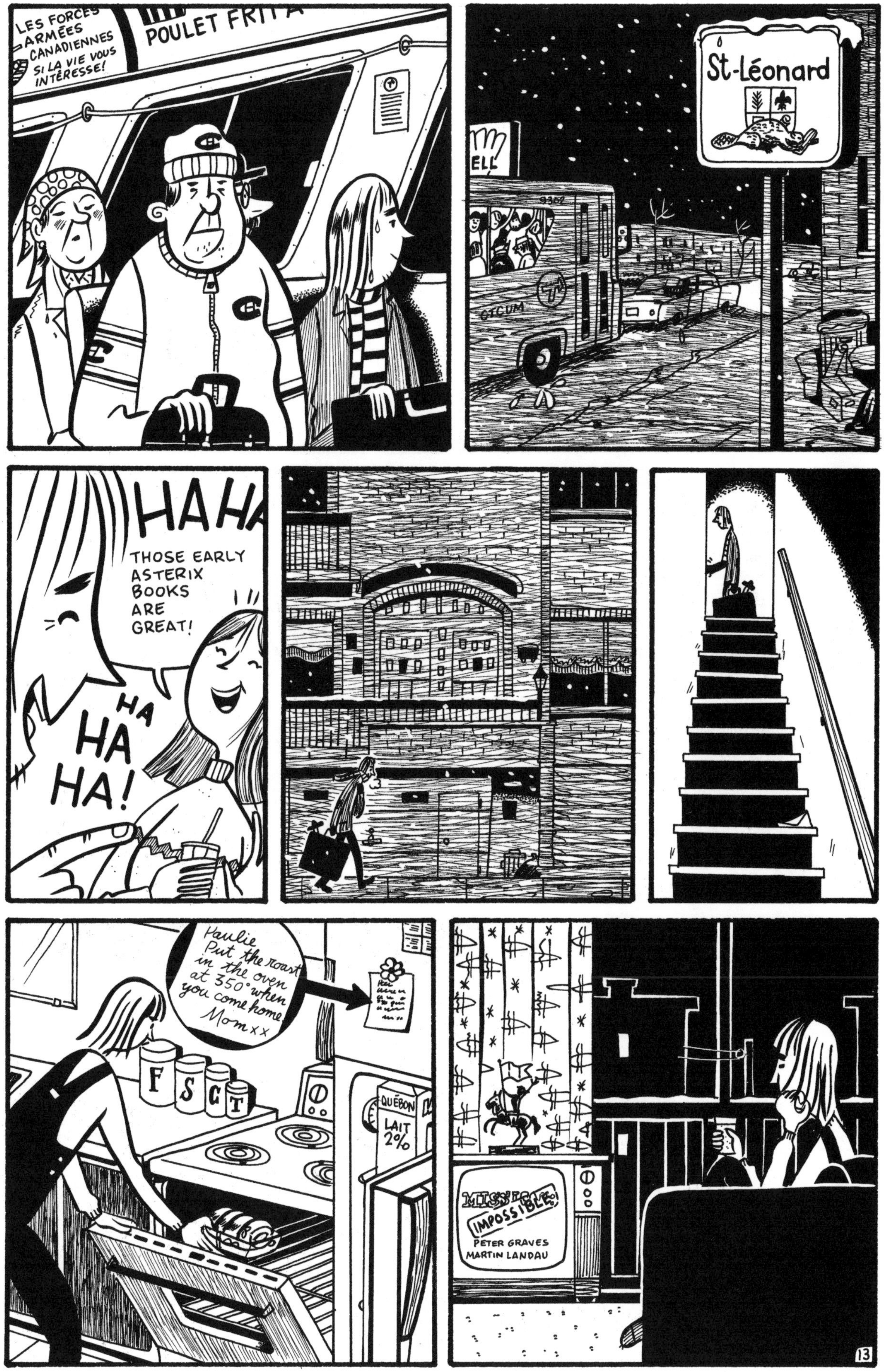
LES FORCES ARMÉES CANADIENNES SI LA VIE VOUS INTÉRESSE!
POULET FRIT
St-Léonard
HAHA
THOSE EARLY ASTERIX BOOKS ARE GREAT!
HA HA HA!
Paulie Put the roast in the oven at 350° when you come home. Mom xx
F S C T
QUÉBON
LAIT 2%
MISSION IMPOSSIBLE
PETER GRAVES
MARTIN LANDAU
13

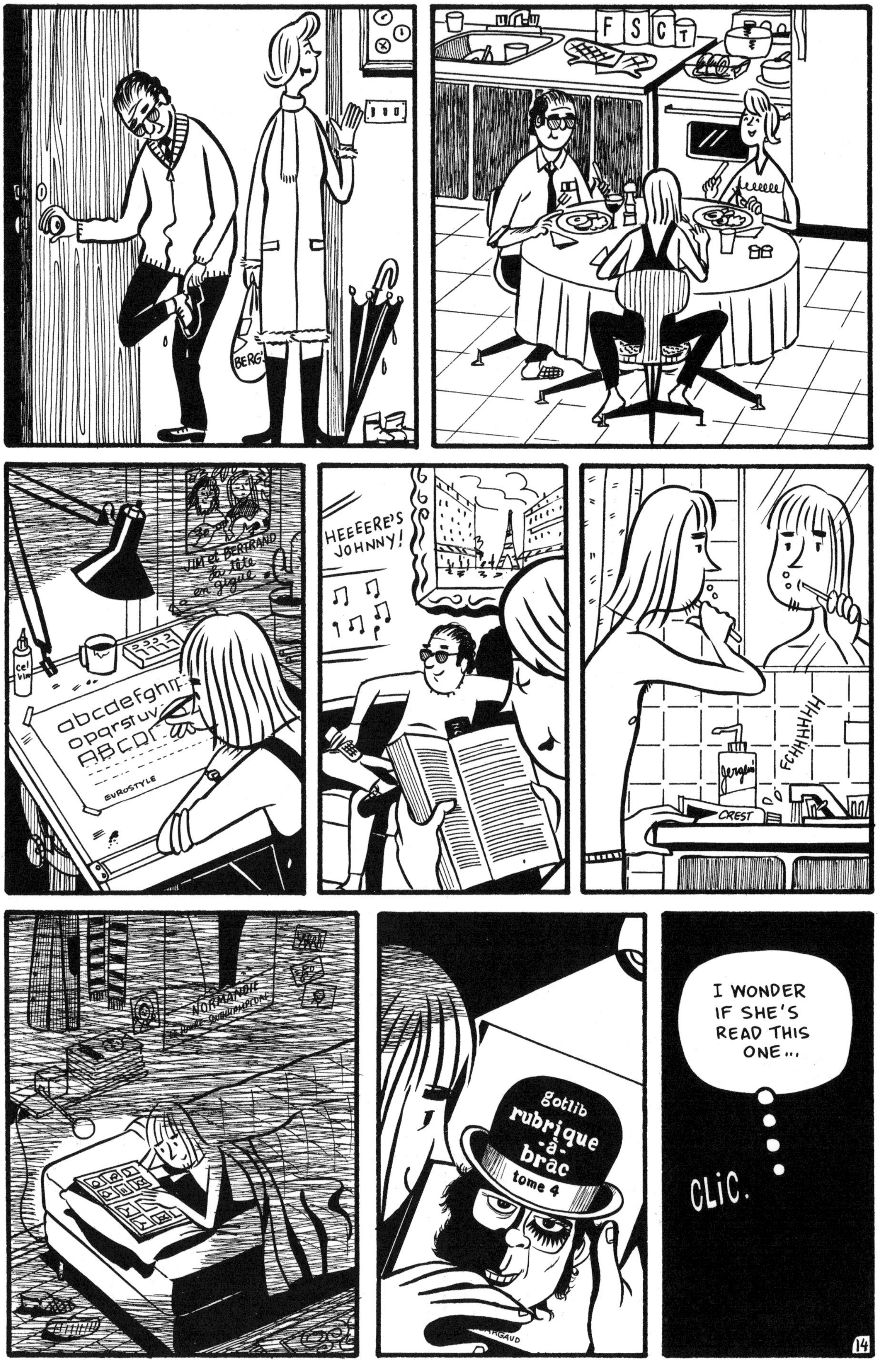

BERG!
F S C T
JIM et BERTRAND
la tête en gigue
cel vim
abcdefghr
opqrstuv
ABCD
EUROSTYLE
HEEEERE'S JOHNNY!
Jergens
FCHHHHHH
CREST
NORMANDIE
I WONDER IF SHE'S READ THIS ONE...
gotlib
rubrique -à- brac
tome 4
CLIC.
14

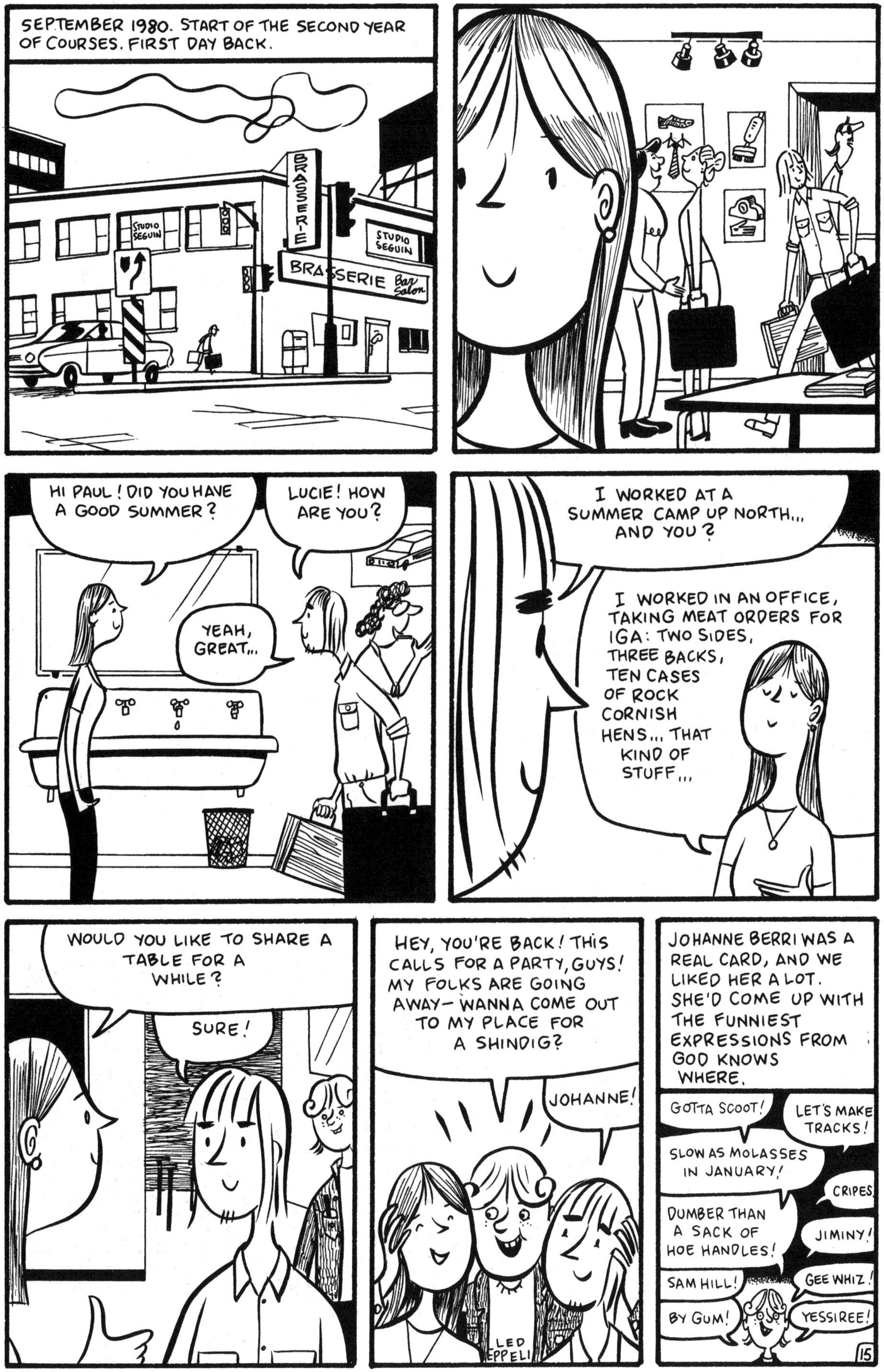
SEPTEMBER 1980. START OF THE SECOND YEAR OF COURSES. FIRST DAY BACK.
BRASSERIE
STUDIO SEGUIN
STUDIO SEGUIN
BRASSERIE Bar Salon
HI PAUL! DID YOU HAVE A GOOD SUMMER?
LUCIE! HOW ARE YOU?
YEAH, GREAT...
I WORKED AT A SUMMER CAMP UP NORTH... AND YOU?
I WORKED IN AN OFFICE, TAKING MEAT ORDERS FOR IGA: TWO SIDES, THREE BACKS, TEN CASES OF ROCK CORNISH HENS... THAT KIND OF STUFF...
WOULD YOU LIKE TO SHARE A TABLE FOR A WHILE?
SURE!
HEY, YOU'RE BACK! THIS CALLS FOR A PARTY, GUYS! MY FOLKS ARE GOING AWAY- WANNA COME OUT TO MY PLACE FOR A SHINDIG?
JOHANNE!
LED EPPELI
JOHANNE BERRI WAS A REAL CARD, AND WE LIKED HER A LOT. SHE'D COME UP WITH THE FUNNIEST EXPRESSIONS FROM GOD KNOWS WHERE.
GOTTA SCOOT!
LET'S MAKE TRACKS!
SLOW AS MOLASSES IN JANUARY!
CRIPES
DUMBER THAN A SACK OF HOE HANDLES!
JIMINY!
SAM HILL!
GEE WHIZ!
BY GUM!
YESSIREE!

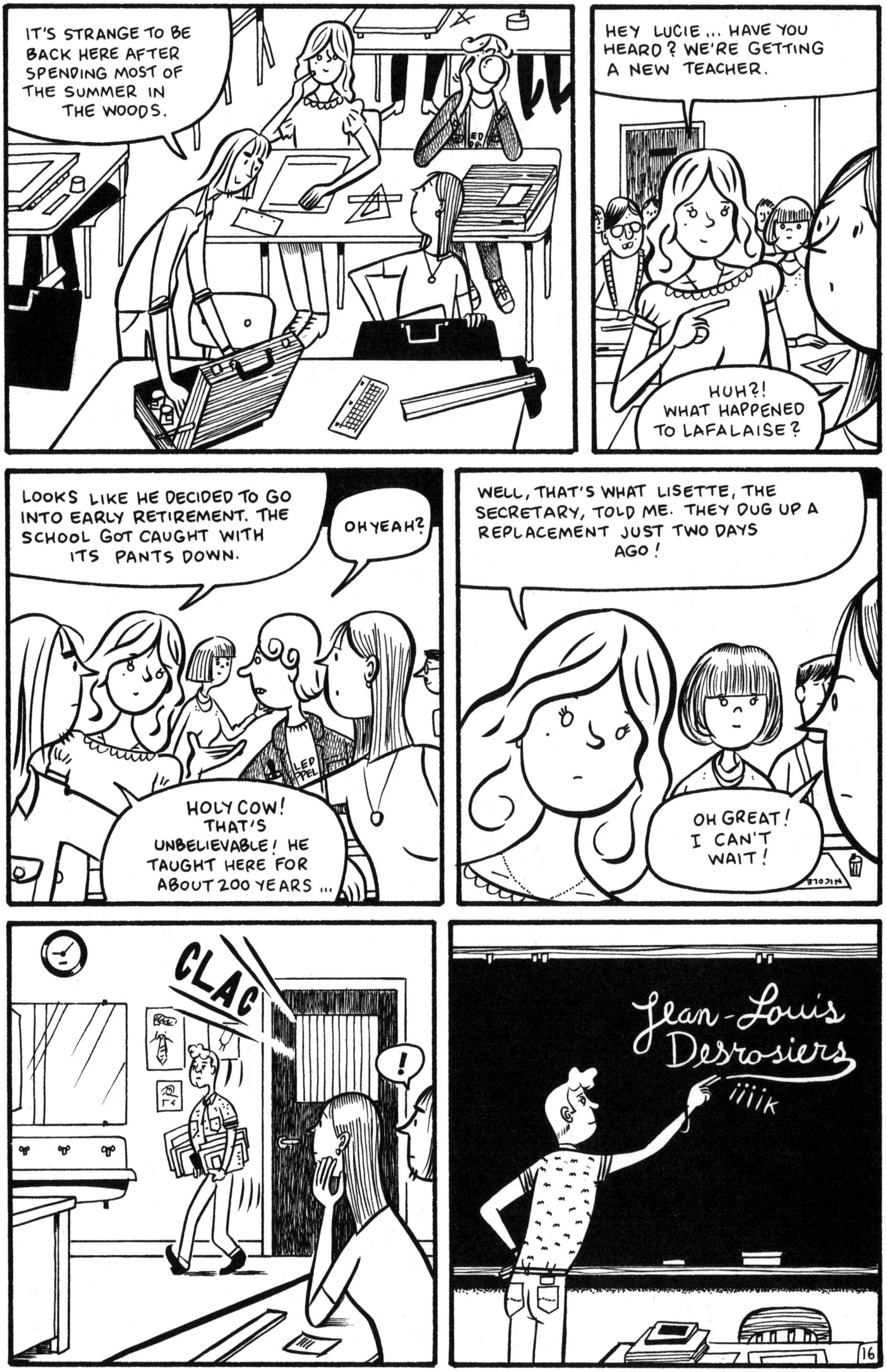
IT'S STRANGE TO BE BACK HERE AFTER SPENDING MOST OF THE SUMMER IN THE WOODS.
HEY LUCIE... HAVE YOU HEARD? WE'RE GETTING A NEW TEACHER.
HUH?! WHAT HAPPENED TO LAFALAISE?
LOOKS LIKE HE DECIDED TO GO INTO EARLY RETIREMENT. THE SCHOOL GOT CAUGHT WITH ITS PANTS DOWN.
OH YEAH?
HOLY COW! THAT'S UNBELIEVABLE! HE TAUGHT HERE FOR ABOUT 200 YEARS...
WELL, THAT'S WHAT LISETTE, THE SECRETARY, TOLD ME. THEY DUG UP A REPLACEMENT JUST TWO DAYS AGO!
OH GREAT! I CAN'T WAIT!
CLAC
!
Jean-Louis Desrosiers
iiiik

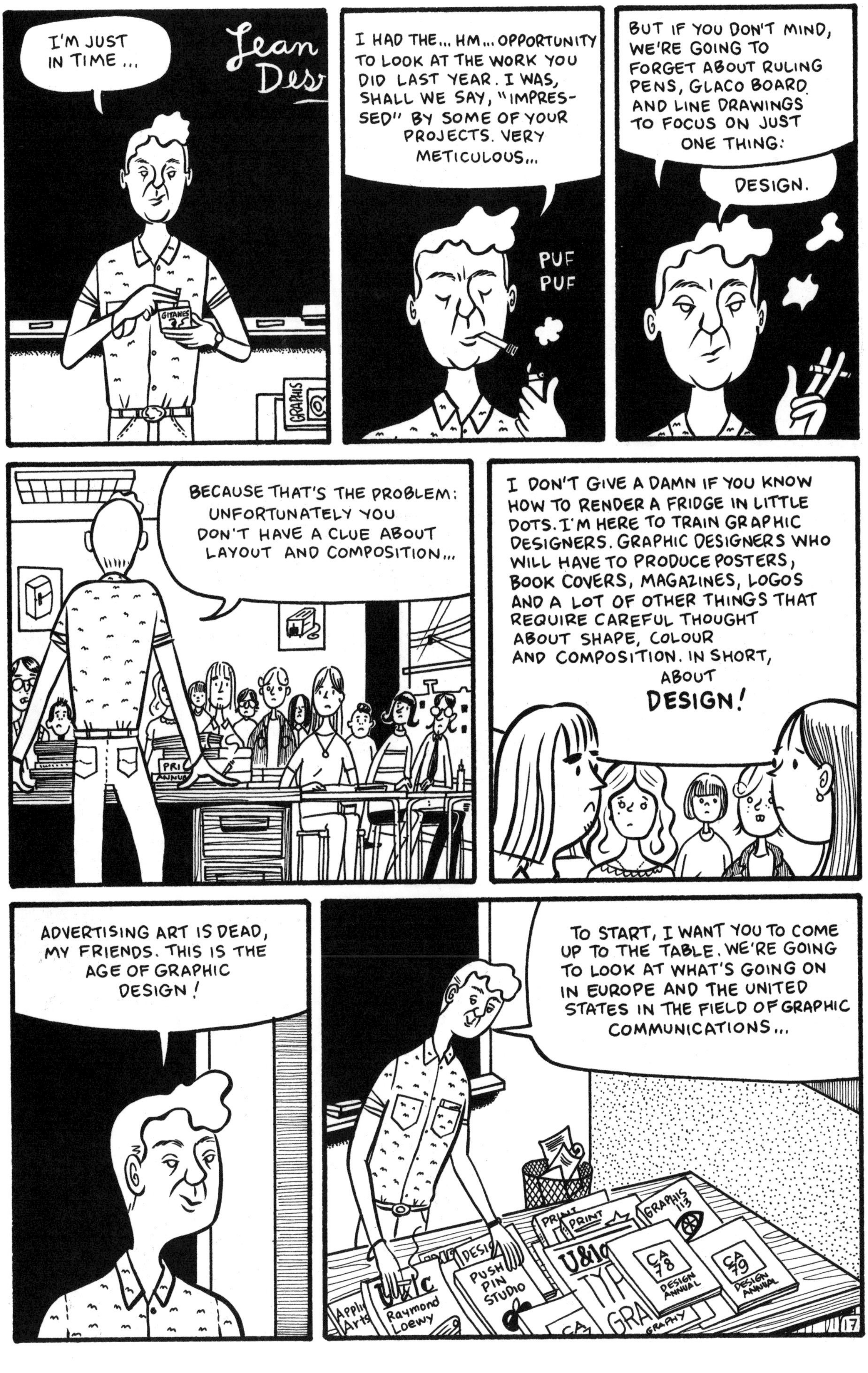
I'M JUST IN TIME ...
Jean Des
GITANES
GRAPHIS
I HAD THE ... HM ... OPPORTUNITY TO LOOK AT THE WORK YOU DID LAST YEAR. I WAS, SHALL WE SAY, "IMPRESSED" BY SOME OF YOUR PROJECTS. VERY METICULOUS ...
PUF PUF
BUT IF YOU DON'T MIND, WE'RE GOING TO FORGET ABOUT RULING PENS, GLACO BOARD AND LINE DRAWINGS TO FOCUS ON JUST ONE THING:
DESIGN.
BECAUSE THAT'S THE PROBLEM: UNFORTUNATELY YOU DON'T HAVE A CLUE ABOUT LAYOUT AND COMPOSITION ...
I DON'T GIVE A DAMN IF YOU KNOW HOW TO RENDER A FRIDGE IN LITTLE DOTS. I'M HERE TO TRAIN GRAPHIC DESIGNERS. GRAPHIC DESIGNERS WHO WILL HAVE TO PRODUCE POSTERS, BOOK COVERS, MAGAZINES, LOGOS AND A LOT OF OTHER THINGS THAT REQUIRE CAREFUL THOUGHT ABOUT SHAPE, COLOUR AND COMPOSITION. IN SHORT, ABOUT DESIGN!
ADVERTISING ART IS DEAD, MY FRIENDS. THIS IS THE AGE OF GRAPHIC DESIGN!
TO START, I WANT YOU TO COME UP TO THE TABLE. WE'RE GOING TO LOOK AT WHAT'S GOING ON IN EUROPE AND THE UNITED STATES IN THE FIELD OF GRAPHIC COMMUNICATIONS ...
PRINT
GRAPHIS 113
PUSH PIN STUDIO
Raymond Loewy
CA 78 DESIGN ANNUAL
CA 79 DESIGN ANNUAL

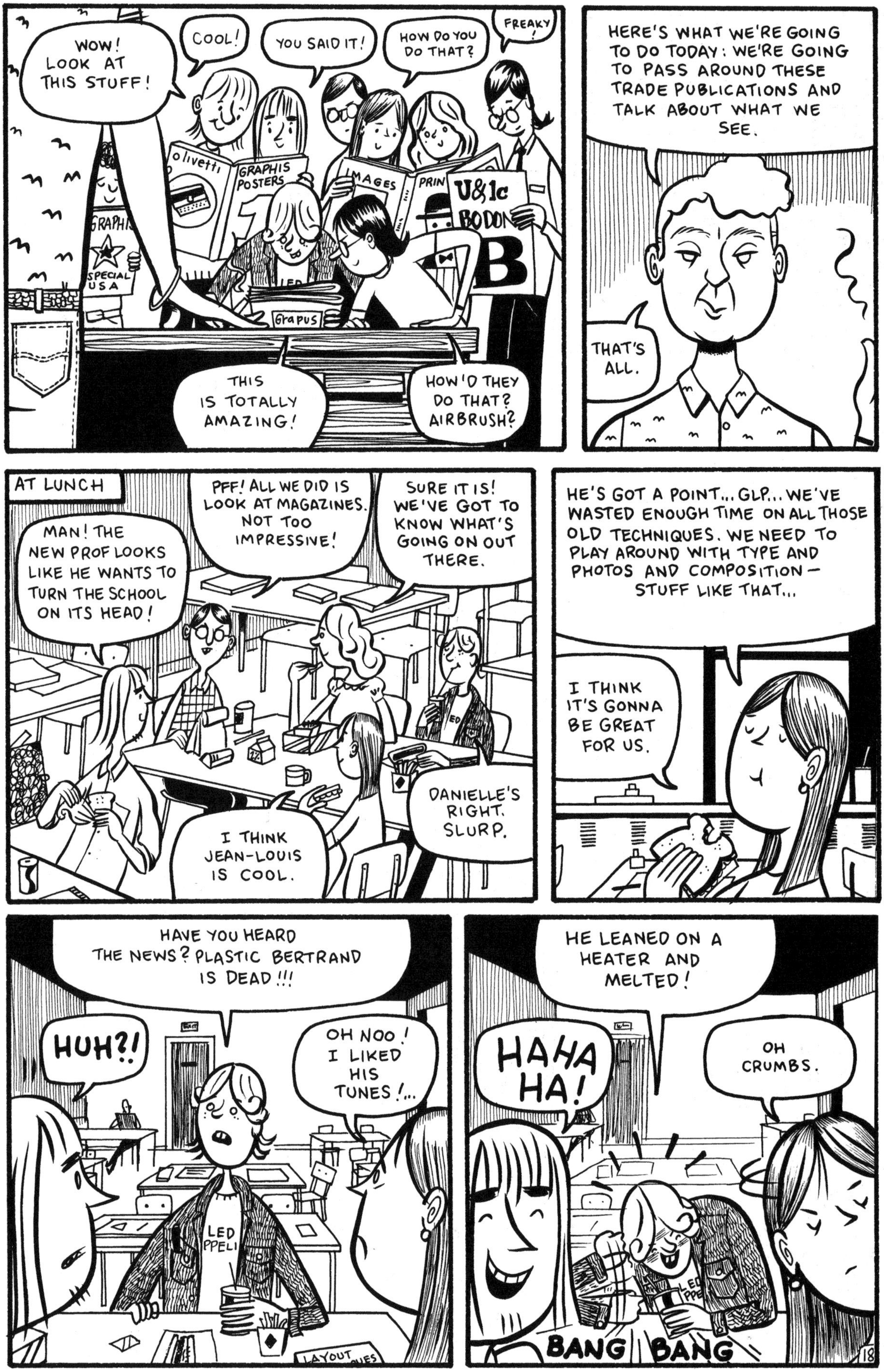
WOW! LOOK AT THIS STUFF!
COOL!
YOU SAID IT!
HOW DO YOU DO THAT?
FREAKY!
olivetti
GRAPHIS POSTERS
IMAGES
PRIN
U&lc BODONI B
GRAPHIS SPECIAL USA
Grapus
THIS IS TOTALLY AMAZING!
HOW'D THEY DO THAT? AIRBRUSH?
HERE'S WHAT WE'RE GOING TO DO TODAY: WE'RE GOING TO PASS AROUND THESE TRADE PUBLICATIONS AND TALK ABOUT WHAT WE SEE.
THAT'S ALL.
AT LUNCH
MAN! THE NEW PROF LOOKS LIKE HE WANTS TO TURN THE SCHOOL ON ITS HEAD!
PFF! ALL WE DID IS LOOK AT MAGAZINES. NOT TOO IMPRESSIVE!
SURE IT IS! WE'VE GOT TO KNOW WHAT'S GOING ON OUT THERE.
I THINK JEAN-LOUIS IS COOL.
DANIELLE'S RIGHT. SLURP.
HE'S GOT A POINT... GLP... WE'VE WASTED ENOUGH TIME ON ALL THOSE OLD TECHNIQUES. WE NEED TO PLAY AROUND WITH TYPE AND PHOTOS AND COMPOSITION — STUFF LIKE THAT...
I THINK IT'S GONNA BE GREAT FOR US.
HAVE YOU HEARD THE NEWS? PLASTIC BERTRAND IS DEAD!!!
HUH?!
OH NOO! I LIKED HIS TUNES!...
LED PPELI
HE LEANED ON A HEATER AND MELTED!
HAHA HA!
OH CRUMBS.
BANG BANG

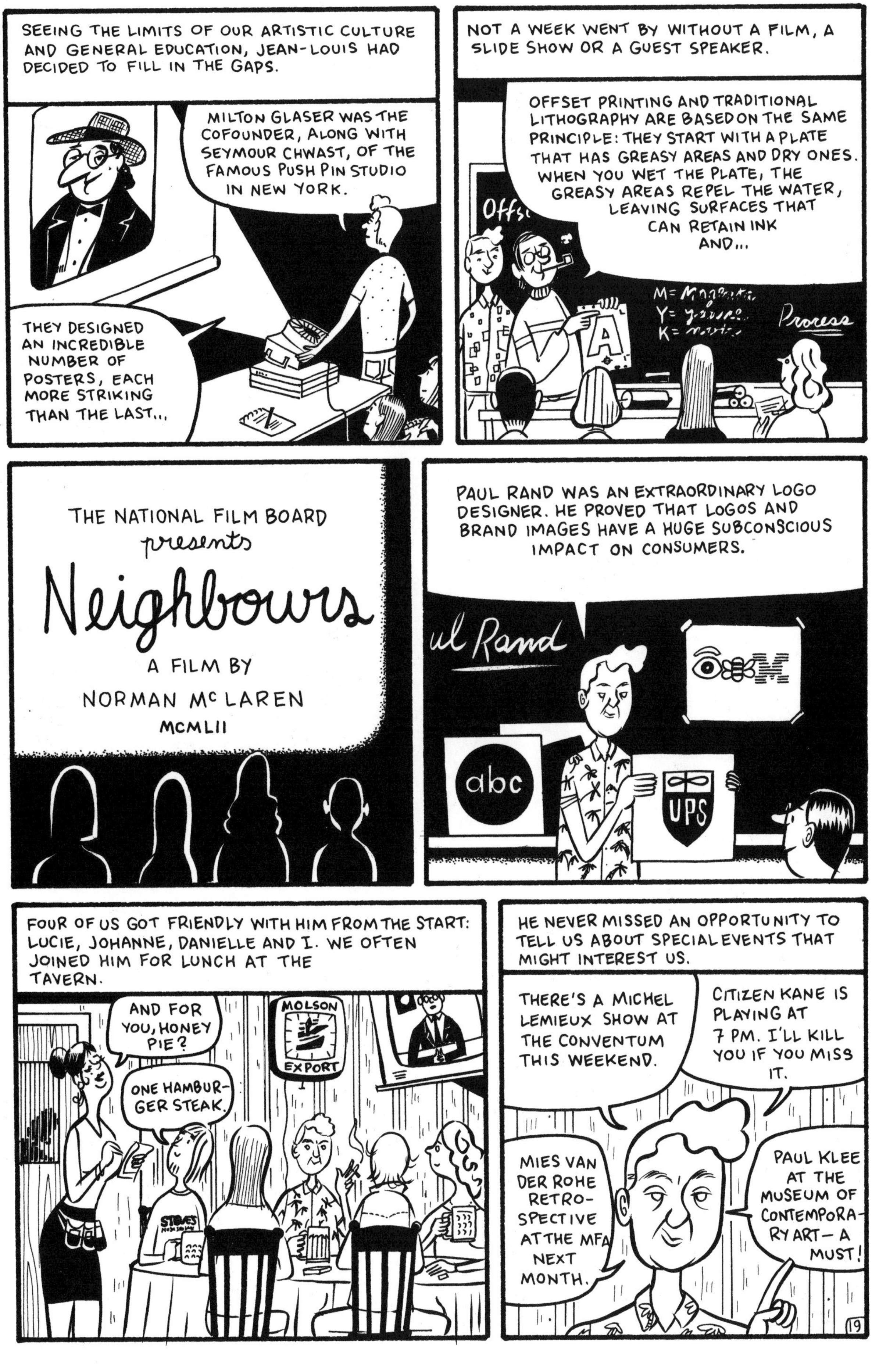

SEEING THE LIMITS OF OUR ARTISTIC CULTURE AND GENERAL EDUCATION, JEAN-LOUIS HAD DECIDED TO FILL IN THE GAPS.
MILTON GLASER WAS THE COFOUNDER, ALONG WITH SEYMOUR CHWAST, OF THE FAMOUS PUSH PIN STUDIO IN NEW YORK.
THEY DESIGNED AN INCREDIBLE NUMBER OF POSTERS, EACH MORE STRIKING THAN THE LAST...
NOT A WEEK WENT BY WITHOUT A FILM, A SLIDE SHOW OR A GUEST SPEAKER.
OFFSET PRINTING AND TRADITIONAL LITHOGRAPHY ARE BASED ON THE SAME PRINCIPLE: THEY START WITH A PLATE THAT HAS GREASY AREAS AND DRY ONES. WHEN YOU WET THE PLATE, THE GREASY AREAS REPEL THE WATER, LEAVING SURFACES THAT CAN RETAIN INK AND...
Process
THE NATIONAL FILM BOARD
presents
Neighbours
A FILM BY
NORMAN McLAREN
MCMLII
PAUL RAND WAS AN EXTRAORDINARY LOGO DESIGNER. HE PROVED THAT LOGOS AND BRAND IMAGES HAVE A HUGE SUBCONSCIOUS IMPACT ON CONSUMERS.
ul Rand
abc
UPS
FOUR OF US GOT FRIENDLY WITH HIM FROM THE START: LUCIE, JOHANNE, DANIELLE AND I. WE OFTEN JOINED HIM FOR LUNCH AT THE TAVERN.
AND FOR YOU, HONEY PIE?
ONE HAMBURGER STEAK.
MOLSON EXPORT
HE NEVER MISSED AN OPPORTUNITY TO TELL US ABOUT SPECIAL EVENTS THAT MIGHT INTEREST US.
THERE'S A MICHEL LEMIEUX SHOW AT THE CONVENTUM THIS WEEKEND.
CITIZEN KANE IS PLAYING AT 7 PM. I'LL KILL YOU IF YOU MISS IT.
MIES VAN DER ROHE RETROSPECTIVE AT THE MFA NEXT MONTH.
PAUL KLEE AT THE MUSEUM OF CONTEMPORARY ART— A MUST!

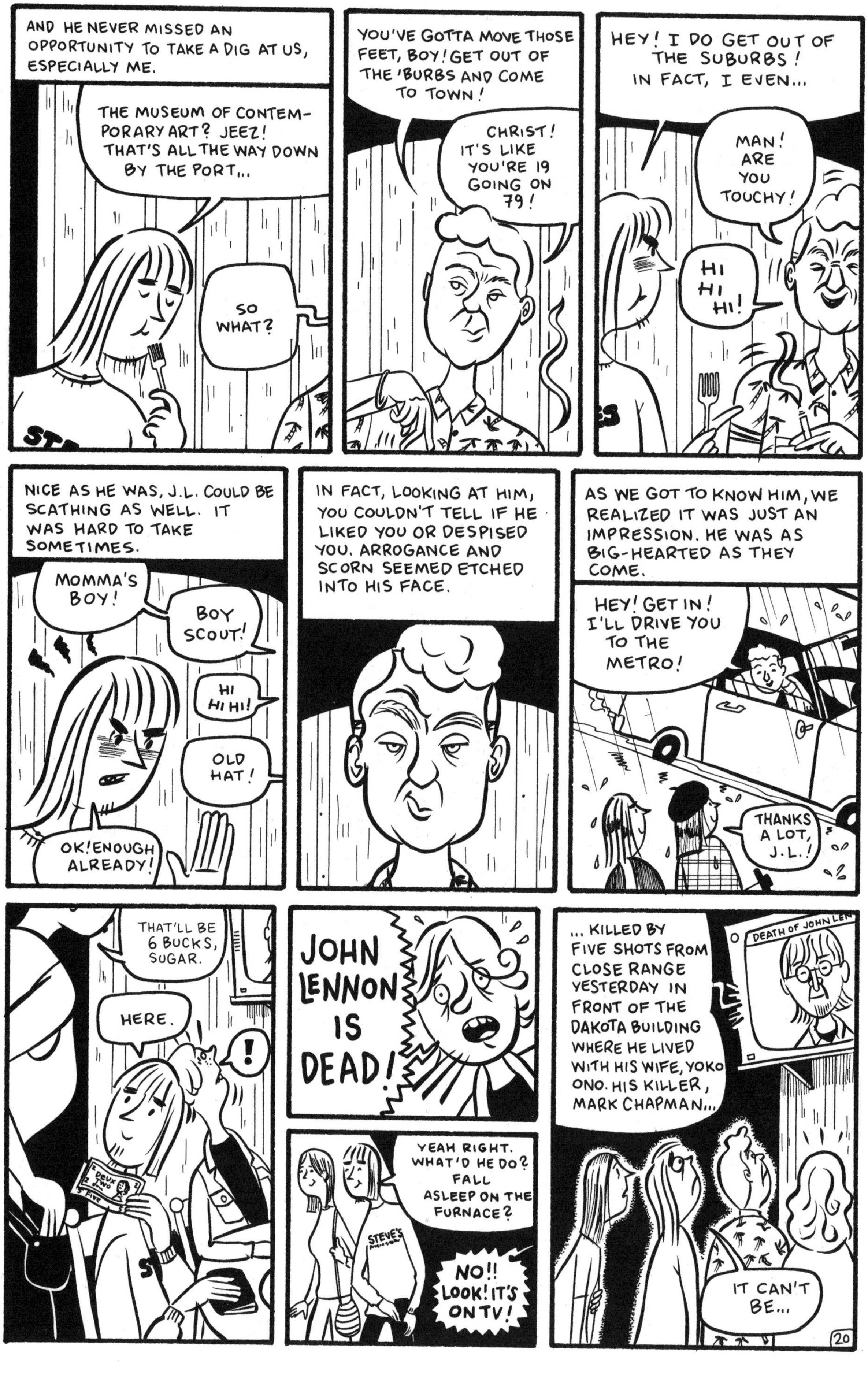
AND HE NEVER MISSED AN OPPORTUNITY TO TAKE A DIG AT US, ESPECIALLY ME.
THE MUSEUM OF CONTEMPORARY ART? JEEZ! THAT'S ALL THE WAY DOWN BY THE PORT...
SO WHAT?
YOU'VE GOTTA MOVE THOSE FEET, BOY! GET OUT OF THE 'BURBS AND COME TO TOWN!
CHRIST! IT'S LIKE YOU'RE 19 GOING ON 79!
HEY! I DO GET OUT OF THE SUBURBS! IN FACT, I EVEN...
MAN! ARE YOU TOUCHY!
HI HI HI!
NICE AS HE WAS, J.L. COULD BE SCATHING AS WELL. IT WAS HARD TO TAKE SOMETIMES.
MOMMA'S BOY!
BOY SCOUT!
HI HI HI!
OLD HAT!
OK! ENOUGH ALREADY!
IN FACT, LOOKING AT HIM, YOU COULDN'T TELL IF HE LIKED YOU OR DESPISED YOU. ARROGANCE AND SCORN SEEMED ETCHED INTO HIS FACE.
AS WE GOT TO KNOW HIM, WE REALIZED IT WAS JUST AN IMPRESSION. HE WAS AS BIG-HEARTED AS THEY COME.
HEY! GET IN! I'LL DRIVE YOU TO THE METRO!
THANKS A LOT, J.L.!
THAT'LL BE 6 BUCKS, SUGAR.
HERE.
!
JOHN LENNON IS DEAD!
YEAH RIGHT. WHAT'D HE DO? FALL ASLEEP ON THE FURNACE?
NO!! LOOK! IT'S ON TV!
... KILLED BY FIVE SHOTS FROM CLOSE RANGE YESTERDAY IN FRONT OF THE DAKOTA BUILDING WHERE HE LIVED WITH HIS WIFE, YOKO ONO. HIS KILLER, MARK CHAPMAN...
IT CAN'T BE...

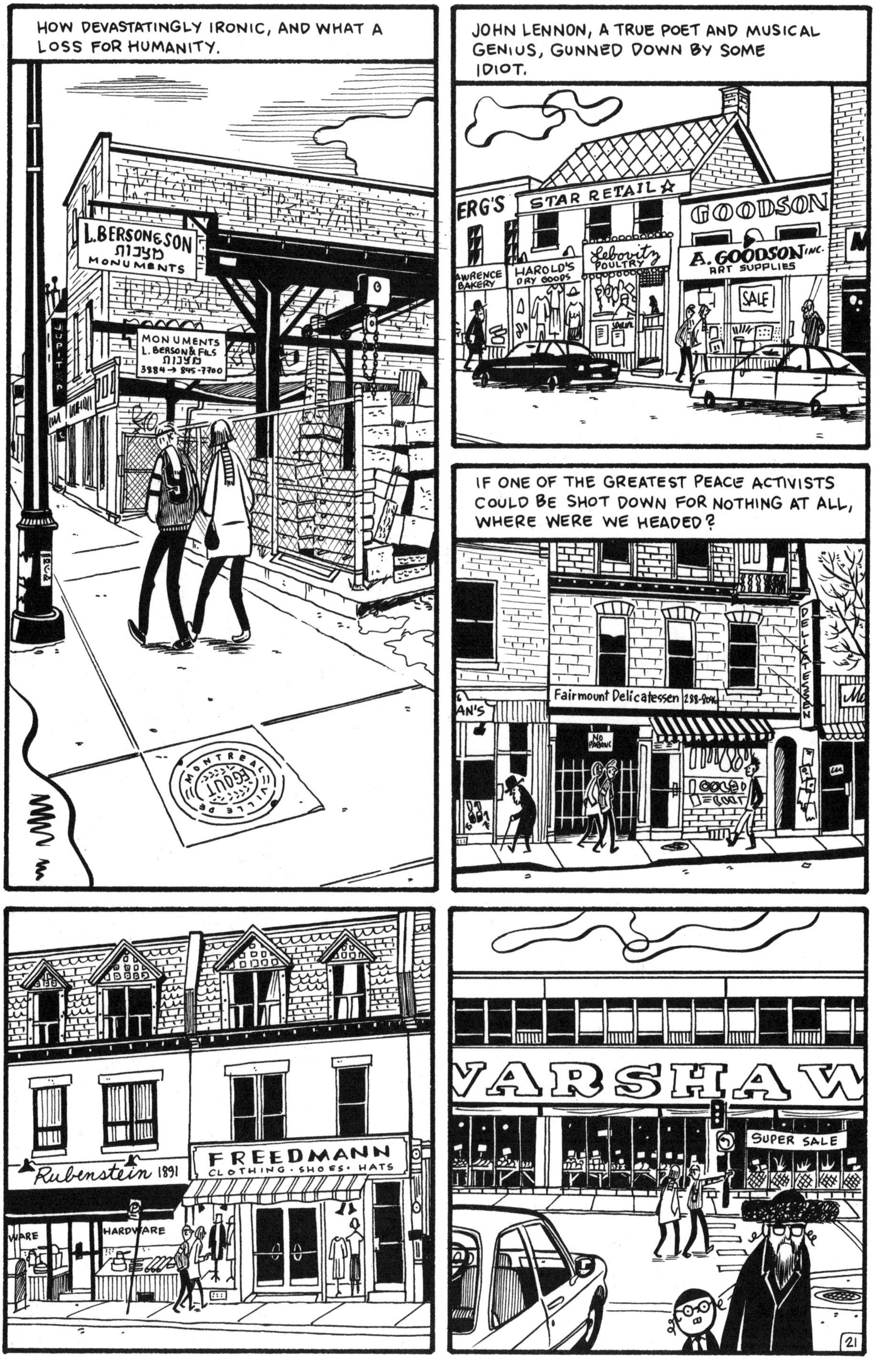
HOW DEVASTATINGLY IRONIC, AND WHAT A LOSS FOR HUMANITY.
L.BERSON&SON
מצבות
MONUMENTS
MONUMENTS
L. BERSON & FILS
מצבות
JOHN LENNON, A TRUE POET AND MUSICAL GENIUS, GUNNED DOWN BY SOME IDIOT.
STAR RETAIL
GOODSON
A. GOODSON INC.
ART SUPPLIES
SALE
HAROLD'S
DRY GOODS
Lebovitz
POULTRY
IF ONE OF THE GREATEST PEACE ACTIVISTS COULD BE SHOT DOWN FOR NOTHING AT ALL, WHERE WERE WE HEADED?
Fairmount Delicatessen
DELICATESSEN
Rubenstein 1891
FREEDMANN
CLOTHING · SHOES · HATS
HARDWARE
VARSHAW
SUPER SALE

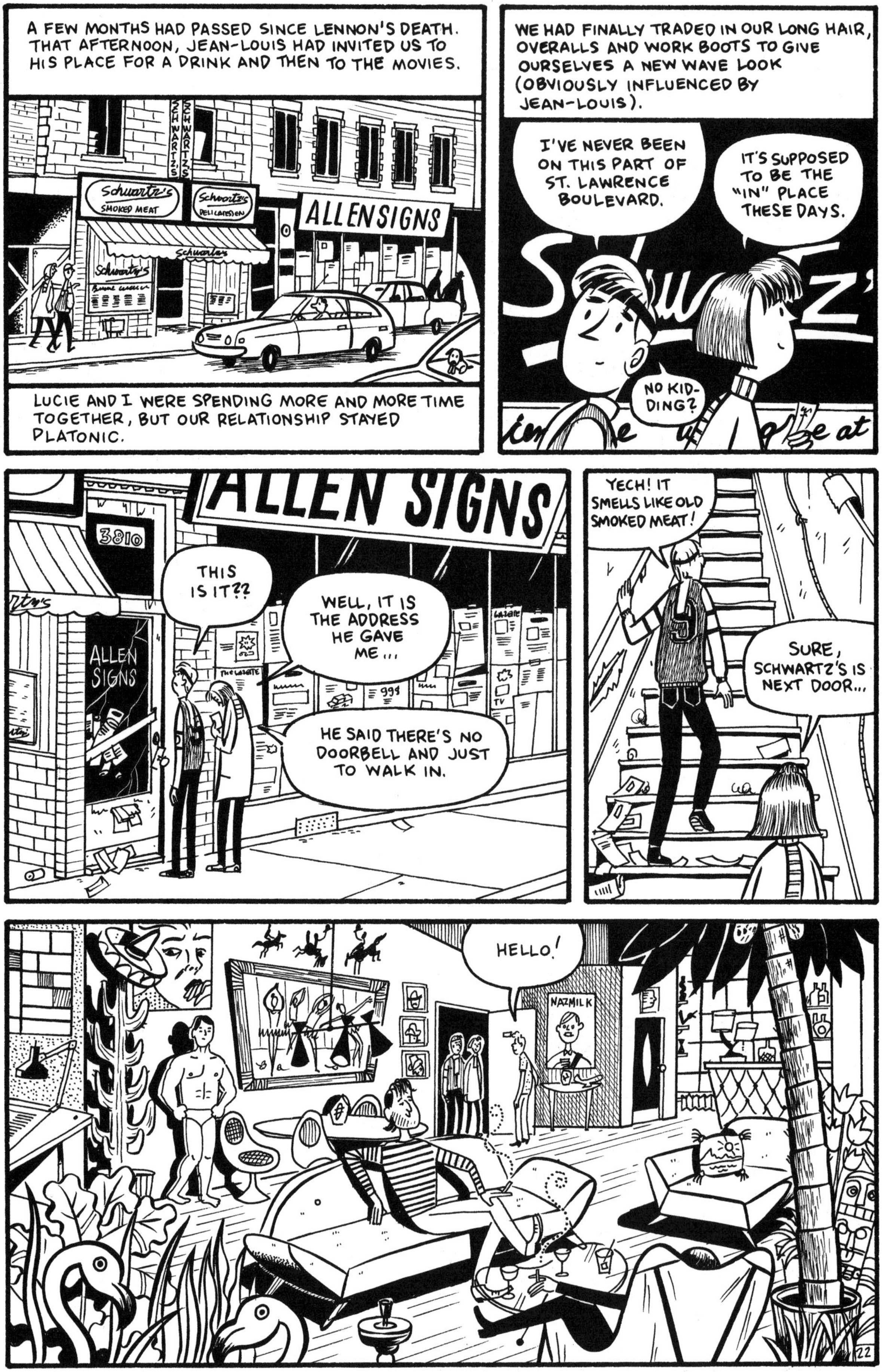
A FEW MONTHS HAD PASSED SINCE LENNON'S DEATH. THAT AFTERNOON, JEAN-LOUIS HAD INVITED US TO HIS PLACE FOR A DRINK AND THEN TO THE MOVIES.
SCHWARTZ'S
Schwartz's SMOKED MEAT
Schwartz's DELICATESSEN
ALLENSIGNS
LUCIE AND I WERE SPENDING MORE AND MORE TIME TOGETHER, BUT OUR RELATIONSHIP STAYED PLATONIC.
WE HAD FINALLY TRADED IN OUR LONG HAIR, OVERALLS AND WORK BOOTS TO GIVE OURSELVES A NEW WAVE LOOK (OBVIOUSLY INFLUENCED BY JEAN-LOUIS).
I'VE NEVER BEEN ON THIS PART OF ST. LAWRENCE BOULEVARD.
IT'S SUPPOSED TO BE THE "IN" PLACE THESE DAYS.
NO KIDDING?
ALLEN SIGNS
3810
ALLEN SIGNS
THIS IS IT??
WELL, IT IS THE ADDRESS HE GAVE ME...
HE SAID THERE'S NO DOORBELL AND JUST TO WALK IN.
YECH! IT SMELLS LIKE OLD SMOKED MEAT!
SURE, SCHWARTZ'S IS NEXT DOOR...
HELLO!
NAZMILK

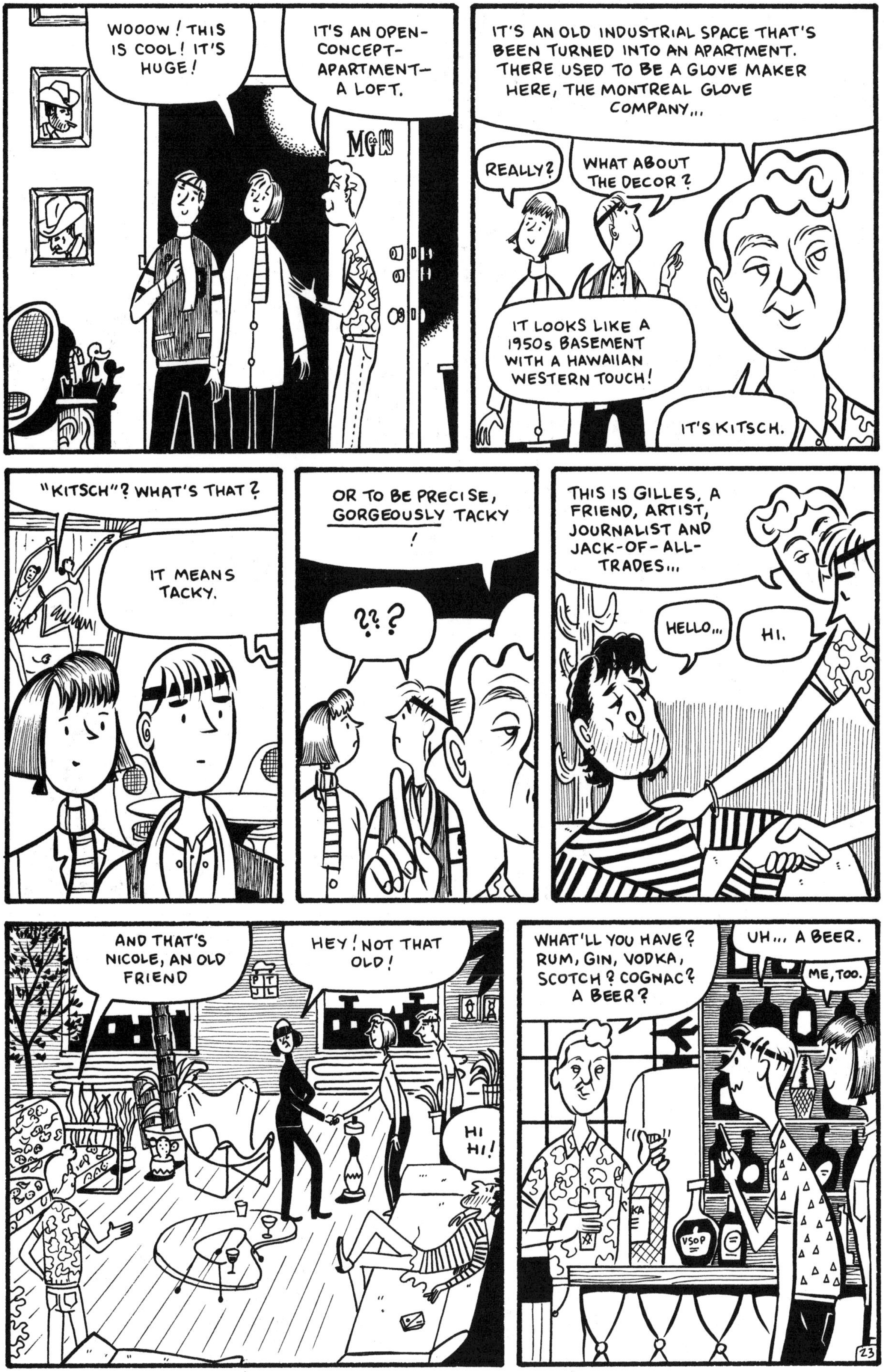
WOOOW! THIS IS COOL! IT'S HUGE!
IT'S AN OPEN-CONCEPT-APARTMENT— A LOFT.
MG CO.
IT'S AN OLD INDUSTRIAL SPACE THAT'S BEEN TURNED INTO AN APARTMENT. THERE USED TO BE A GLOVE MAKER HERE, THE MONTREAL GLOVE COMPANY...
REALLY?
WHAT ABOUT THE DECOR?
IT LOOKS LIKE A 1950s BASEMENT WITH A HAWAIIAN WESTERN TOUCH!
IT'S KITSCH.
"KITSCH"? WHAT'S THAT?
IT MEANS TACKY.
OR TO BE PRECISE, GORGEOUSLY TACKY!
???
THIS IS GILLES, A FRIEND, ARTIST, JOURNALIST AND JACK-OF-ALL-TRADES...
HELLO...
HI.
AND THAT'S NICOLE, AN OLD FRIEND
HEY! NOT THAT OLD!
HI HI!
WHAT'LL YOU HAVE? RUM, GIN, VODKA, SCOTCH? COGNAC? A BEER?
UH... A BEER.
ME, TOO.
VSOP

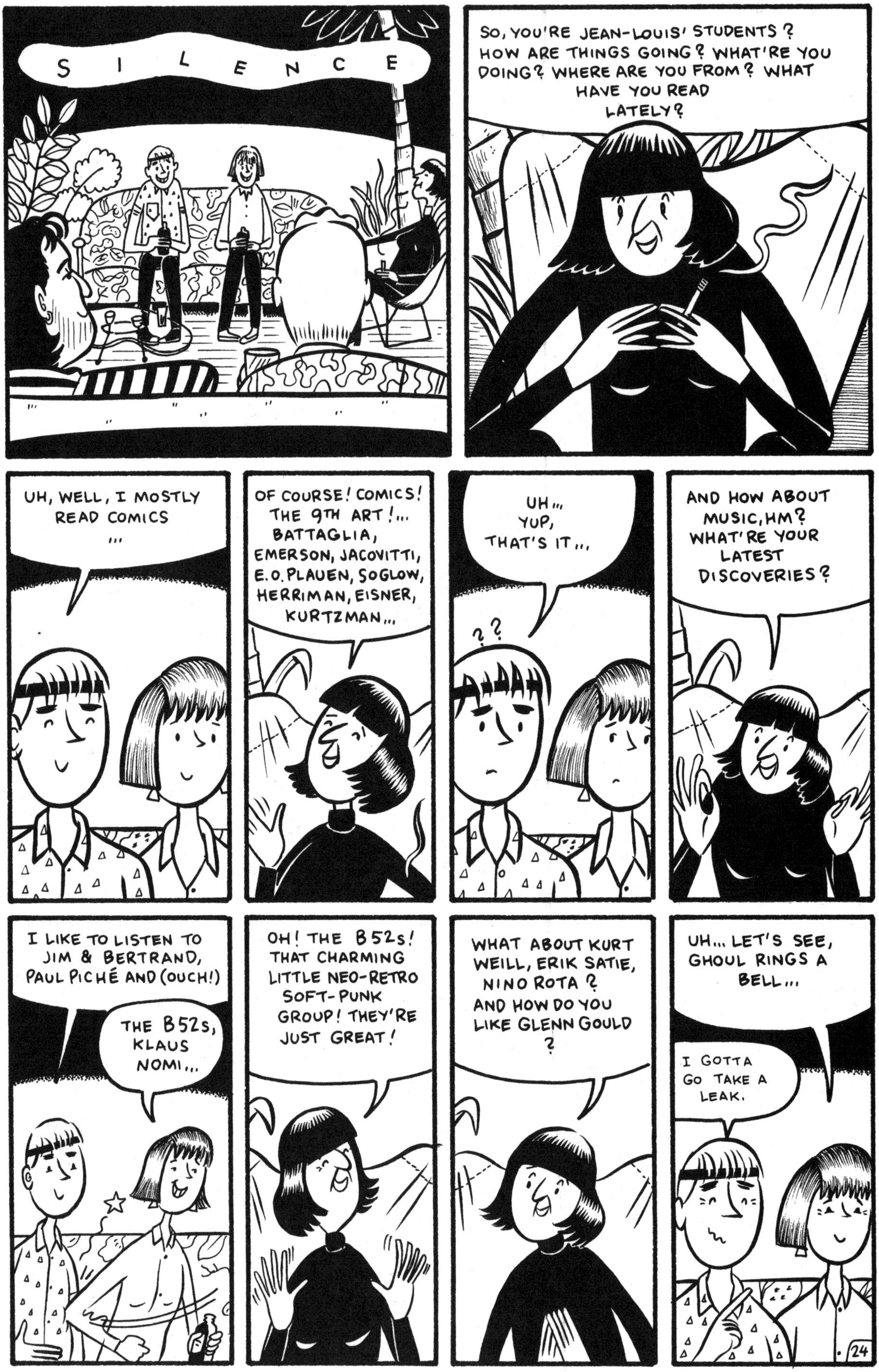
SILENCE
SO, YOU'RE JEAN-LOUIS' STUDENTS? HOW ARE THINGS GOING? WHAT'RE YOU DOING? WHERE ARE YOU FROM? WHAT HAVE YOU READ LATELY?
UH, WELL, I MOSTLY READ COMICS ...
OF COURSE! COMICS! THE 9TH ART!... BATTAGLIA, EMERSON, JACOVITTI, E.O. PLAUEN, SOGLOW, HERRIMAN, EISNER, KURTZMAN...
UH... YUP, THAT'S IT...
AND HOW ABOUT MUSIC, HM? WHAT'RE YOUR LATEST DISCOVERIES?
I LIKE TO LISTEN TO JIM & BERTRAND, PAUL PICHÉ AND (OUCH!)
THE B52s, KLAUS NOMI...
OH! THE B52s! THAT CHARMING LITTLE NEO-RETRO SOFT-PUNK GROUP! THEY'RE JUST GREAT!
WHAT ABOUT KURT WEILL, ERIK SATIE, NINO ROTA? AND HOW DO YOU LIKE GLENN GOULD?
UH... LET'S SEE, GHOUL RINGS A BELL...
I GOTTA GO TAKE A LEAK.
24

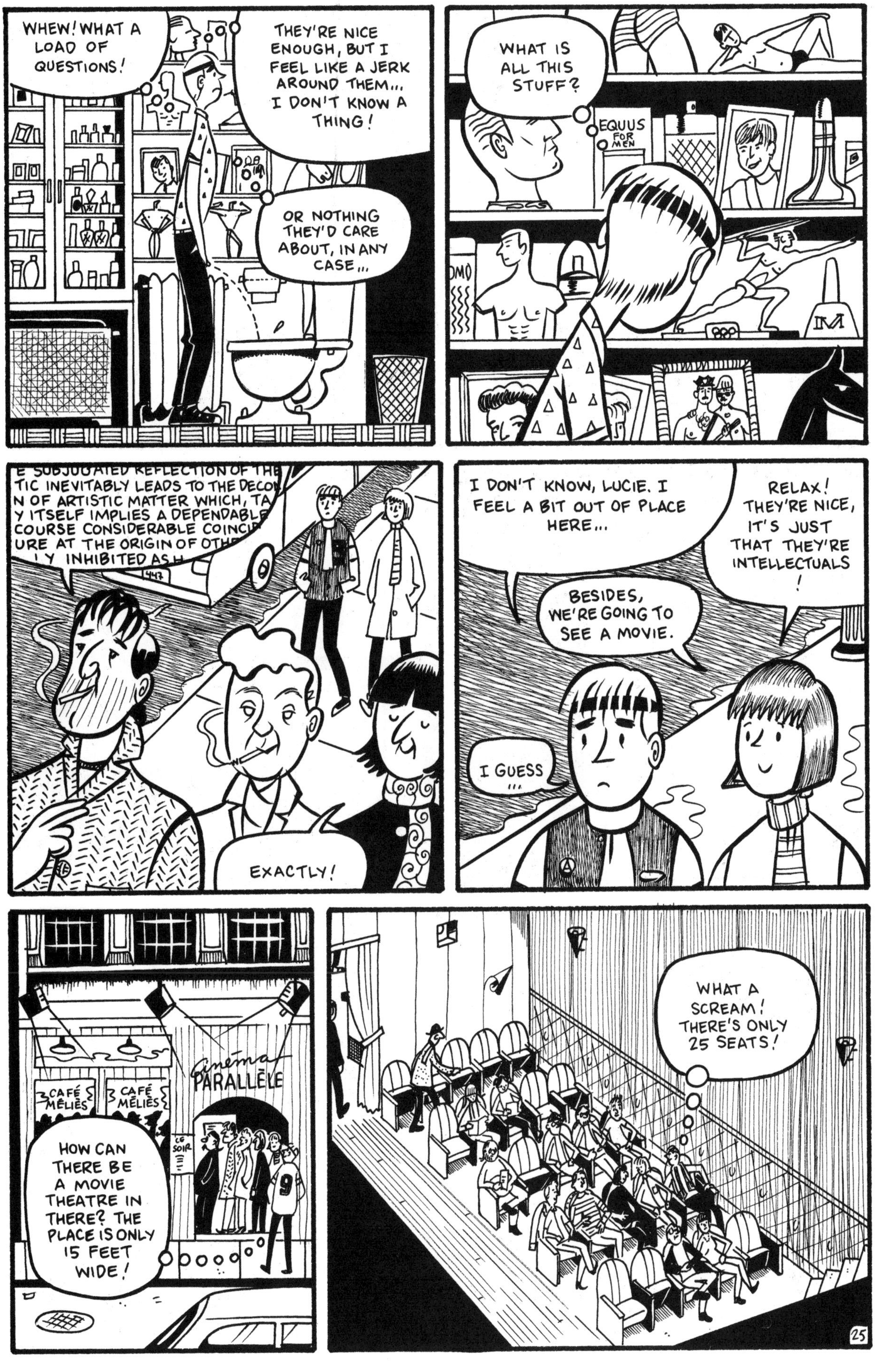
WHEW! WHAT A LOAD OF QUESTIONS!
THEY'RE NICE ENOUGH, BUT I FEEL LIKE A JERK AROUND THEM... I DON'T KNOW A THING!
OR NOTHING THEY'D CARE ABOUT, IN ANY CASE...
WHAT IS ALL THIS STUFF?
EQUUS FOR MEN
TIC INEVITABLY LEADS TO THE DECON
N OF ARTISTIC MATTER WHICH, TA
Y ITSELF IMPLIES A DEPENDABLE
COURSE CONSIDERABLE COINCID
URE AT THE ORIGIN OF OTH
EXACTLY!
I DON'T KNOW, LUCIE. I FEEL A BIT OUT OF PLACE HERE...
RELAX! THEY'RE NICE, IT'S JUST THAT THEY'RE INTELLECTUALS!
BESIDES, WE'RE GOING TO SEE A MOVIE.
I GUESS...
CAFÉ MÉLIÈS
CAFÉ MÉLIÈS
Cinéma PARALLÈLE
CE SOIR
HOW CAN THERE BE A MOVIE THEATRE IN THERE? THE PLACE IS ONLY 15 FEET WIDE!
WHAT A SCREAM! THERE'S ONLY 25 SEATS!

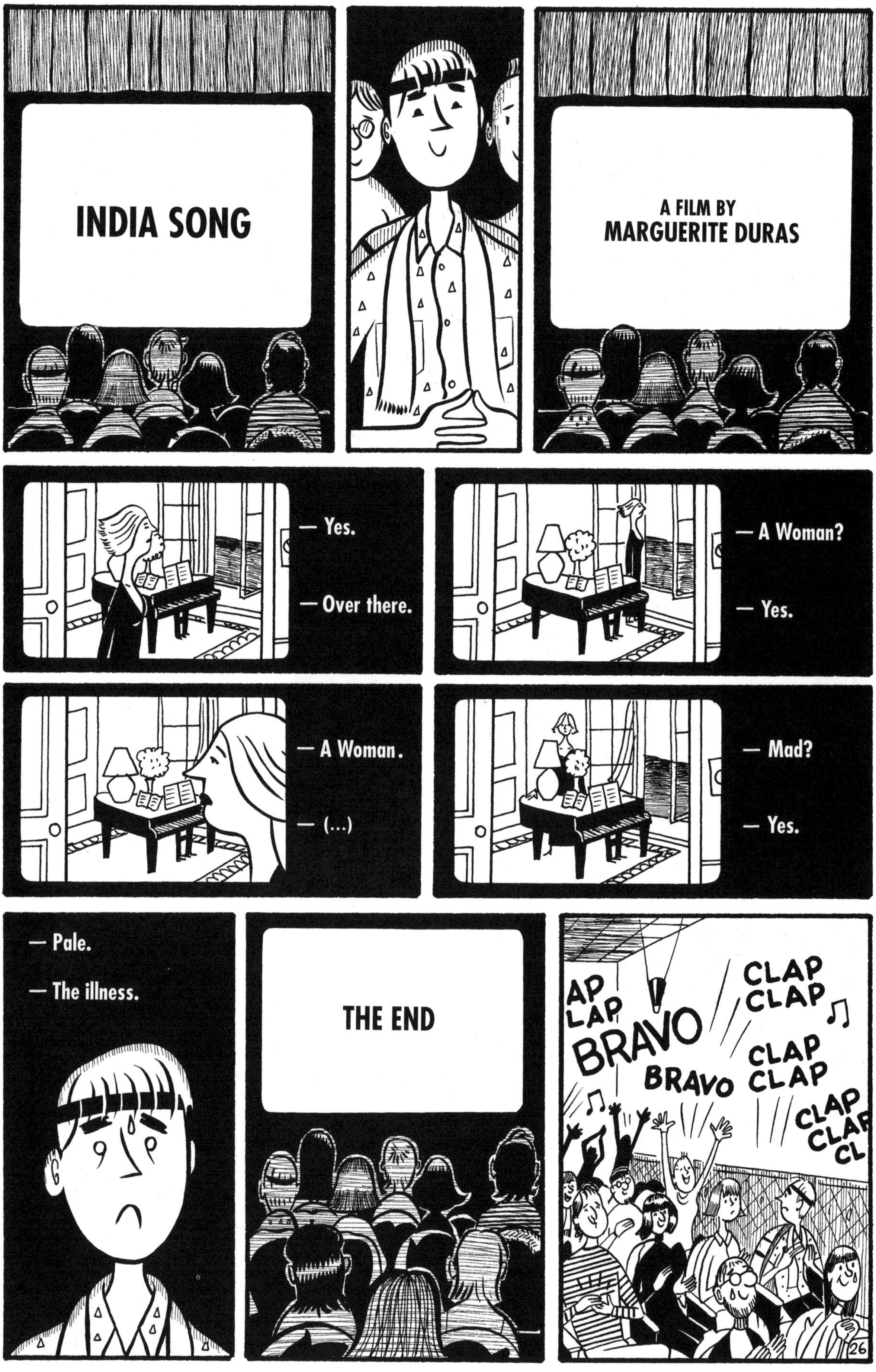
INDIA SONG
A FILM BY
MARGUERITE DURAS
— Yes.
— Over there.
— A Woman?
— Yes.
— A Woman.
— (...)
— Mad?
— Yes.
— Pale.
— The illness.
THE END
AP
LAP
BRAVO
CLAP
CLAP
CLAP
CLAP
BRAVO
CLAP
26

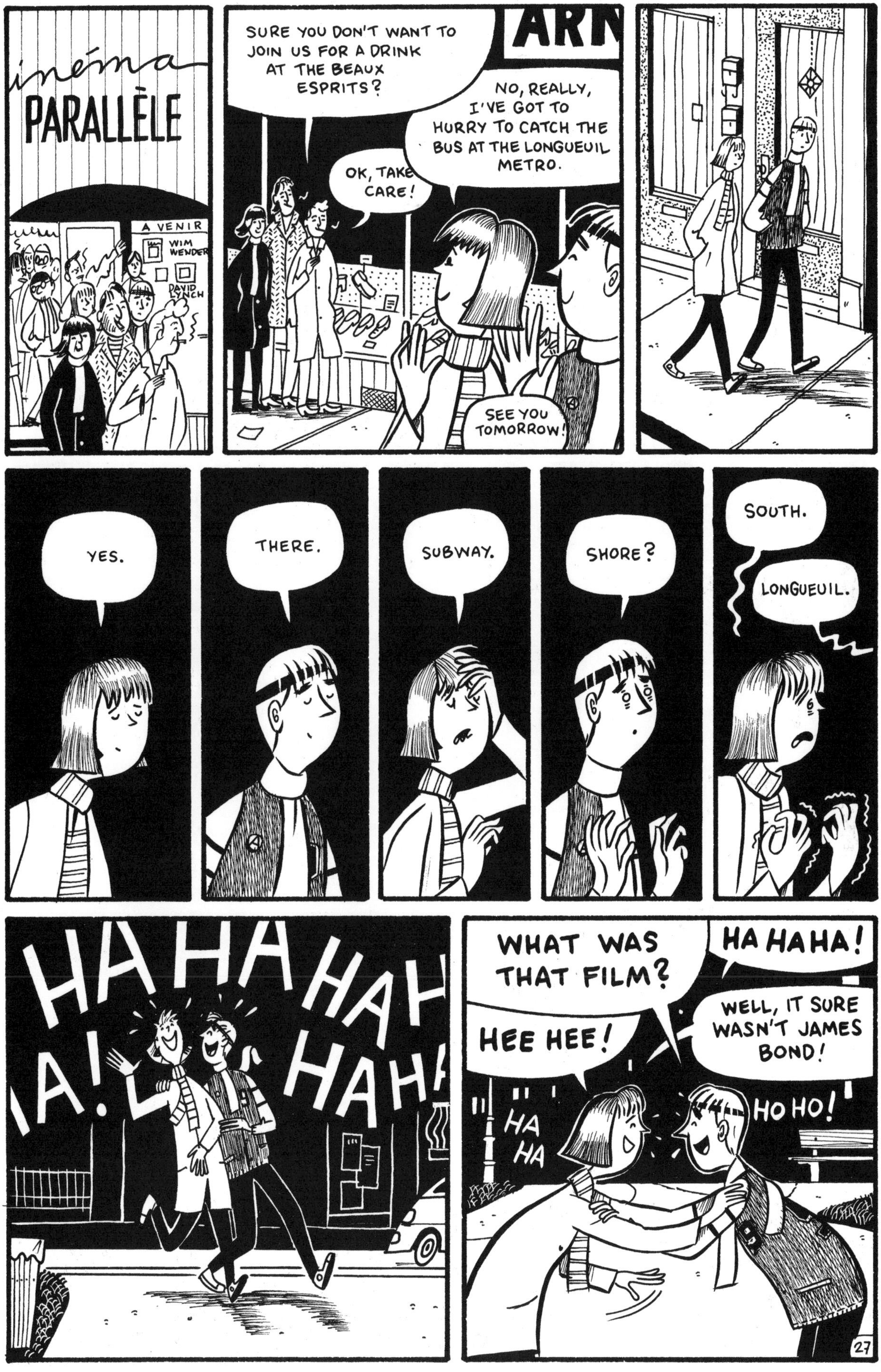
inéma
PARALLÈLE
A VENIR
WIM WENDER
DAVID LYNCH
ARN
SURE YOU DON'T WANT TO JOIN US FOR A DRINK AT THE BEAUX ESPRITS?
NO, REALLY, I'VE GOT TO HURRY TO CATCH THE BUS AT THE LONGUEUIL METRO.
OK, TAKE CARE!
SEE YOU TOMORROW!
YES.
THERE.
SUBWAY.
SHORE?
SOUTH.
LONGUEUIL.
HAHAHAHAH
A!
HAHAH
WHAT WAS THAT FILM?
HA HAHA!
HEE HEE!
WELL, IT SURE WASN'T JAMES BOND!
HA HA
HO HO!

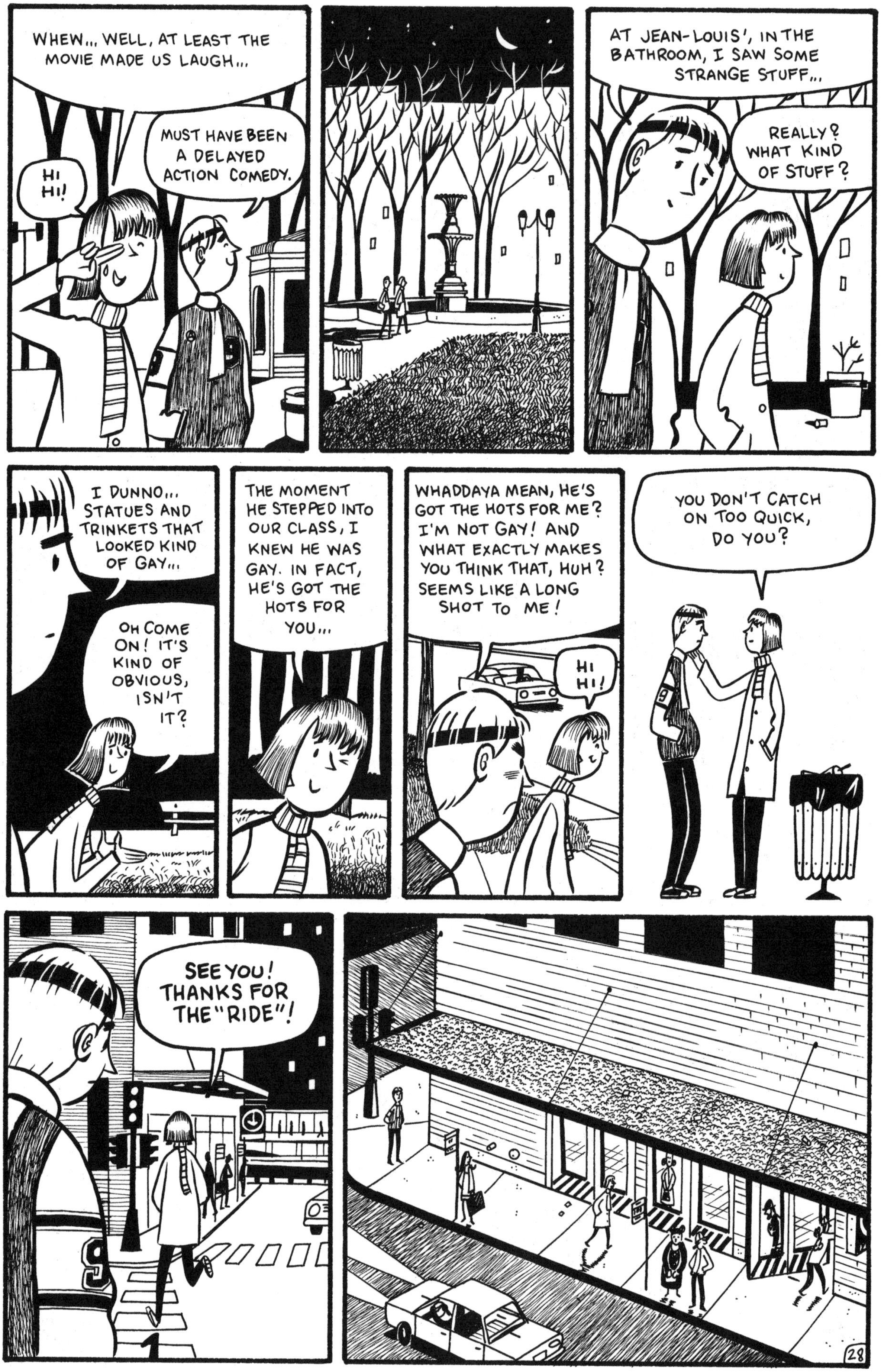
WHEW... WELL, AT LEAST THE MOVIE MADE US LAUGH...
HI HI!
MUST HAVE BEEN A DELAYED ACTION COMEDY.
AT JEAN-LOUIS', IN THE BATHROOM, I SAW SOME STRANGE STUFF...
REALLY? WHAT KIND OF STUFF?
I DUNNO... STATUES AND TRINKETS THAT LOOKED KIND OF GAY...
OH COME ON! IT'S KIND OF OBVIOUS, ISN'T IT?
THE MOMENT HE STEPPED INTO OUR CLASS, I KNEW HE WAS GAY. IN FACT, HE'S GOT THE HOTS FOR YOU...
WHADDAYA MEAN, HE'S GOT THE HOTS FOR ME? I'M NOT GAY! AND WHAT EXACTLY MAKES YOU THINK THAT, HUH? SEEMS LIKE A LONG SHOT TO ME!
HI HI!
YOU DON'T CATCH ON TOO QUICK, DO YOU?
SEE YOU! THANKS FOR THE "RIDE"!
28

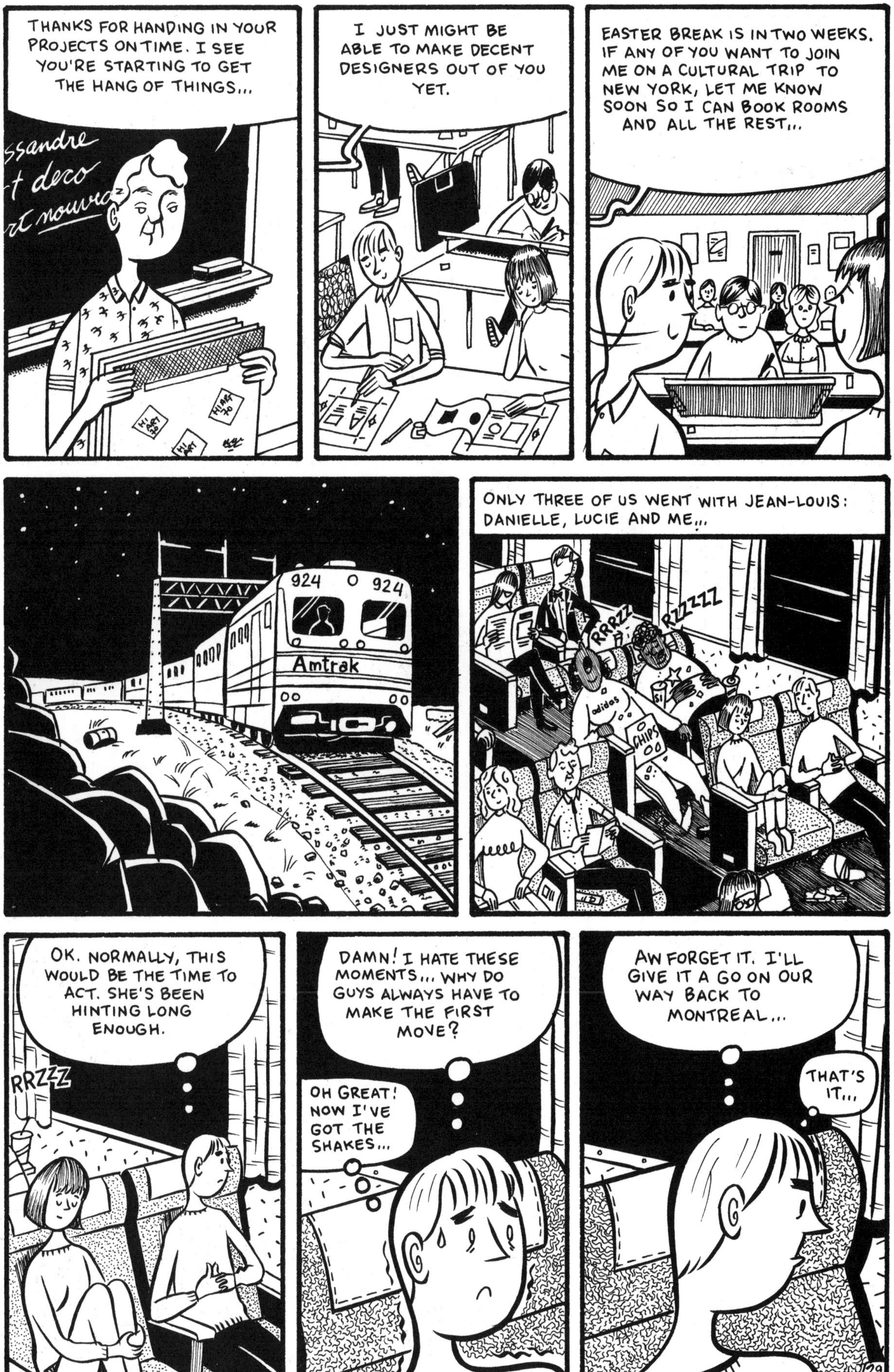
THANKS FOR HANDING IN YOUR PROJECTS ON TIME. I SEE YOU'RE STARTING TO GET THE HANG OF THINGS...
I JUST MIGHT BE ABLE TO MAKE DECENT DESIGNERS OUT OF YOU YET.
EASTER BREAK IS IN TWO WEEKS. IF ANY OF YOU WANT TO JOIN ME ON A CULTURAL TRIP TO NEW YORK, LET ME KNOW SOON SO I CAN BOOK ROOMS AND ALL THE REST...
924 924
Amtrak
ONLY THREE OF US WENT WITH JEAN-LOUIS: DANIELLE, LUCIE AND ME...
RRRZZ
RZZZZZ
adidas
CHIPS
OK. NORMALLY, THIS WOULD BE THE TIME TO ACT. SHE'S BEEN HINTING LONG ENOUGH.
RRZZZ
DAMN! I HATE THESE MOMENTS... WHY DO GUYS ALWAYS HAVE TO MAKE THE FIRST MOVE?
OH GREAT! NOW I'VE GOT THE SHAKES...
AW FORGET IT. I'LL GIVE IT A GO ON OUR WAY BACK TO MONTREAL...
THAT'S IT...

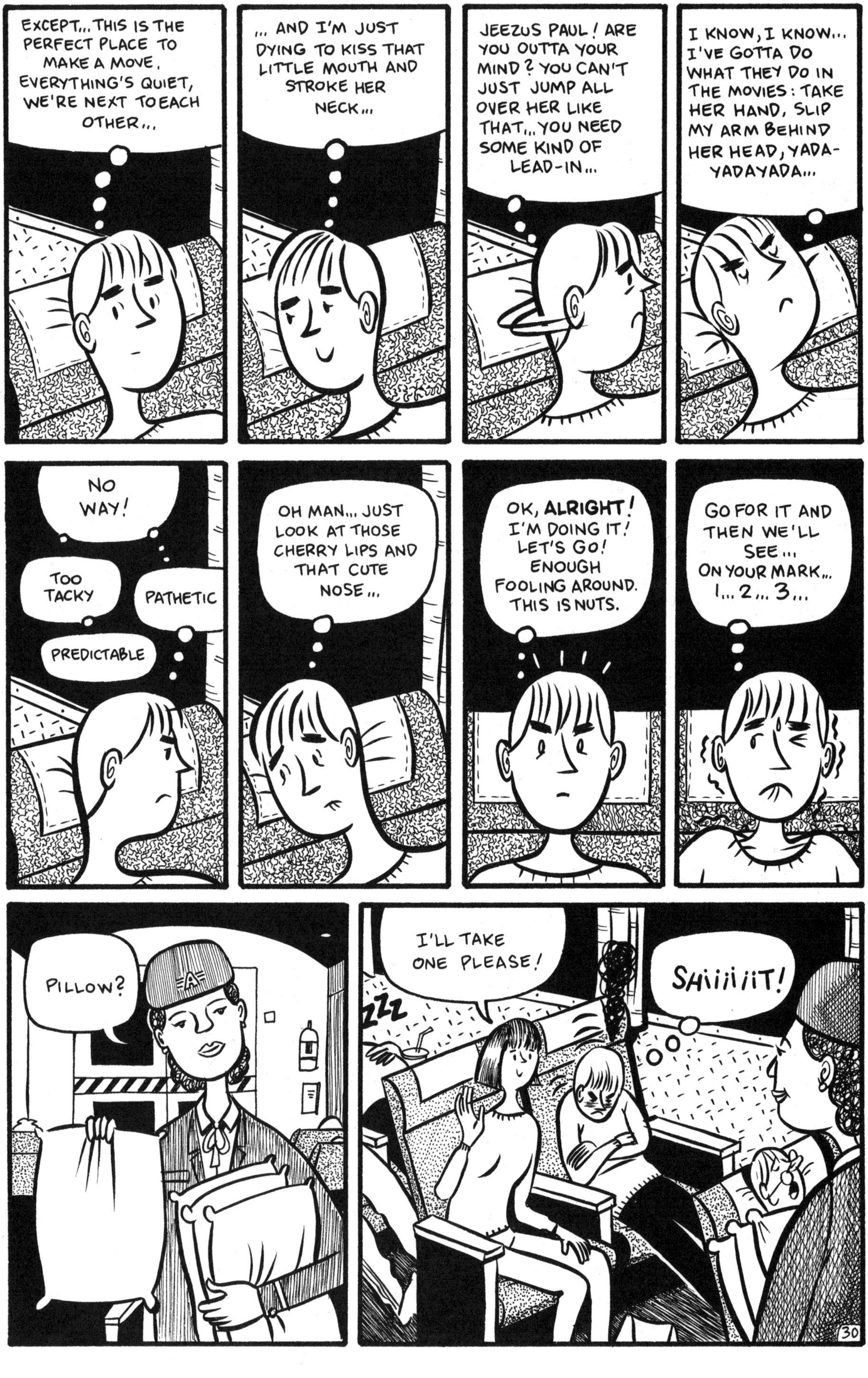
EXCEPT... THIS IS THE PERFECT PLACE TO MAKE A MOVE. EVERYTHING'S QUIET, WE'RE NEXT TO EACH OTHER...
... AND I'M JUST DYING TO KISS THAT LITTLE MOUTH AND STROKE HER NECK...
JEEZUS PAUL! ARE YOU OUTTA YOUR MIND? YOU CAN'T JUST JUMP ALL OVER HER LIKE THAT... YOU NEED SOME KIND OF LEAD-IN...
I KNOW, I KNOW... I'VE GOTTA DO WHAT THEY DO IN THE MOVIES: TAKE HER HAND, SLIP MY ARM BEHIND HER HEAD, YADA-YADAYADA...
NO WAY!
TOO TACKY
PATHETIC
PREDICTABLE
OH MAN... JUST LOOK AT THOSE CHERRY LIPS AND THAT CUTE NOSE...
OK, **ALRIGHT**! I'M DOING IT! LET'S GO! ENOUGH FOOLING AROUND. THIS IS NUTS.
GO FOR IT AND THEN WE'LL SEE... ON YOUR MARK... 1... 2... 3...
PILLOW?
I'LL TAKE ONE PLEASE!
ZZZ
SHIIIIIIT!

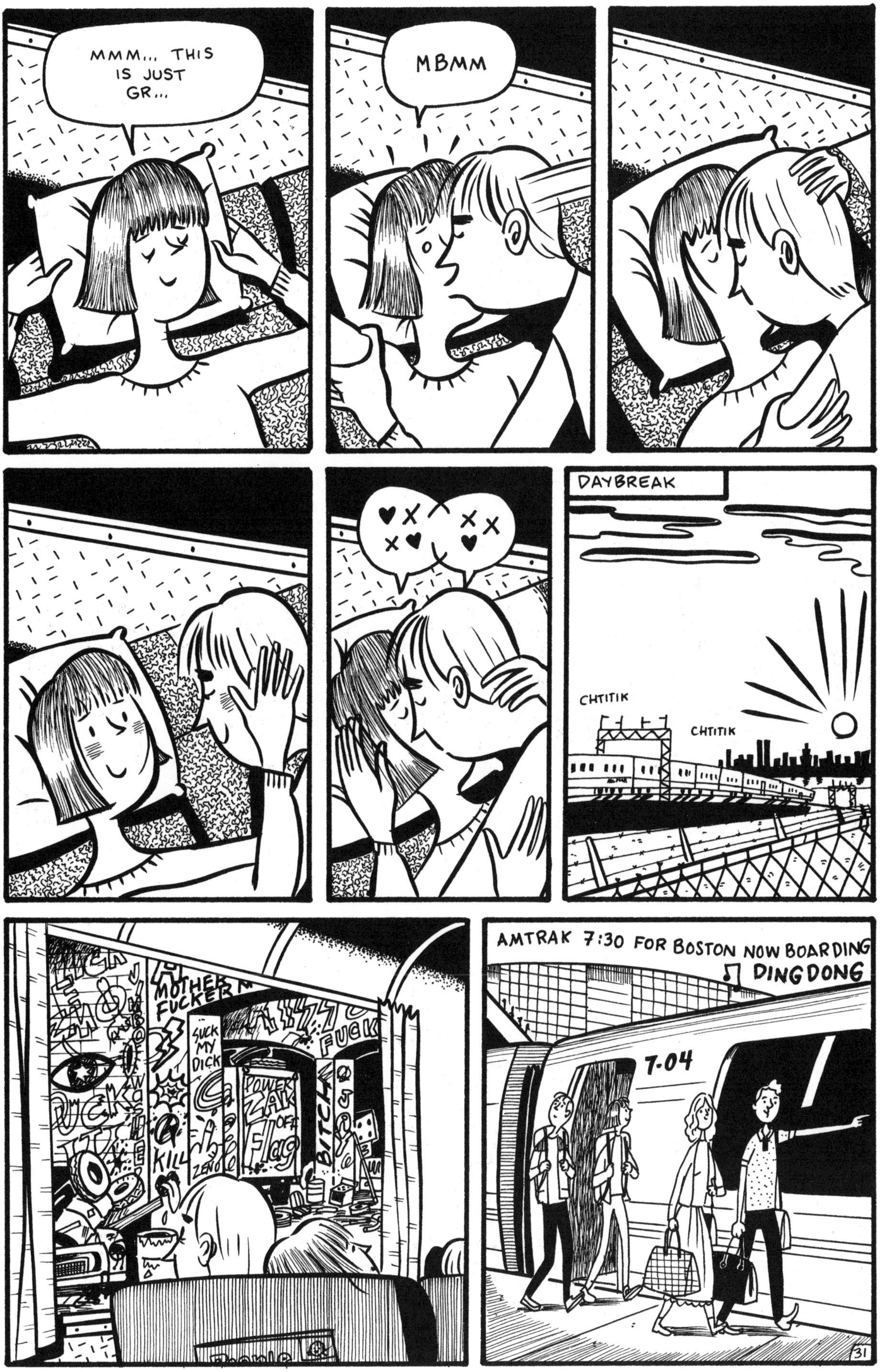
MMM... THIS IS JUST GR...
MBMM
DAYBREAK
CHTITIK
CHTITIK
MOTHER FUCKER
SUCK MY DICK
FUCK
POWER
KILL
BITCH
AMTRAK 7:30 FOR BOSTON NOW BOARDING
DING DONG
7-04

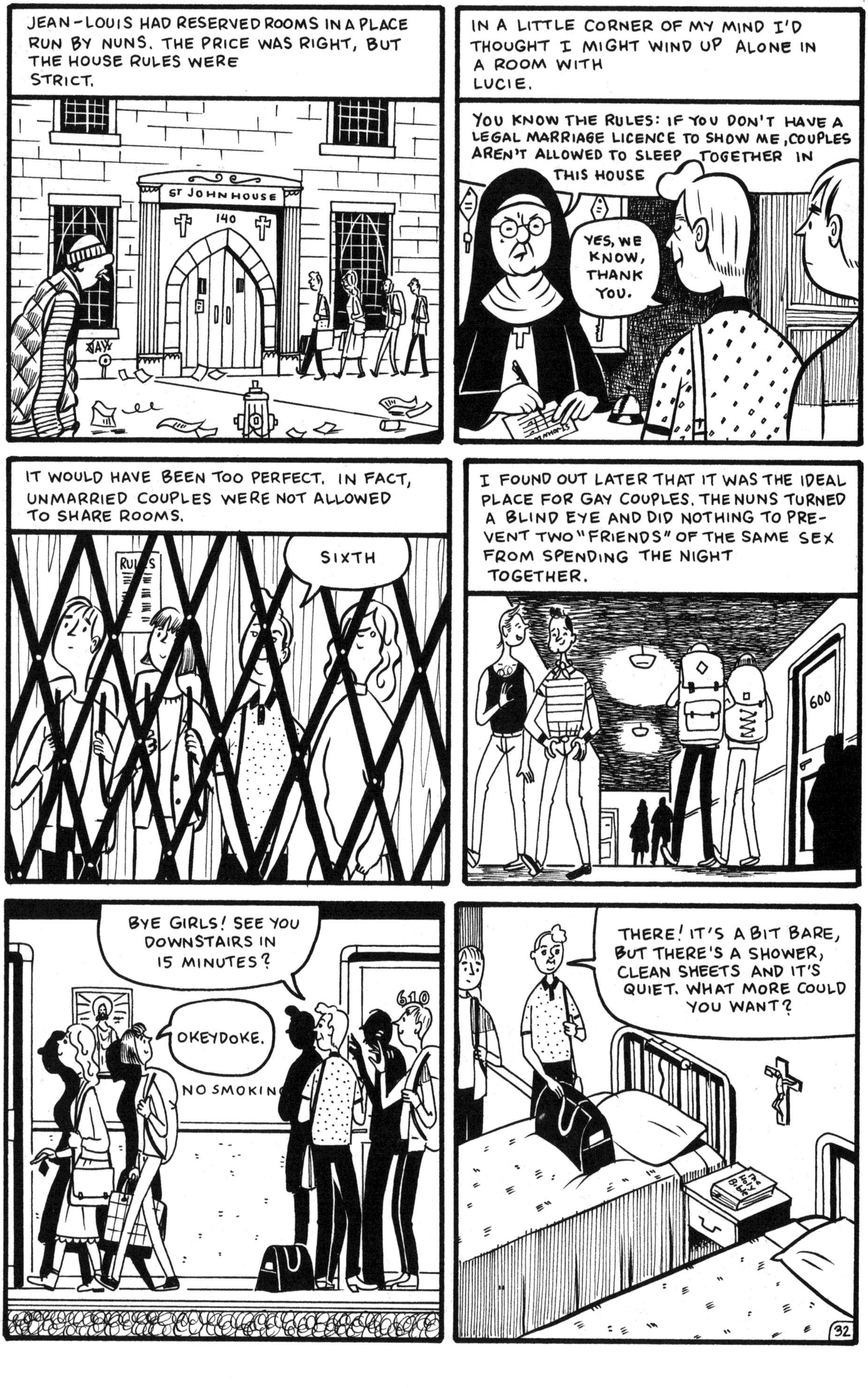

JEAN-LOUIS HAD RESERVED ROOMS IN A PLACE RUN BY NUNS. THE PRICE WAS RIGHT, BUT THE HOUSE RULES WERE STRICT.
ST JOHN HOUSE
140
IN A LITTLE CORNER OF MY MIND I'D THOUGHT I MIGHT WIND UP ALONE IN A ROOM WITH LUCIE.
YOU KNOW THE RULES: IF YOU DON'T HAVE A LEGAL MARRIAGE LICENCE TO SHOW ME, COUPLES AREN'T ALLOWED TO SLEEP TOGETHER IN THIS HOUSE
YES, WE KNOW, THANK YOU.
IT WOULD HAVE BEEN TOO PERFECT. IN FACT, UNMARRIED COUPLES WERE NOT ALLOWED TO SHARE ROOMS.
SIXTH
I FOUND OUT LATER THAT IT WAS THE IDEAL PLACE FOR GAY COUPLES. THE NUNS TURNED A BLIND EYE AND DID NOTHING TO PREVENT TWO "FRIENDS" OF THE SAME SEX FROM SPENDING THE NIGHT TOGETHER.
600
BYE GIRLS! SEE YOU DOWNSTAIRS IN 15 MINUTES?
OKEYDOKE.
NO SMOKIN
610
THERE! IT'S A BIT BARE, BUT THERE'S A SHOWER, CLEAN SHEETS AND IT'S QUIET. WHAT MORE COULD YOU WANT?
The Holy Bible

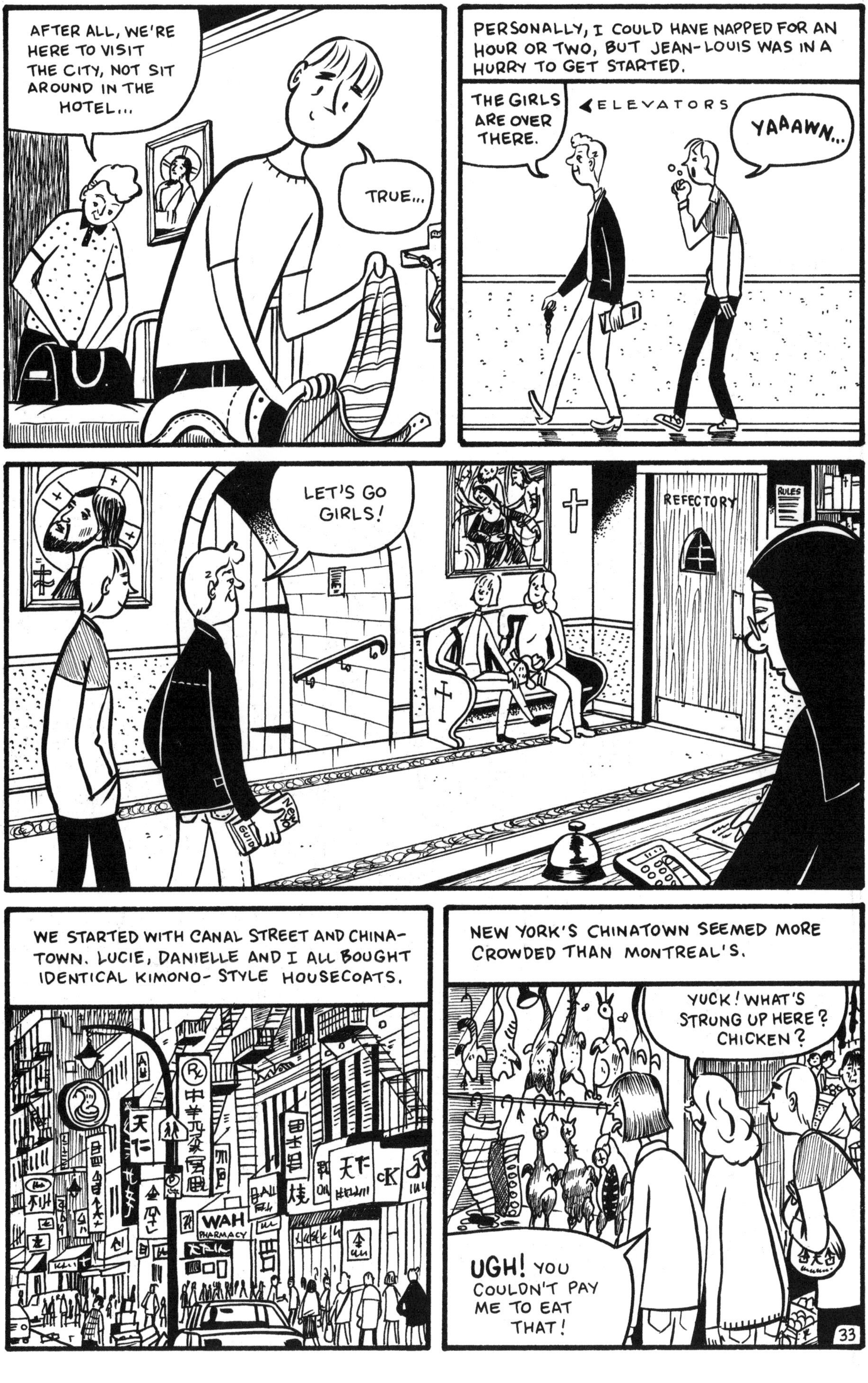
AFTER ALL, WE'RE HERE TO VISIT THE CITY, NOT SIT AROUND IN THE HOTEL...
TRUE...
PERSONALLY, I COULD HAVE NAPPED FOR AN HOUR OR TWO, BUT JEAN-LOUIS WAS IN A HURRY TO GET STARTED.
THE GIRLS ARE OVER THERE.
ELEVATORS
YAAAWN...
LET'S GO GIRLS!
REFECTORY
RULES
WE STARTED WITH CANAL STREET AND CHINA-TOWN. LUCIE, DANIELLE AND I ALL BOUGHT IDENTICAL KIMONO-STYLE HOUSECOATS.
WAH
PHARMACY
NEW YORK'S CHINATOWN SEEMED MORE CROWDED THAN MONTREAL'S.
YUCK! WHAT'S STRUNG UP HERE? CHICKEN?
UGH! YOU COULDN'T PAY ME TO EAT THAT!

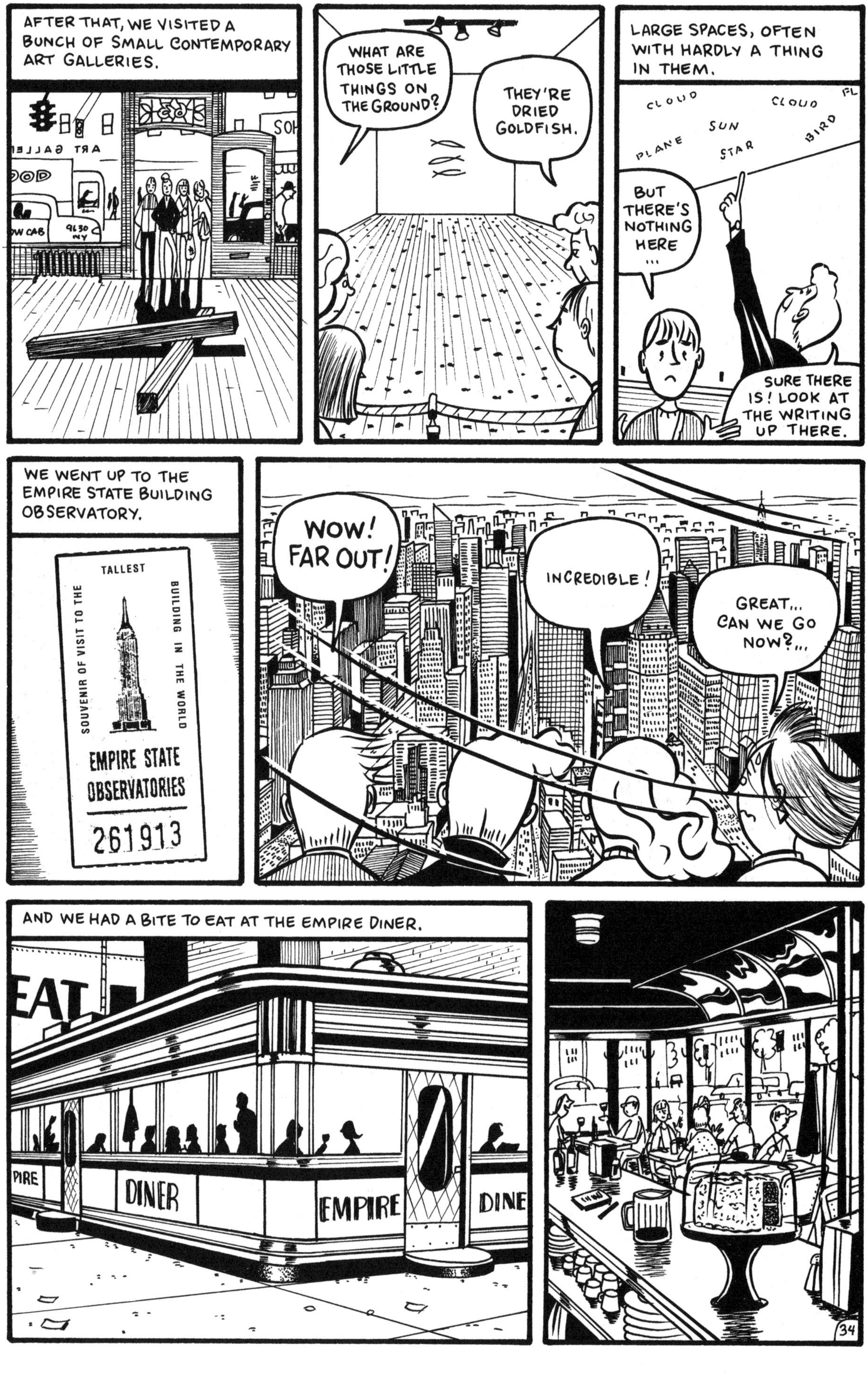

AFTER THAT, WE VISITED A BUNCH OF SMALL CONTEMPORARY ART GALLERIES.
ART GALLE
SOH
9630 NY
WHAT ARE THOSE LITTLE THINGS ON THE GROUND?
THEY'RE DRIED GOLDFISH.
LARGE SPACES, OFTEN WITH HARDLY A THING IN THEM.
CLOUD
CLOUD
SUN
PLANE
STAR
BIRD
BUT THERE'S NOTHING HERE...
SURE THERE IS! LOOK AT THE WRITING UP THERE.
WE WENT UP TO THE EMPIRE STATE BUILDING OBSERVATORY.
SOUVENIR OF VISIT TO THE TALLEST BUILDING IN THE WORLD
EMPIRE STATE OBSERVATORIES
261913
WOW! FAR OUT!
INCREDIBLE!
GREAT... CAN WE GO NOW?...
AND WE HAD A BITE TO EAT AT THE EMPIRE DINER.
EAT
PIRE
DINER
EMPIRE
DINE

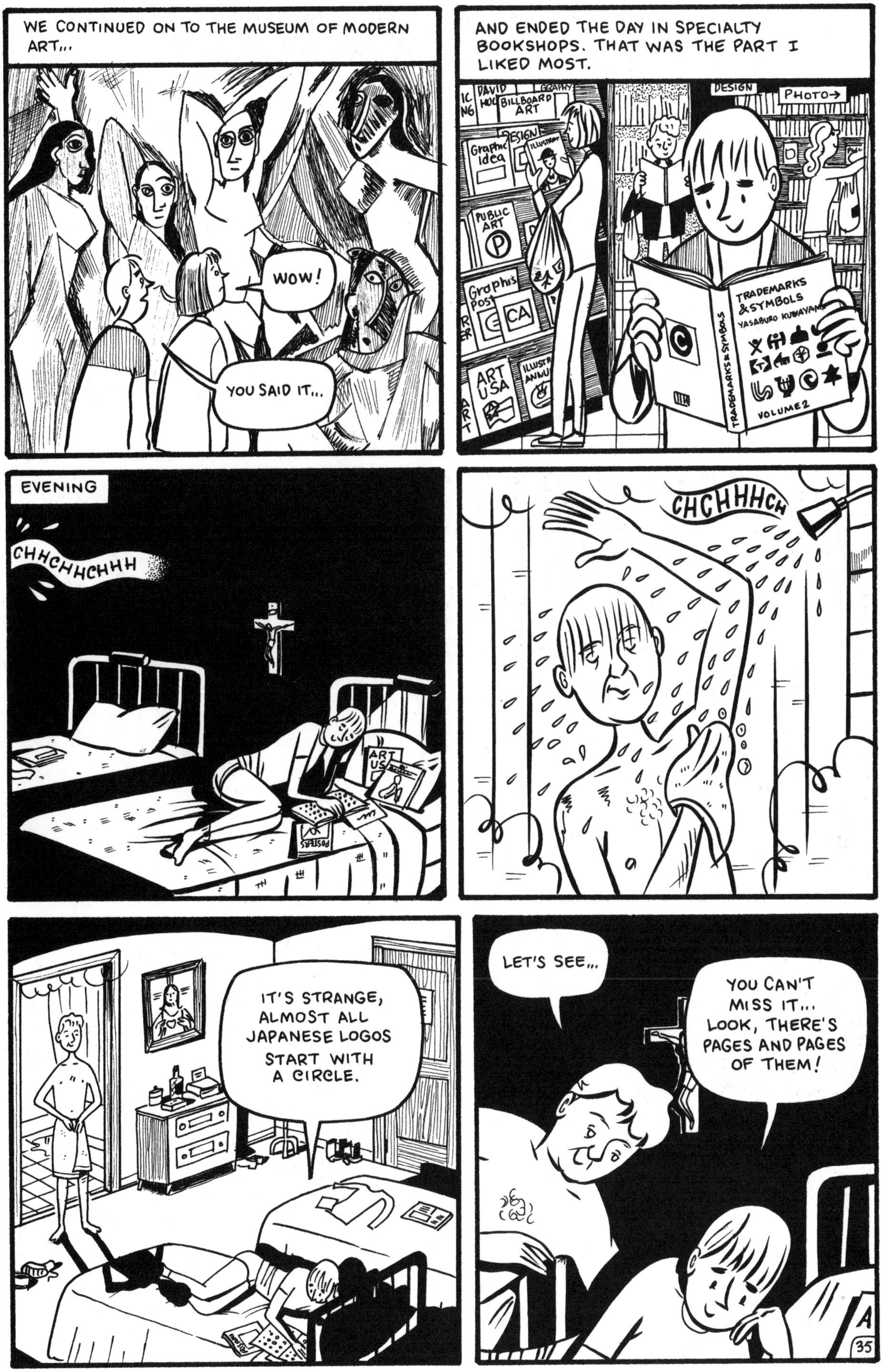
WE CONTINUED ON TO THE MUSEUM OF MODERN ART...
WOW!
YOU SAID IT...
AND ENDED THE DAY IN SPECIALTY BOOKSHOPS. THAT WAS THE PART I LIKED MOST.
DESIGN
PHOTO→
BILLBOARD ART
PUBLIC ART
CA
ART USA
TRADEMARKS & SYMBOLS
YASABURO KUWAYAMA
VOLUME 2
EVENING
CHHCHHCHHH
ART US
POSTERS
CHCHHHCH
IT'S STRANGE, ALMOST ALL JAPANESE LOGOS START WITH A CIRCLE.
LET'S SEE...
YOU CAN'T MISS IT... LOOK, THERE'S PAGES AND PAGES OF THEM!

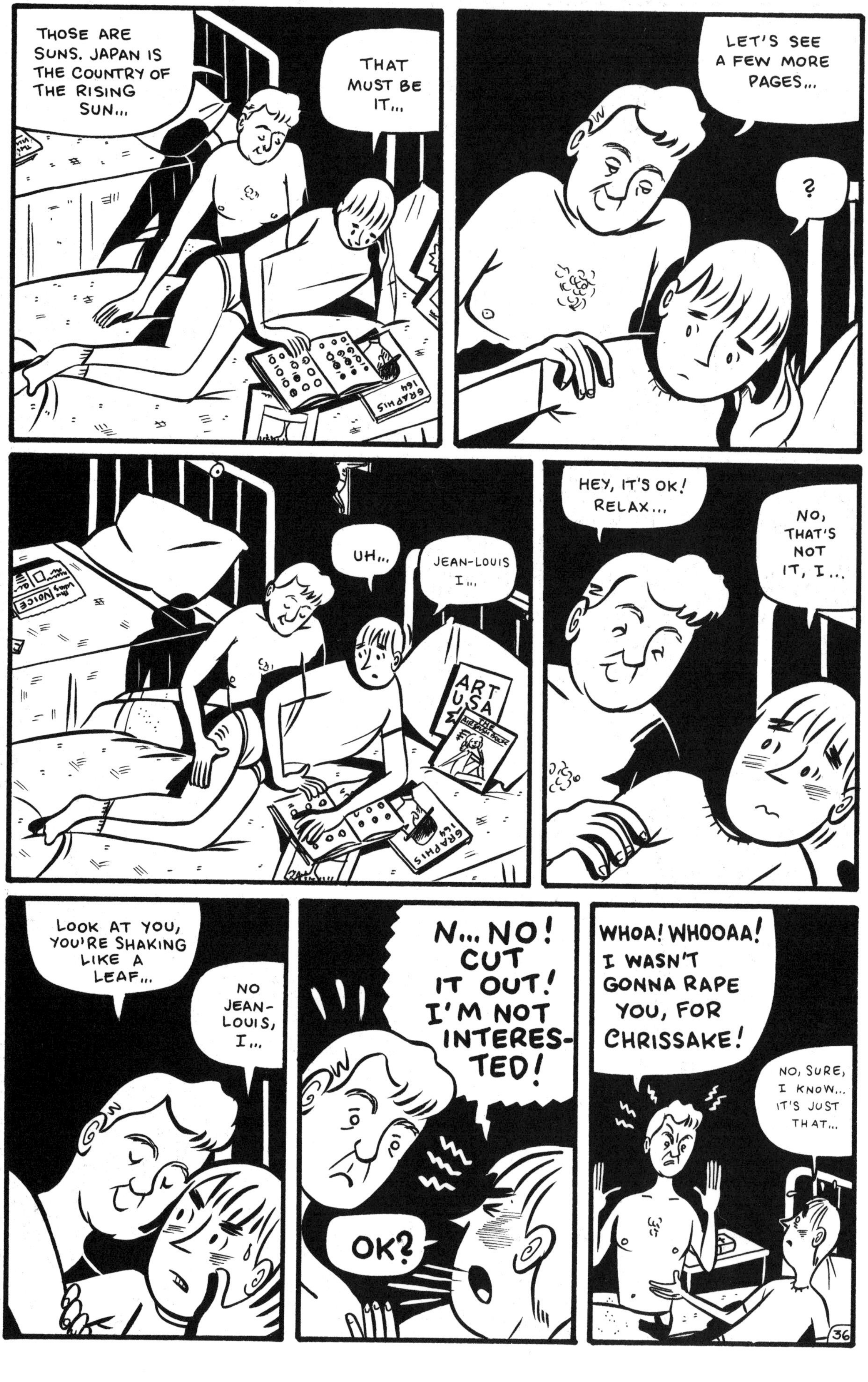
THOSE ARE SUNS. JAPAN IS THE COUNTRY OF THE RISING SUN...
THAT MUST BE IT...
GRAPHIS 164
LET'S SEE A FEW MORE PAGES...
?
UH...
JEAN-LOUIS I...
ART USA
GRAPHIS 164
HEY, IT'S OK! RELAX...
NO, THAT'S NOT IT, I...
LOOK AT YOU, YOU'RE SHAKING LIKE A LEAF...
NO JEAN-LOUIS, I...
N... NO! CUT IT OUT! I'M NOT INTERESTED!
OK?
WHOA! WHOOAA! I WASN'T GONNA RAPE YOU, FOR CHRISSAKE!
NO, SURE, I KNOW... IT'S JUST THAT...

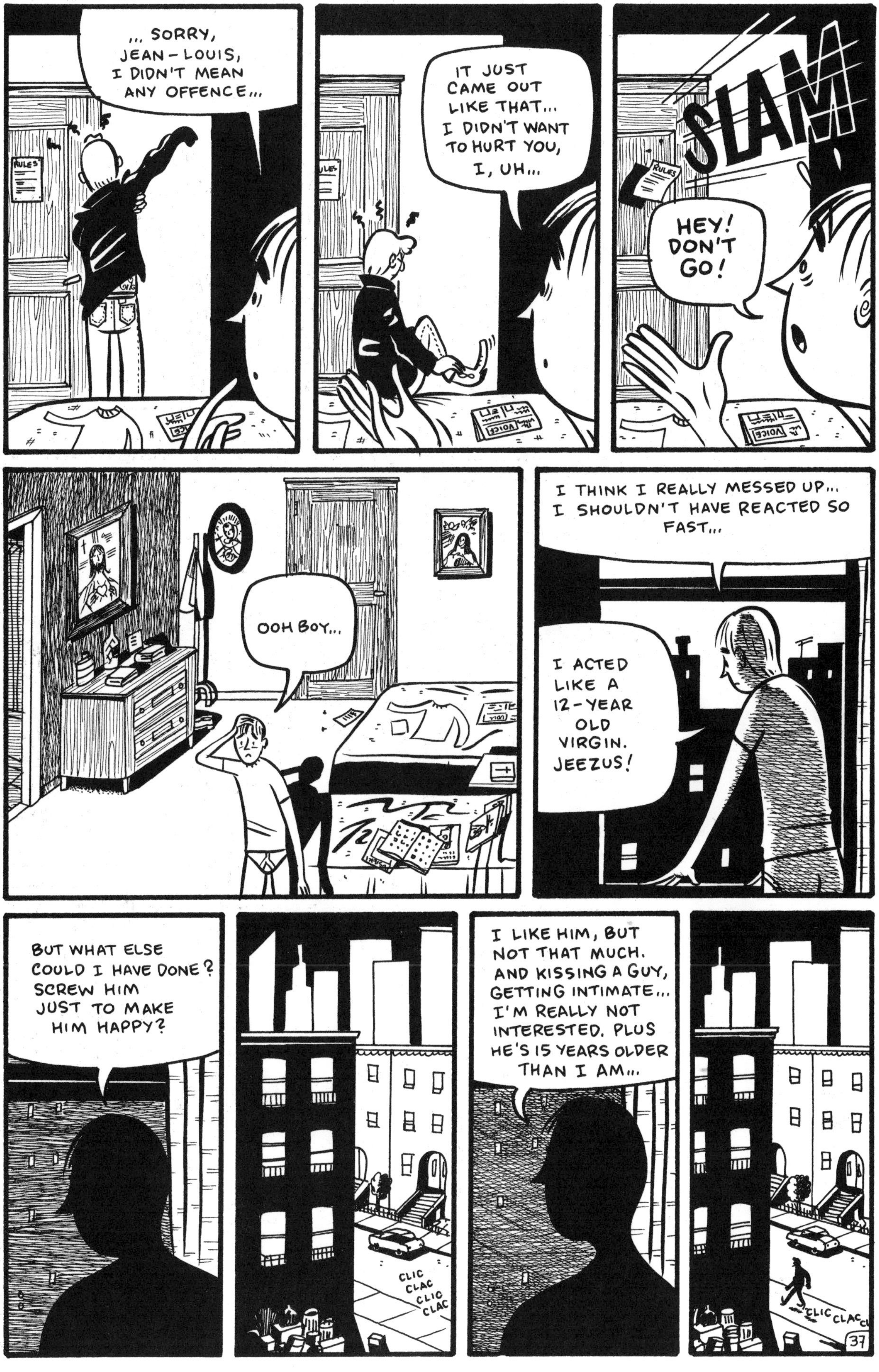
... SORRY, JEAN-LOUIS, I DIDN'T MEAN ANY OFFENCE...
IT JUST CAME OUT LIKE THAT... I DIDN'T WANT TO HURT YOU, I, UH...
SLAM
HEY! DON'T GO!
OOH BOY...
I THINK I REALLY MESSED UP... I SHOULDN'T HAVE REACTED SO FAST...
I ACTED LIKE A 12-YEAR OLD VIRGIN. JEEZUS!
BUT WHAT ELSE COULD I HAVE DONE? SCREW HIM JUST TO MAKE HIM HAPPY?
CLIC CLAC CLIC CLAC
I LIKE HIM, BUT NOT THAT MUCH. AND KISSING A GUY, GETTING INTIMATE... I'M REALLY NOT INTERESTED. PLUS HE'S 15 YEARS OLDER THAN I AM...
CLIC CLAC

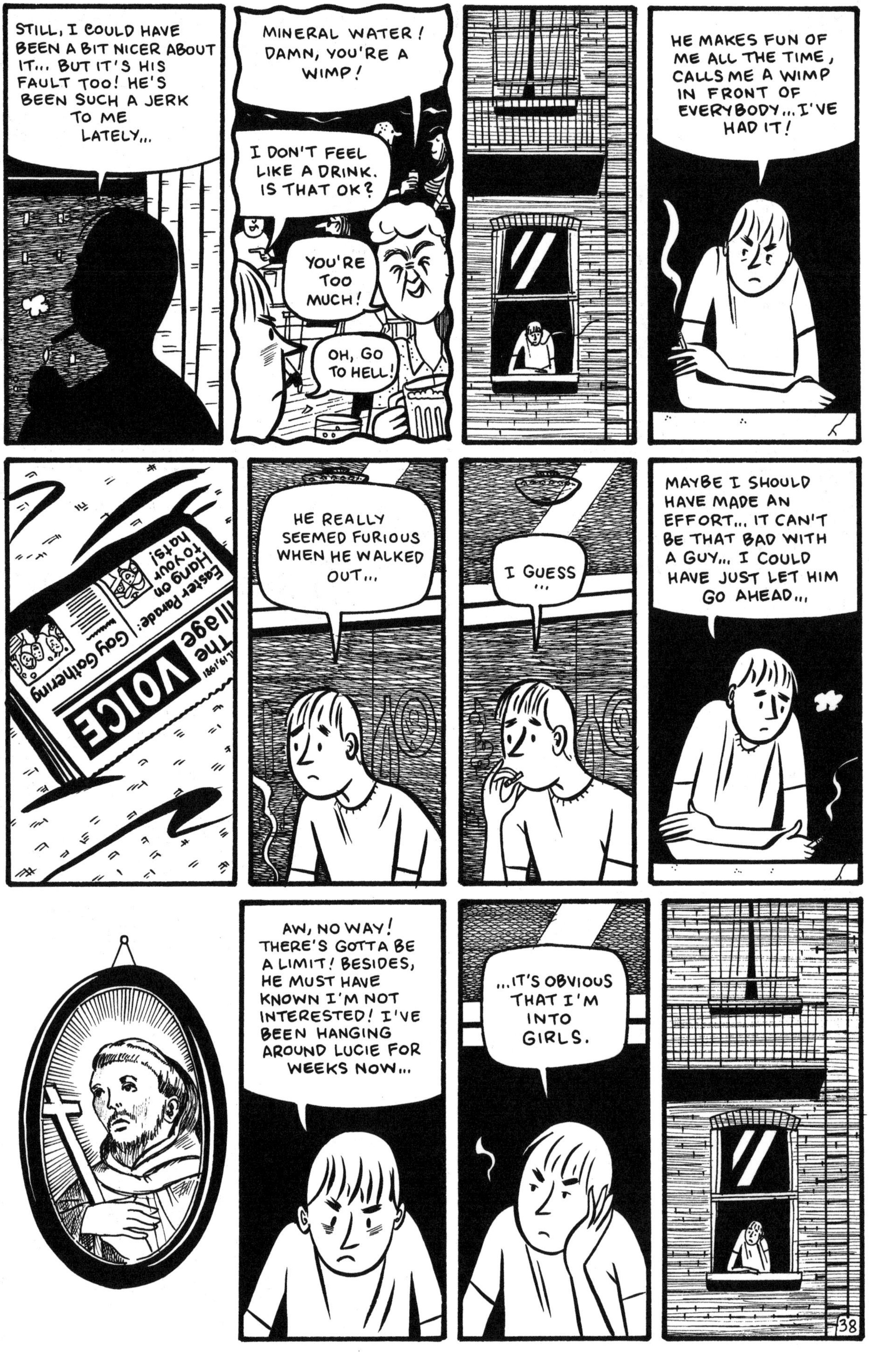
STILL, I COULD HAVE BEEN A BIT NICER ABOUT IT... BUT IT'S HIS FAULT TOO! HE'S BEEN SUCH A JERK TO ME LATELY...
MINERAL WATER! DAMN, YOU'RE A WIMP!
I DON'T FEEL LIKE A DRINK. IS THAT OK?
YOU'RE TOO MUCH!
OH, GO TO HELL!
HE MAKES FUN OF ME ALL THE TIME, CALLS ME A WIMP IN FRONT OF EVERYBODY... I'VE HAD IT!
The Village VOICE
Gay Gathering
Easter Parade: Hang on to your hats!
HE REALLY SEEMED FURIOUS WHEN HE WALKED OUT...
I GUESS ...
MAYBE I SHOULD HAVE MADE AN EFFORT... IT CAN'T BE THAT BAD WITH A GUY... I COULD HAVE JUST LET HIM GO AHEAD...
AW, NO WAY! THERE'S GOTTA BE A LIMIT! BESIDES, HE MUST HAVE KNOWN I'M NOT INTERESTED! I'VE BEEN HANGING AROUND LUCIE FOR WEEKS NOW...
...IT'S OBVIOUS THAT I'M INTO GIRLS.

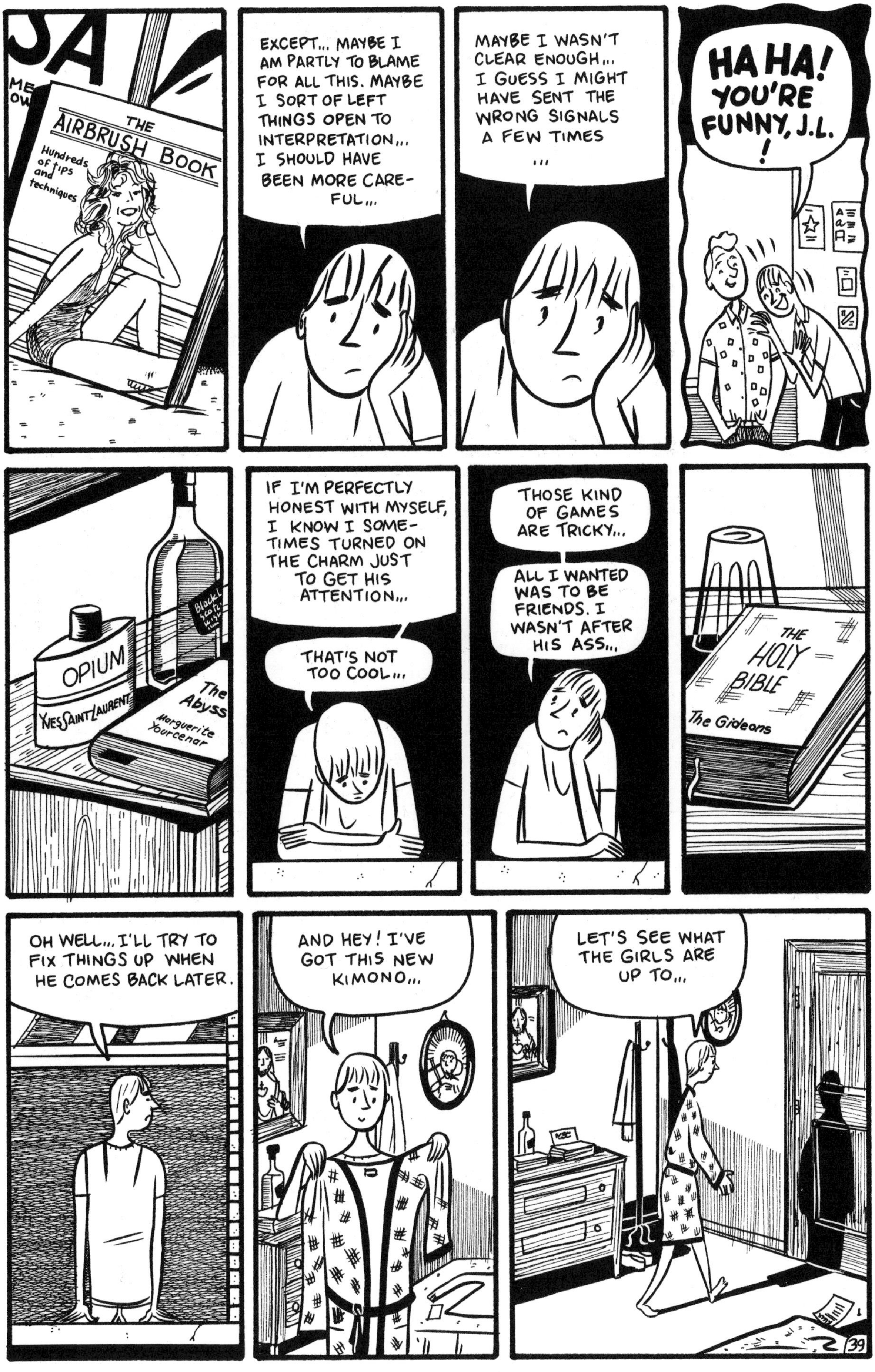
THE AIRBRUSH BOOK
Hundreds of tips and techniques
EXCEPT... MAYBE I AM PARTLY TO BLAME FOR ALL THIS. MAYBE I SORT OF LEFT THINGS OPEN TO INTERPRETATION... I SHOULD HAVE BEEN MORE CARE-FUL...
MAYBE I WASN'T CLEAR ENOUGH... I GUESS I MIGHT HAVE SENT THE WRONG SIGNALS A FEW TIMES ...
HA HA! YOU'RE FUNNY, J.L.!
OPIUM
YVES SAINT LAURENT
The Abyss
Marguerite Yourcenar
IF I'M PERFECTLY HONEST WITH MYSELF, I KNOW I SOME-TIMES TURNED ON THE CHARM JUST TO GET HIS ATTENTION...
THAT'S NOT TOO COOL...
THOSE KIND OF GAMES ARE TRICKY...
ALL I WANTED WAS TO BE FRIENDS. I WASN'T AFTER HIS ASS...
THE HOLY BIBLE
The Gideons
OH WELL... I'LL TRY TO FIX THINGS UP WHEN HE COMES BACK LATER.
AND HEY! I'VE GOT THIS NEW KIMONO...
LET'S SEE WHAT THE GIRLS ARE UP TO...

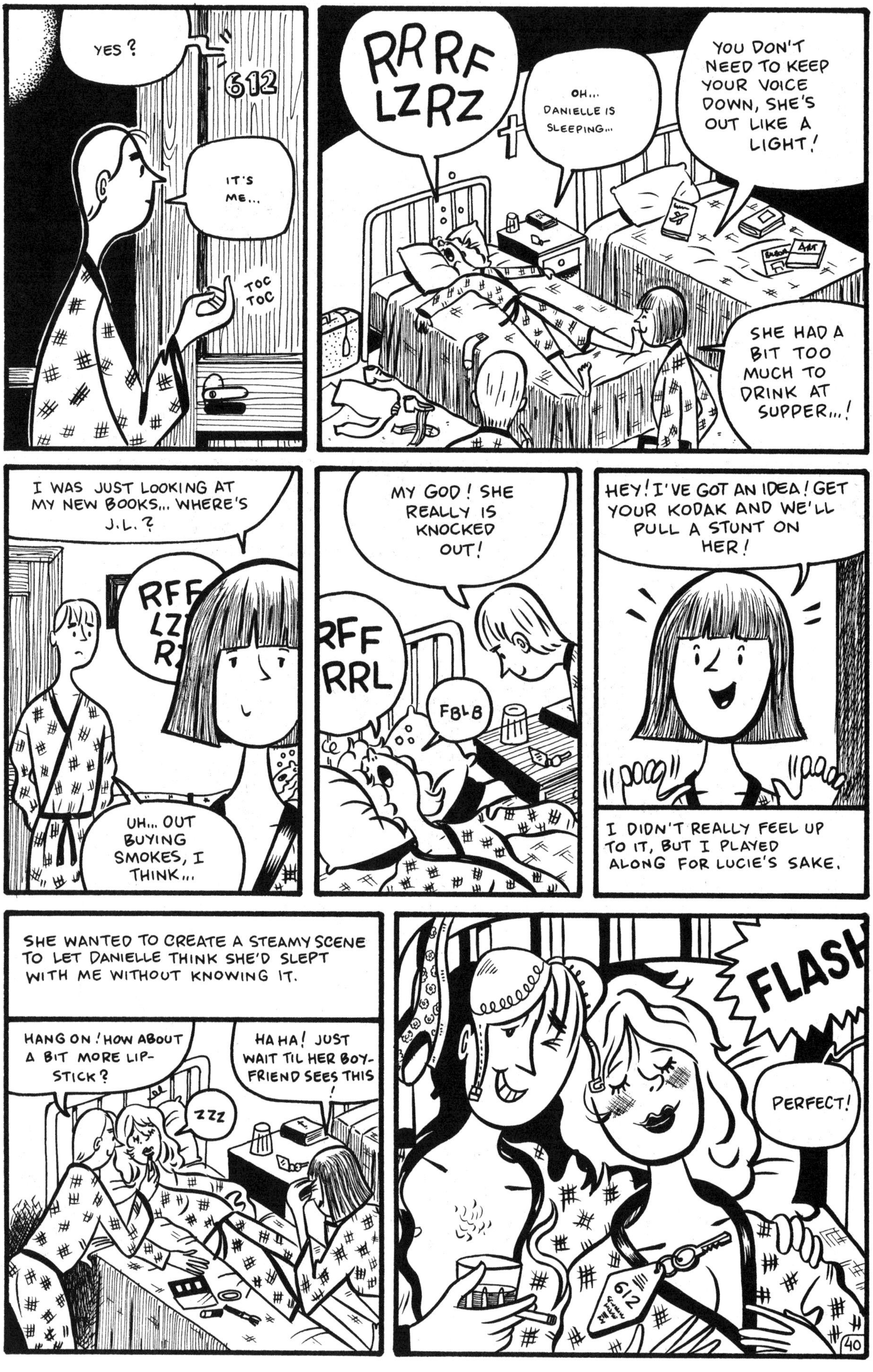
YES ?
612
IT'S ME...
TOC TOC
RRRF LZRZ
OH... DANIELLE IS SLEEPING...
YOU DON'T NEED TO KEEP YOUR VOICE DOWN, SHE'S OUT LIKE A LIGHT!
SHE HAD A BIT TOO MUCH TO DRINK AT SUPPER...!
I WAS JUST LOOKING AT MY NEW BOOKS... WHERE'S J.L. ?
UH... OUT BUYING SMOKES, I THINK...
MY GOD! SHE REALLY IS KNOCKED OUT!
RFF RRL
FBLB
HEY! I'VE GOT AN IDEA! GET YOUR KODAK AND WE'LL PULL A STUNT ON HER!
I DIDN'T REALLY FEEL UP TO IT, BUT I PLAYED ALONG FOR LUCIE'S SAKE.
SHE WANTED TO CREATE A STEAMY SCENE TO LET DANIELLE THINK SHE'D SLEPT WITH ME WITHOUT KNOWING IT.
HANG ON! HOW ABOUT A BIT MORE LIP-STICK ?
ZZZ
HA HA! JUST WAIT TIL HER BOY-FRIEND SEES THIS!
FLASH
PERFECT!
612
40

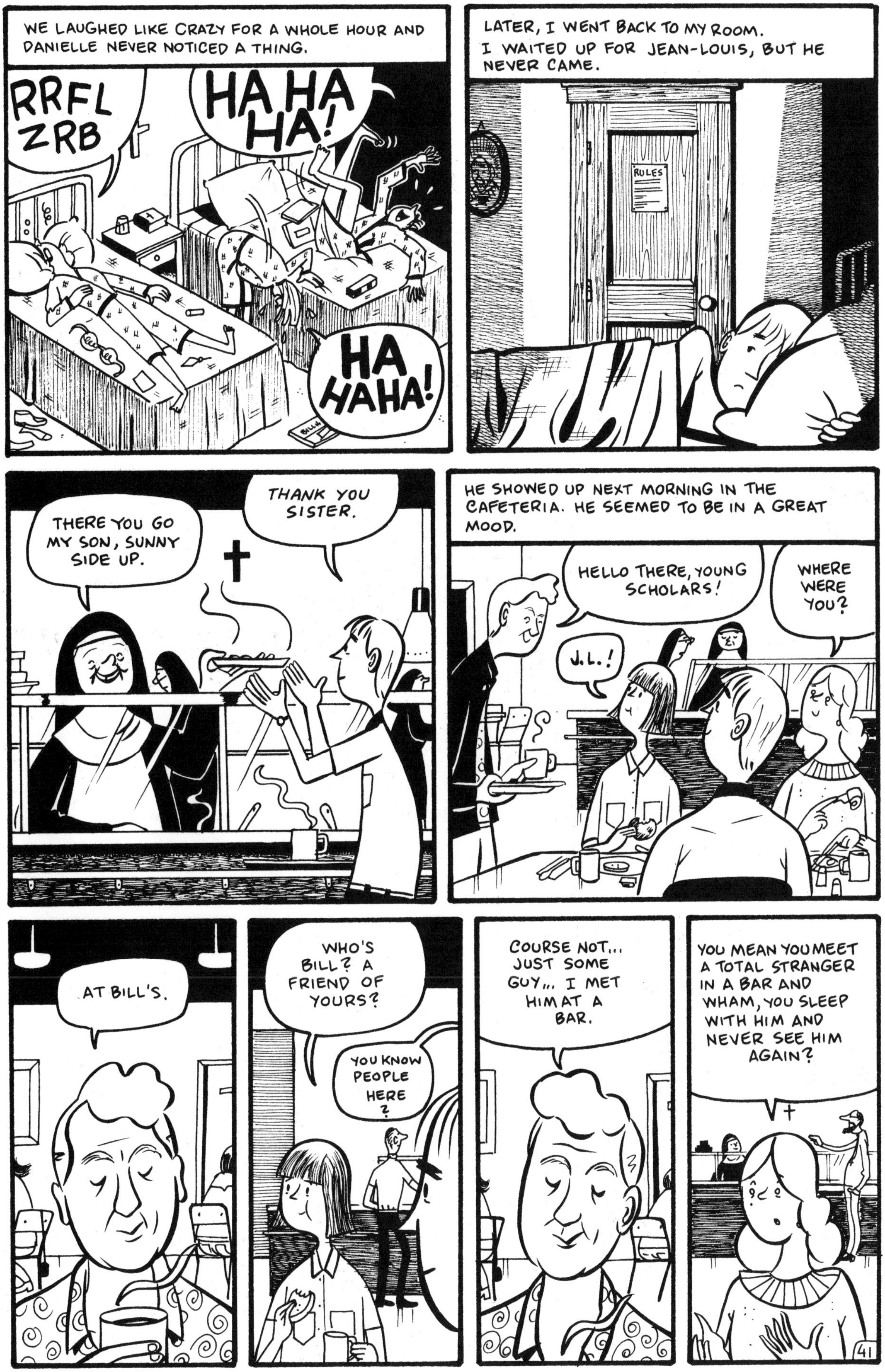

WE LAUGHED LIKE CRAZY FOR A WHOLE HOUR AND DANIELLE NEVER NOTICED A THING.
RRFL ZRB
HA HA HA!
HA HAHA!
LATER, I WENT BACK TO MY ROOM. I WAITED UP FOR JEAN-LOUIS, BUT HE NEVER CAME.
RULES
THERE YOU GO MY SON, SUNNY SIDE UP.
THANK YOU SISTER.
HE SHOWED UP NEXT MORNING IN THE CAFETERIA. HE SEEMED TO BE IN A GREAT MOOD.
HELLO THERE, YOUNG SCHOLARS!
J.L.!
WHERE WERE YOU?
AT BILL'S.
WHO'S BILL? A FRIEND OF YOURS?
YOU KNOW PEOPLE HERE?
COURSE NOT... JUST SOME GUY... I MET HIM AT A BAR.
YOU MEAN YOU MEET A TOTAL STRANGER IN A BAR AND WHAM, YOU SLEEP WITH HIM AND NEVER SEE HIM AGAIN?

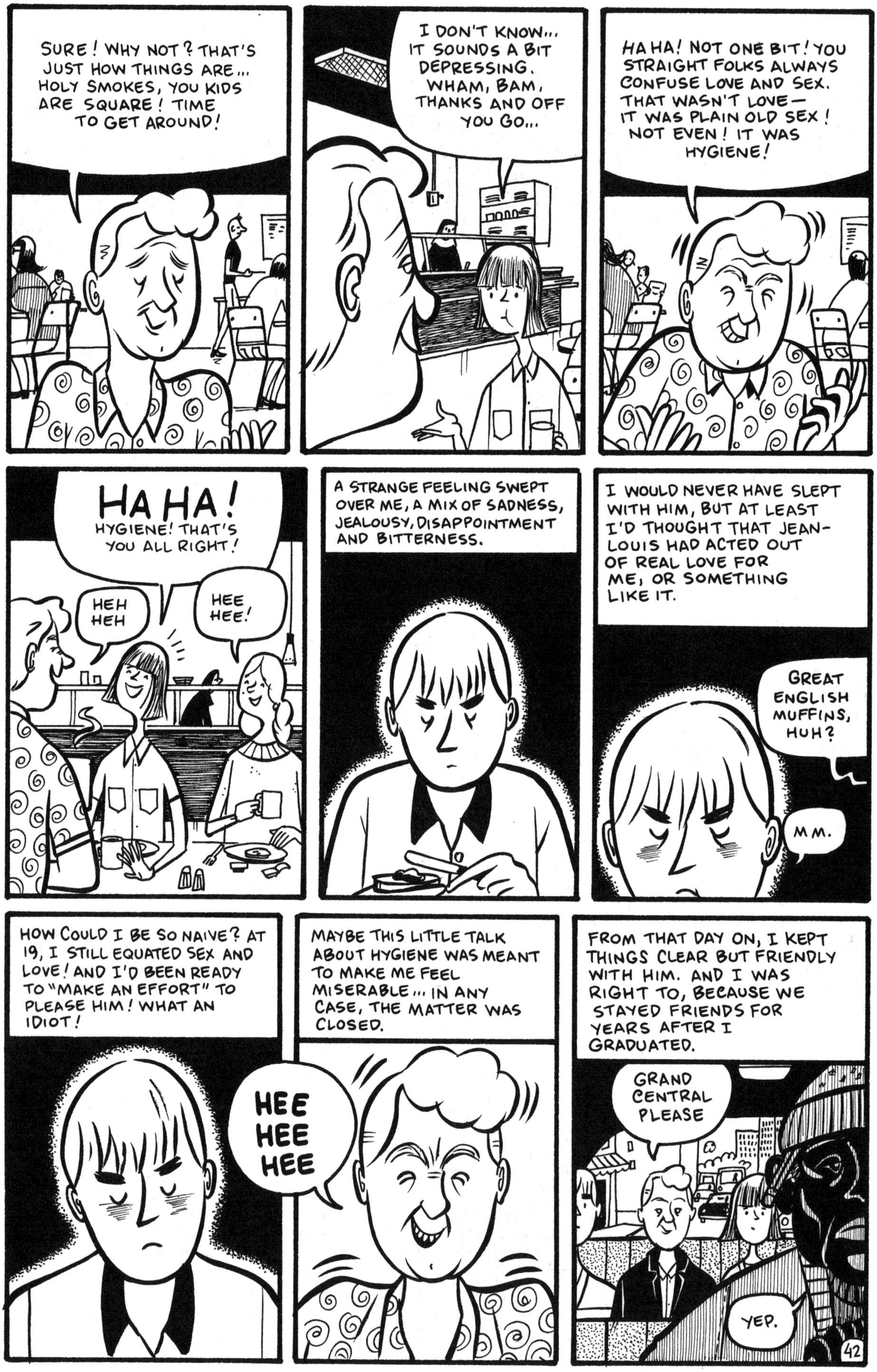
SURE! WHY NOT? THAT'S JUST HOW THINGS ARE... HOLY SMOKES, YOU KIDS ARE SQUARE! TIME TO GET AROUND!
I DON'T KNOW... IT SOUNDS A BIT DEPRESSING. WHAM, BAM, THANKS AND OFF YOU GO...
HA HA! NOT ONE BIT! YOU STRAIGHT FOLKS ALWAYS CONFUSE LOVE AND SEX. THAT WASN'T LOVE— IT WAS PLAIN OLD SEX! NOT EVEN! IT WAS HYGIENE!
HA HA! HYGIENE! THAT'S YOU ALL RIGHT!
HEH HEH
HEE HEE!
A STRANGE FEELING SWEPT OVER ME, A MIX OF SADNESS, JEALOUSY, DISAPPOINTMENT AND BITTERNESS.
I WOULD NEVER HAVE SLEPT WITH HIM, BUT AT LEAST I'D THOUGHT THAT JEAN-LOUIS HAD ACTED OUT OF REAL LOVE FOR ME, OR SOMETHING LIKE IT.
GREAT ENGLISH MUFFINS, HUH?
MM.
HOW COULD I BE SO NAIVE? AT 19, I STILL EQUATED SEX AND LOVE! AND I'D BEEN READY TO "MAKE AN EFFORT" TO PLEASE HIM! WHAT AN IDIOT!
HEE HEE HEE
MAYBE THIS LITTLE TALK ABOUT HYGIENE WAS MEANT TO MAKE ME FEEL MISERABLE... IN ANY CASE, THE MATTER WAS CLOSED.
FROM THAT DAY ON, I KEPT THINGS CLEAR BUT FRIENDLY WITH HIM. AND I WAS RIGHT TO, BECAUSE WE STAYED FRIENDS FOR YEARS AFTER I GRADUATED.
GRAND CENTRAL PLEASE
YEP.

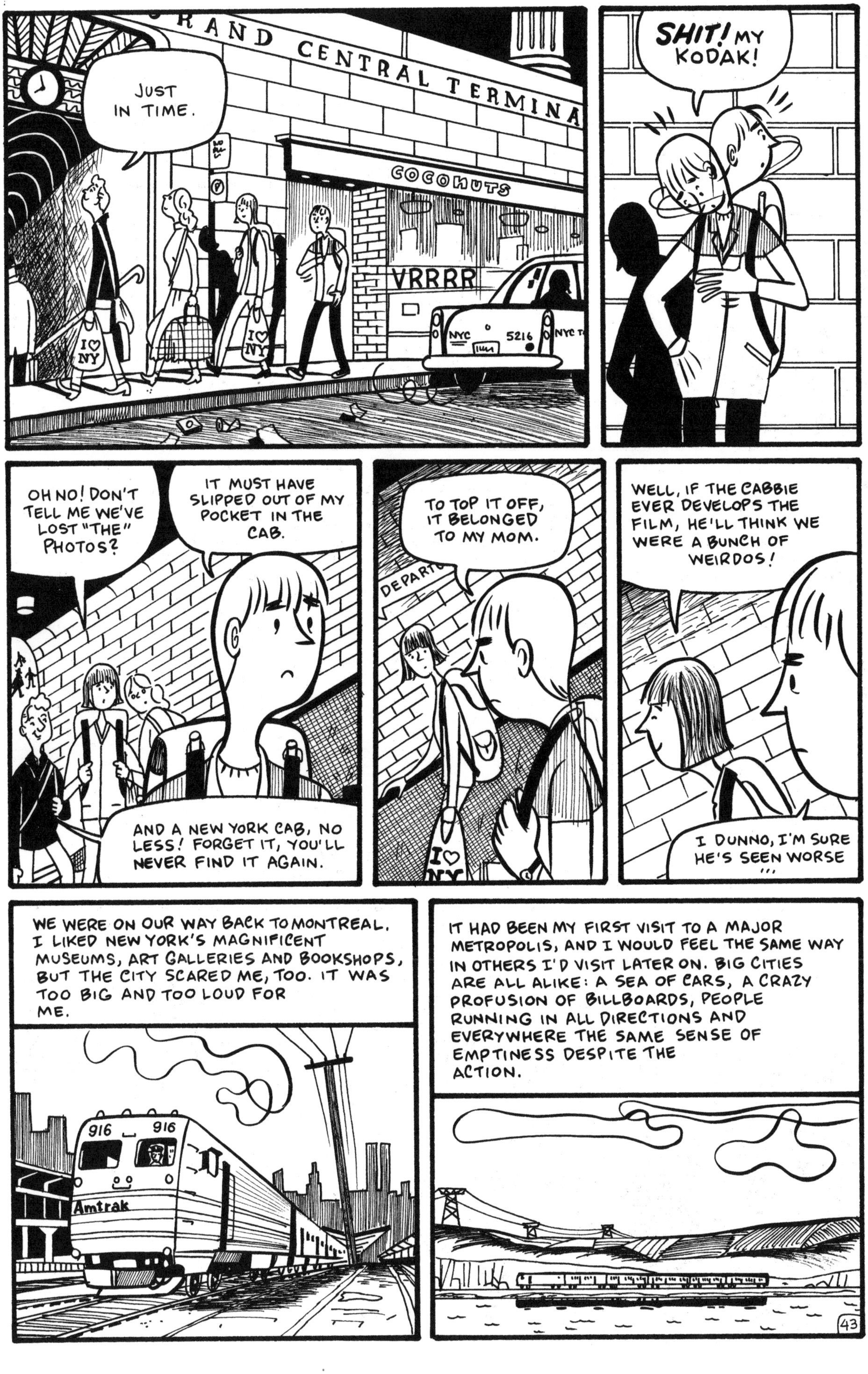

GRAND CENTRAL TERMINA
JUST IN TIME.
COCONUTS
VRRRR
NYC 5216
SHIT! MY KODAK!
OH NO! DON'T TELL ME WE'VE LOST "THE" PHOTOS?
IT MUST HAVE SLIPPED OUT OF MY POCKET IN THE CAB.
AND A NEW YORK CAB, NO LESS! FORGET IT, YOU'LL NEVER FIND IT AGAIN.
TO TOP IT OFF, IT BELONGED TO MY MOM.
WELL, IF THE CABBIE EVER DEVELOPS THE FILM, HE'LL THINK WE WERE A BUNCH OF WEIRDOS!
I DUNNO, I'M SURE HE'S SEEN WORSE ...
WE WERE ON OUR WAY BACK TO MONTREAL. I LIKED NEW YORK'S MAGNIFICENT MUSEUMS, ART GALLERIES AND BOOKSHOPS, BUT THE CITY SCARED ME, TOO. IT WAS TOO BIG AND TOO LOUD FOR ME.
916 916
Amtrak
IT HAD BEEN MY FIRST VISIT TO A MAJOR METROPOLIS, AND I WOULD FEEL THE SAME WAY IN OTHERS I'D VISIT LATER ON. BIG CITIES ARE ALL ALIKE: A SEA OF CARS, A CRAZY PROFUSION OF BILLBOARDS, PEOPLE RUNNING IN ALL DIRECTIONS AND EVERYWHERE THE SAME SENSE OF EMPTINESS DESPITE THE ACTION.

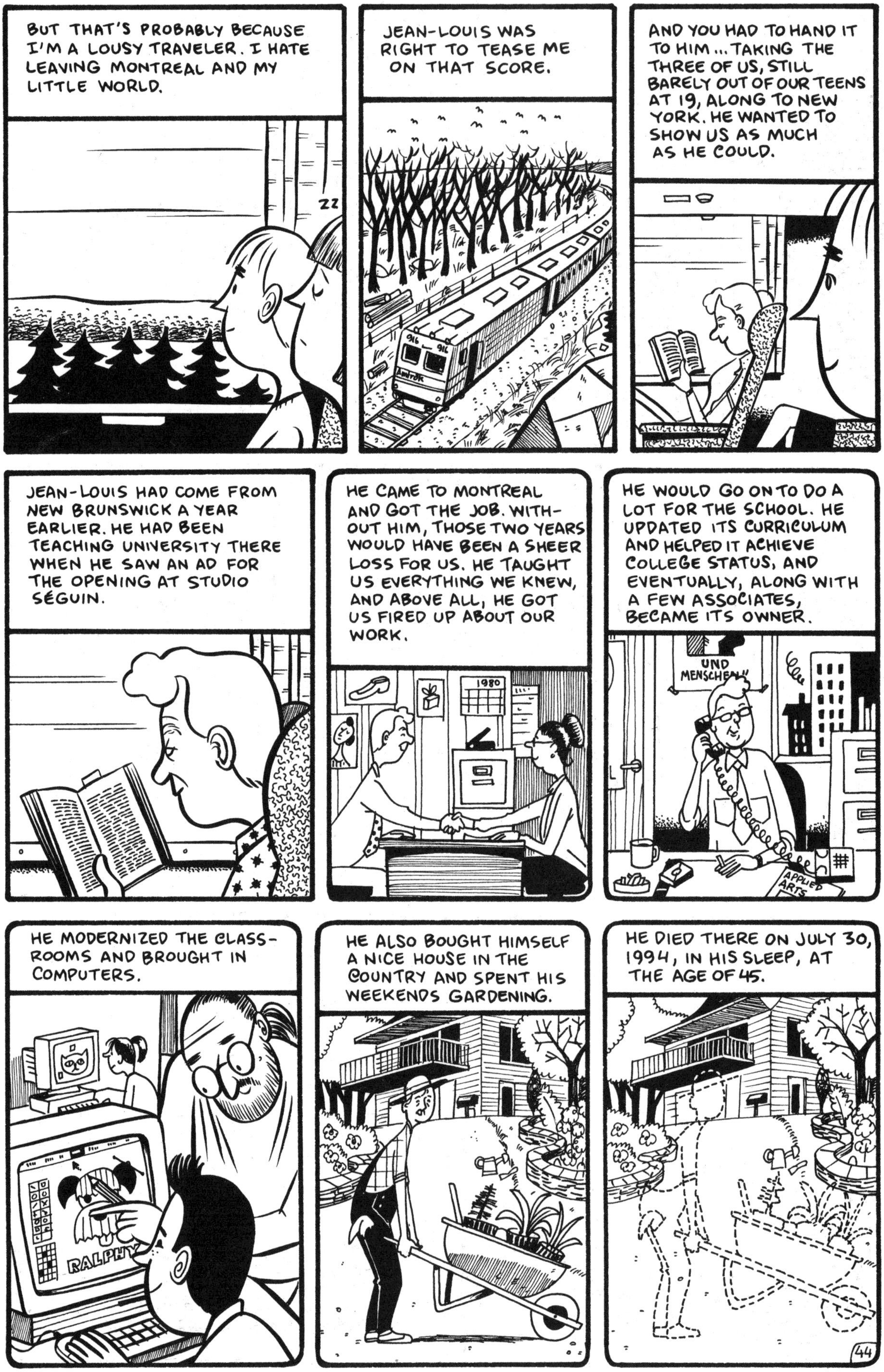
BUT THAT'S PROBABLY BECAUSE I'M A LOUSY TRAVELER. I HATE LEAVING MONTREAL AND MY LITTLE WORLD.
ZZ
JEAN-LOUIS WAS RIGHT TO TEASE ME ON THAT SCORE.
AND YOU HAD TO HAND IT TO HIM ... TAKING THE THREE OF US, STILL BARELY OUT OF OUR TEENS AT 19, ALONG TO NEW YORK. HE WANTED TO SHOW US AS MUCH AS HE COULD.
JEAN-LOUIS HAD COME FROM NEW BRUNSWICK A YEAR EARLIER. HE HAD BEEN TEACHING UNIVERSITY THERE WHEN HE SAW AN AD FOR THE OPENING AT STUDIO SÉGUIN.
HE CAME TO MONTREAL AND GOT THE JOB. WITHOUT HIM, THOSE TWO YEARS WOULD HAVE BEEN A SHEER LOSS FOR US. HE TAUGHT US EVERYTHING WE KNEW, AND ABOVE ALL, HE GOT US FIRED UP ABOUT OUR WORK.
1980
HE WOULD GO ON TO DO A LOT FOR THE SCHOOL. HE UPDATED ITS CURRICULUM AND HELPED IT ACHIEVE COLLEGE STATUS, AND EVENTUALLY, ALONG WITH A FEW ASSOCIATES, BECAME ITS OWNER.
UND MENSCHEN!!
APPLIED ARTS
HE MODERNIZED THE CLASSROOMS AND BROUGHT IN COMPUTERS.
RALPHY
HE ALSO BOUGHT HIMSELF A NICE HOUSE IN THE COUNTRY AND SPENT HIS WEEKENDS GARDENING.
HE DIED THERE ON JULY 30, 1994, IN HIS SLEEP, AT THE AGE OF 45.

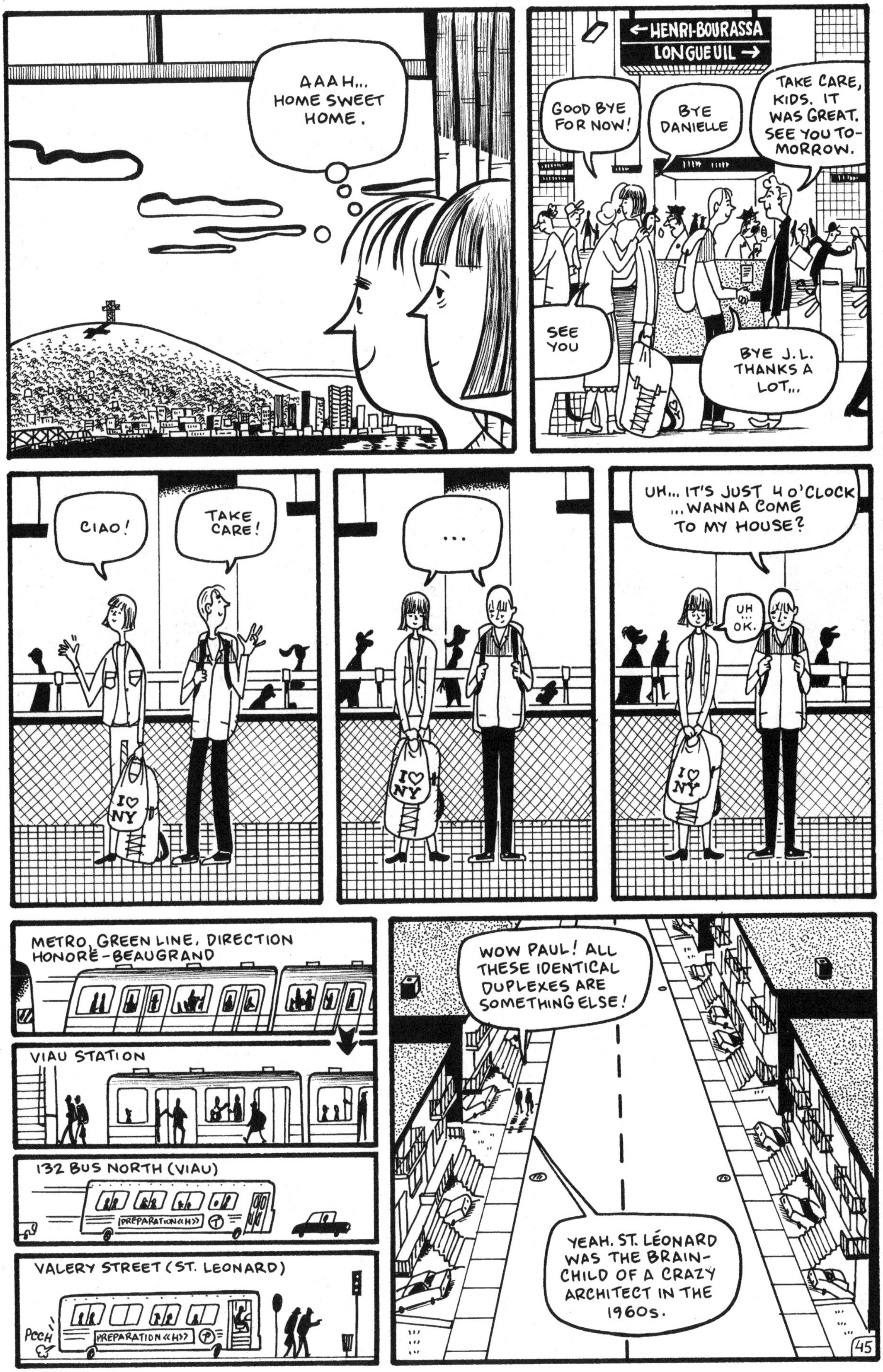
AAAH... HOME SWEET HOME.
← HENRI-BOURASSA
LONGUEUIL →
GOOD BYE FOR NOW!
BYE DANIELLE
TAKE CARE, KIDS. IT WAS GREAT. SEE YOU TO-MORROW.
SEE YOU
BYE J.L. THANKS A LOT...
CIAO!
TAKE CARE!
I ♡ NY
...
UH... IT'S JUST 4 O'CLOCK ...WANNA COME TO MY HOUSE?
UH ... OK.
METRO, GREEN LINE, DIRECTION HONORÉ-BEAUGRAND
VIAU STATION
132 BUS NORTH (VIAU)
PREPARATION «H»
VALERY STREET (ST. LEONARD)
PCCH
PREPARATION «H»
WOW PAUL! ALL THESE IDENTICAL DUPLEXES ARE SOMETHING ELSE!
YEAH. ST. LÉONARD WAS THE BRAIN-CHILD OF A CRAZY ARCHITECT IN THE 1960s.
45

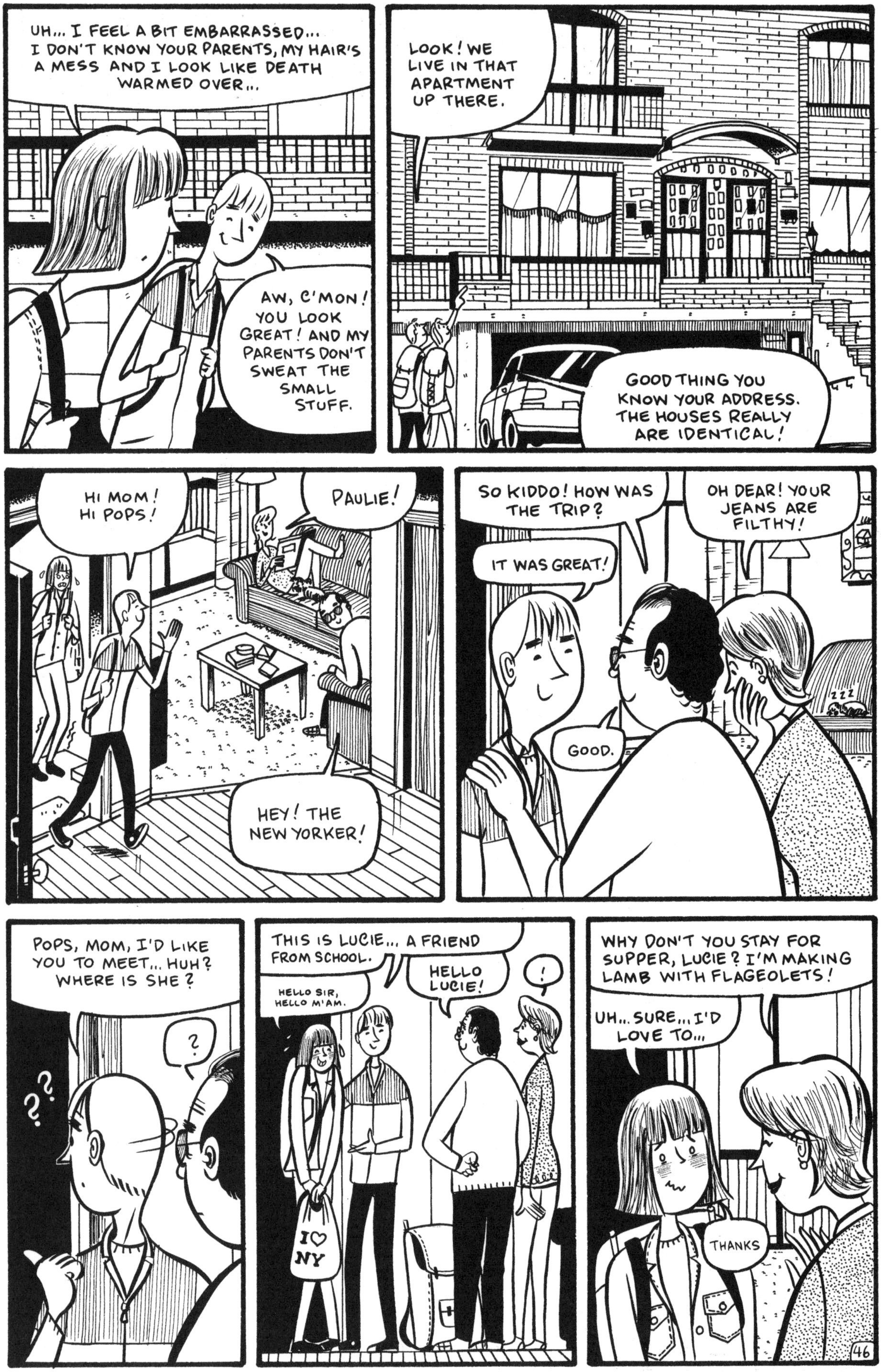
UH... I FEEL A BIT EMBARRASSED... I DON'T KNOW YOUR PARENTS, MY HAIR'S A MESS AND I LOOK LIKE DEATH WARMED OVER...
AW, C'MON! YOU LOOK GREAT! AND MY PARENTS DON'T SWEAT THE SMALL STUFF.
LOOK! WE LIVE IN THAT APARTMENT UP THERE.
GOOD THING YOU KNOW YOUR ADDRESS. THE HOUSES REALLY ARE IDENTICAL!
HI MOM! HI POPS!
PAULIE!
HEY! THE NEW YORKER!
SO KIDDO! HOW WAS THE TRIP?
IT WAS GREAT!
GOOD.
OH DEAR! YOUR JEANS ARE FILTHY!
ZZZ
POPS, MOM, I'D LIKE YOU TO MEET... HUH? WHERE IS SHE?
?
??
THIS IS LUCIE... A FRIEND FROM SCHOOL.
HELLO SIR, HELLO M'AM.
HELLO LUCIE!
!
I ♡ NY
WHY DON'T YOU STAY FOR SUPPER, LUCIE? I'M MAKING LAMB WITH FLAGEOLETS!
UH... SURE... I'D LOVE TO...
THANKS

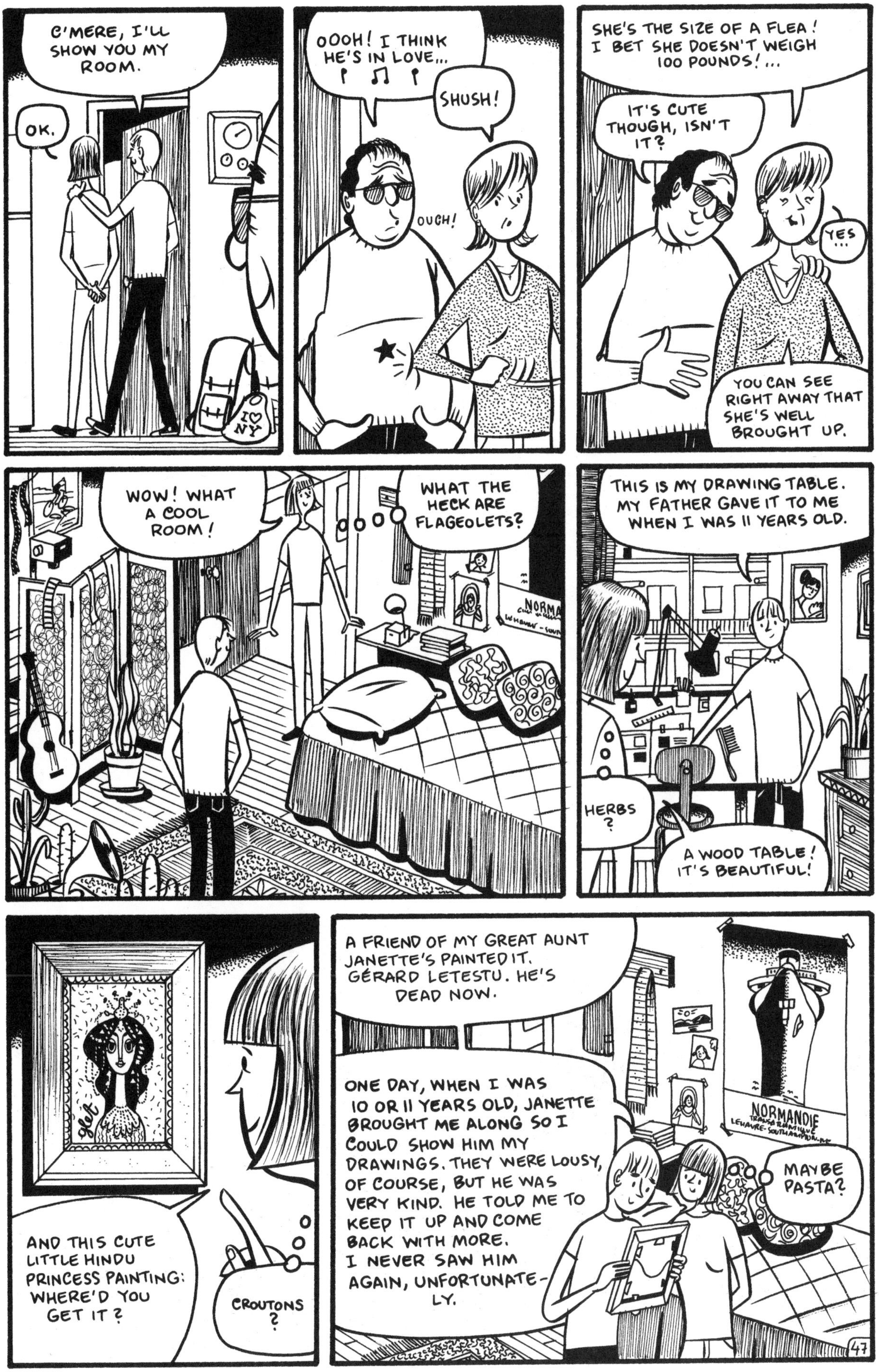
C'MERE, I'LL SHOW YOU MY ROOM.
OK.
OOOH! I THINK HE'S IN LOVE...
SHUSH!
OUCH!
SHE'S THE SIZE OF A FLEA! I BET SHE DOESN'T WEIGH 100 POUNDS!...
IT'S CUTE THOUGH, ISN'T IT?
YES...
YOU CAN SEE RIGHT AWAY THAT SHE'S WELL BROUGHT UP.
WOW! WHAT A COOL ROOM!
WHAT THE HECK ARE FLAGEOLETS?
NORMA
THIS IS MY DRAWING TABLE. MY FATHER GAVE IT TO ME WHEN I WAS 11 YEARS OLD.
HERBS?
A WOOD TABLE! IT'S BEAUTIFUL!
AND THIS CUTE LITTLE HINDU PRINCESS PAINTING: WHERE'D YOU GET IT?
CROUTONS?
A FRIEND OF MY GREAT AUNT JANETTE'S PAINTED IT. GÉRARD LETESTU. HE'S DEAD NOW.
ONE DAY, WHEN I WAS 10 OR 11 YEARS OLD, JANETTE BROUGHT ME ALONG SO I COULD SHOW HIM MY DRAWINGS. THEY WERE LOUSY, OF COURSE, BUT HE WAS VERY KIND. HE TOLD ME TO KEEP IT UP AND COME BACK WITH MORE. I NEVER SAW HIM AGAIN, UNFORTUNATELY.
NORMANDIE
MAYBE PASTA?

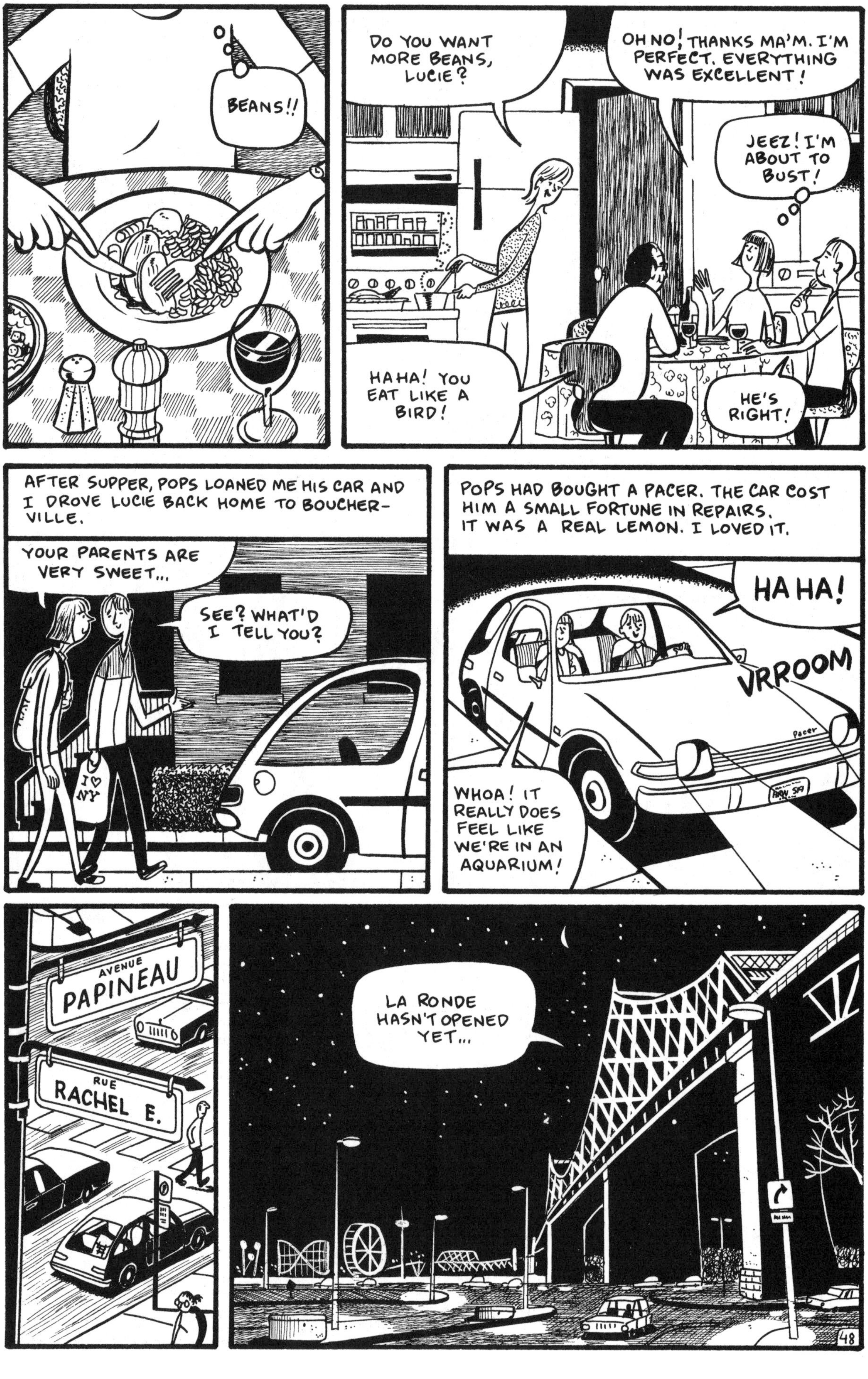

BEANS!!
DO YOU WANT MORE BEANS, LUCIE?
OH NO! THANKS MA'M. I'M PERFECT. EVERYTHING WAS EXCELLENT!
JEEZ! I'M ABOUT TO BUST!
HA HA! YOU EAT LIKE A BIRD!
HE'S RIGHT!
AFTER SUPPER, POPS LOANED ME HIS CAR AND I DROVE LUCIE BACK HOME TO BOUCHER-VILLE.
YOUR PARENTS ARE VERY SWEET...
SEE? WHAT'D I TELL YOU?
I ♥ NY
POPS HAD BOUGHT A PACER. THE CAR COST HIM A SMALL FORTUNE IN REPAIRS. IT WAS A REAL LEMON. I LOVED IT.
HA HA!
VRROOM
Pacer
WHOA! IT REALLY DOES FEEL LIKE WE'RE IN AN AQUARIUM!
AVENUE PAPINEAU
RUE RACHEL E.
LA RONDE HASN'T OPENED YET...

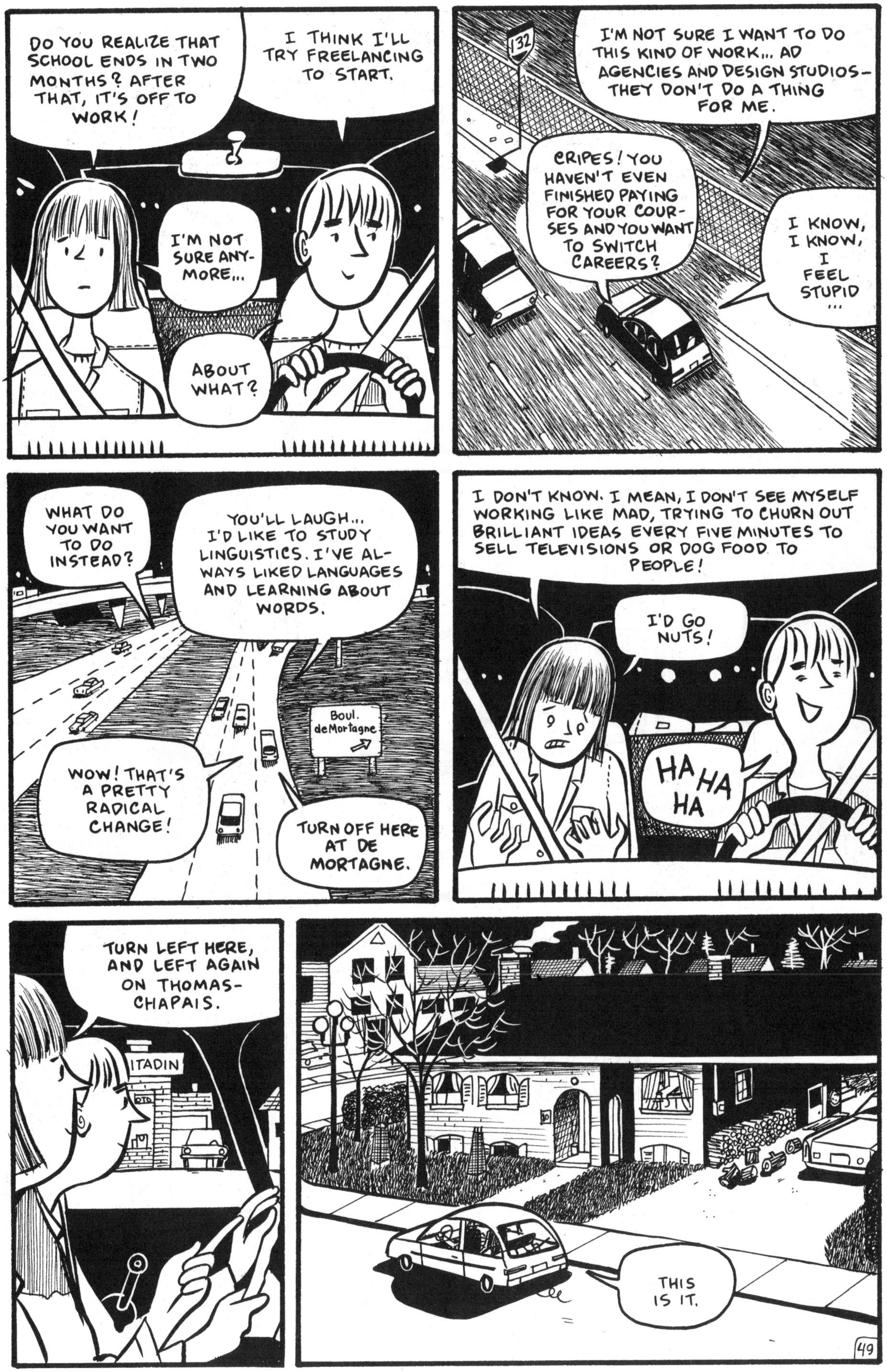
DO YOU REALIZE THAT SCHOOL ENDS IN TWO MONTHS? AFTER THAT, IT'S OFF TO WORK!
I THINK I'LL TRY FREELANCING TO START.
I'M NOT SURE ANYMORE...
ABOUT WHAT?
132
I'M NOT SURE I WANT TO DO THIS KIND OF WORK... AD AGENCIES AND DESIGN STUDIOS- THEY DON'T DO A THING FOR ME.
CRIPES! YOU HAVEN'T EVEN FINISHED PAYING FOR YOUR COURSES AND YOU WANT TO SWITCH CAREERS?
I KNOW, I KNOW, I FEEL STUPID...
WHAT DO YOU WANT TO DO INSTEAD?
YOU'LL LAUGH... I'D LIKE TO STUDY LINGUISTICS. I'VE ALWAYS LIKED LANGUAGES AND LEARNING ABOUT WORDS.
Boul. deMortagne
WOW! THAT'S A PRETTY RADICAL CHANGE!
TURN OFF HERE AT DE MORTAGNE.
I DON'T KNOW. I MEAN, I DON'T SEE MYSELF WORKING LIKE MAD, TRYING TO CHURN OUT BRILLIANT IDEAS EVERY FIVE MINUTES TO SELL TELEVISIONS OR DOG FOOD TO PEOPLE!
I'D GO NUTS!
HA HA HA
TURN LEFT HERE, AND LEFT AGAIN ON THOMAS-CHAPAIS.
ITADIN
THIS IS IT.

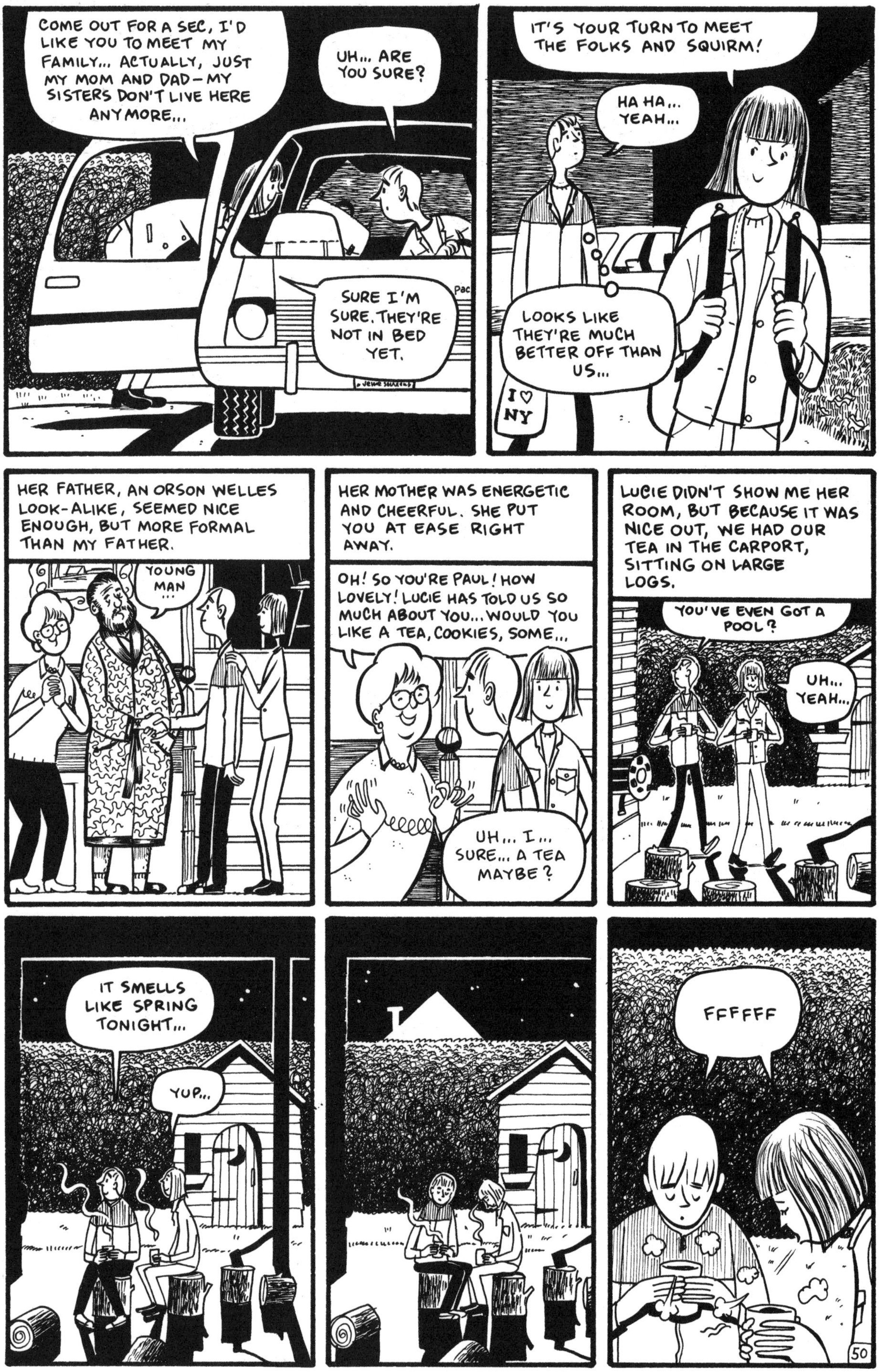
COME OUT FOR A SEC, I'D LIKE YOU TO MEET MY FAMILY... ACTUALLY, JUST MY MOM AND DAD—MY SISTERS DON'T LIVE HERE ANYMORE...
UH... ARE YOU SURE?
SURE I'M SURE. THEY'RE NOT IN BED YET.
IT'S YOUR TURN TO MEET THE FOLKS AND SQUIRM!
HA HA... YEAH...
LOOKS LIKE THEY'RE MUCH BETTER OFF THAN US...
I ♡ NY
HER FATHER, AN ORSON WELLES LOOK-ALIKE, SEEMED NICE ENOUGH, BUT MORE FORMAL THAN MY FATHER.
YOUNG MAN ...
HER MOTHER WAS ENERGETIC AND CHEERFUL. SHE PUT YOU AT EASE RIGHT AWAY.
OH! SO YOU'RE PAUL! HOW LOVELY! LUCIE HAS TOLD US SO MUCH ABOUT YOU... WOULD YOU LIKE A TEA, COOKIES, SOME...
UH... I... SURE... A TEA MAYBE?
LUCIE DIDN'T SHOW ME HER ROOM, BUT BECAUSE IT WAS NICE OUT, WE HAD OUR TEA IN THE CARPORT, SITTING ON LARGE LOGS.
YOU'VE EVEN GOT A POOL?
UH... YEAH...
IT SMELLS LIKE SPRING TONIGHT...
YUP...
FFFFFF
50

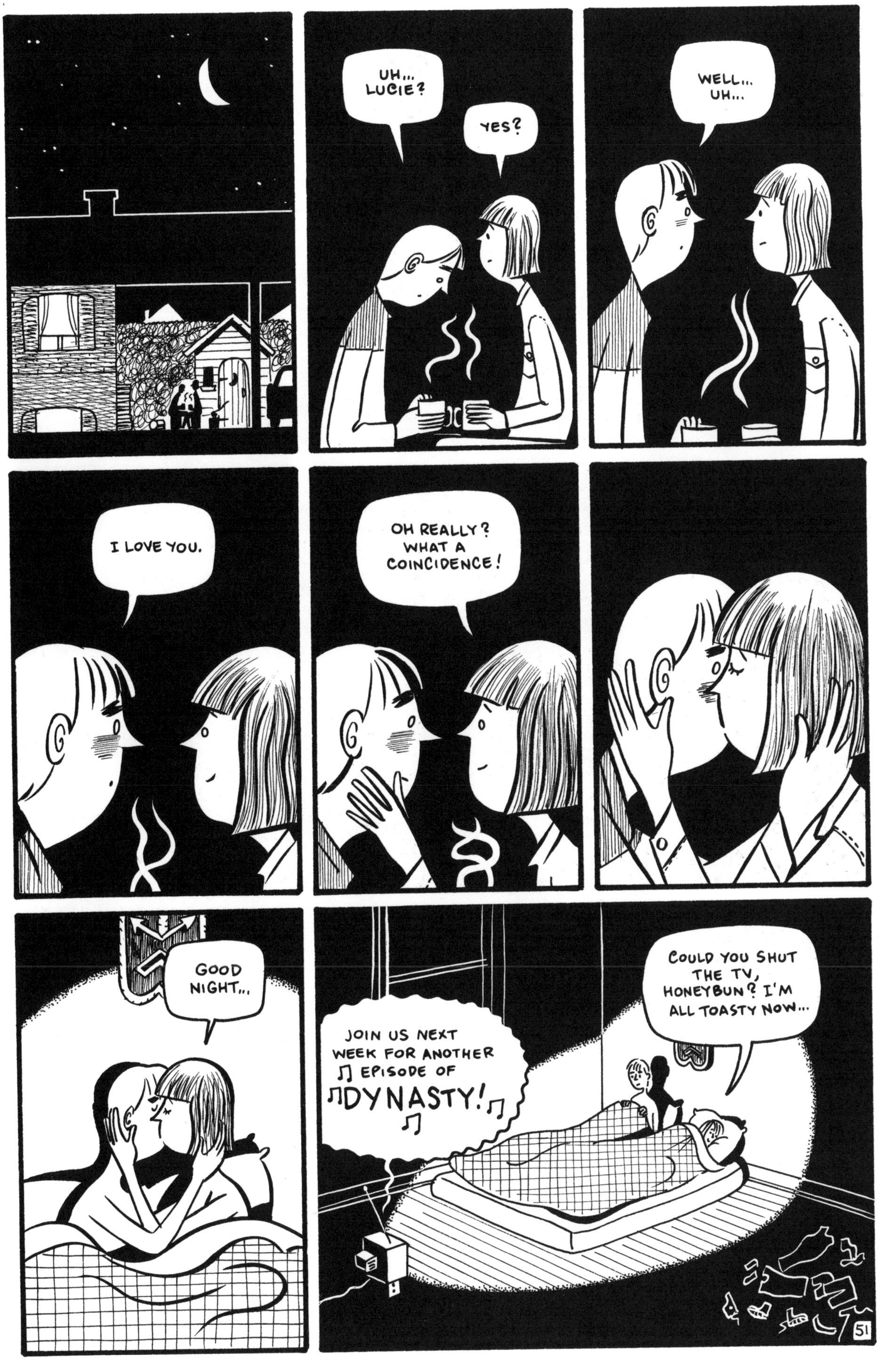
UH... LUCIE?
YES?
WELL... UH...
I LOVE YOU.
OH REALLY? WHAT A COINCIDENCE!
GOOD NIGHT...
JOIN US NEXT WEEK FOR ANOTHER ♫ EPISODE OF ♫DYNASTY! ♫ ♫
COULD YOU SHUT THE TV, HONEYBUN? I'M ALL TOASTY NOW...

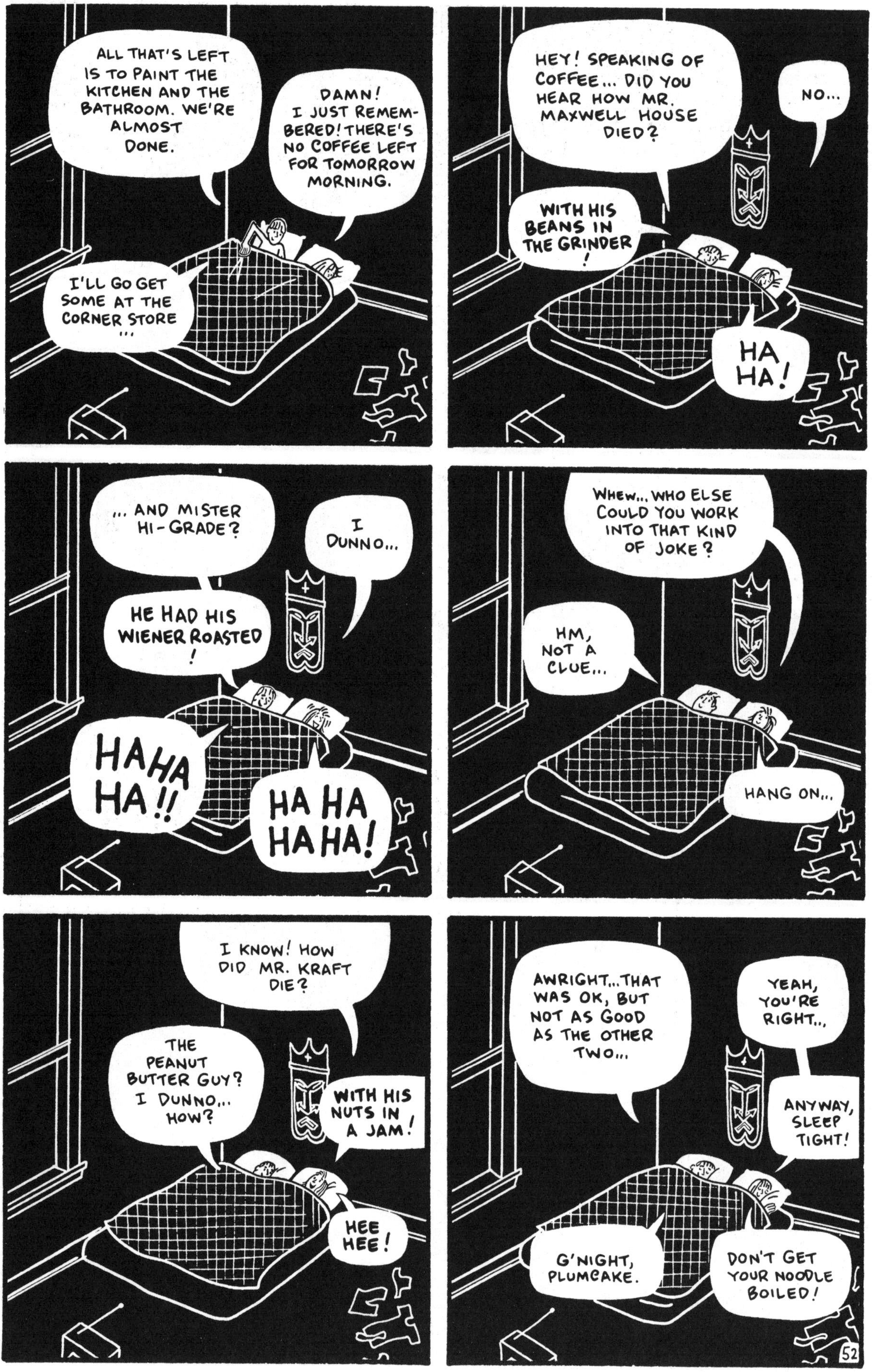
ALL THAT'S LEFT IS TO PAINT THE KITCHEN AND THE BATHROOM. WE'RE ALMOST DONE.
DAMN! I JUST REMEMBERED! THERE'S NO COFFEE LEFT FOR TOMORROW MORNING.
I'LL GO GET SOME AT THE CORNER STORE ...
HEY! SPEAKING OF COFFEE... DID YOU HEAR HOW MR. MAXWELL HOUSE DIED?
NO...
WITH HIS BEANS IN THE GRINDER!
HA HA!
... AND MISTER HI-GRADE?
I DUNNO...
HE HAD HIS WIENER ROASTED!
HAHAHA HA!!
HA HA HAHA!
WHEW... WHO ELSE COULD YOU WORK INTO THAT KIND OF JOKE?
HM, NOT A CLUE...
HANG ON...
I KNOW! HOW DID MR. KRAFT DIE?
THE PEANUT BUTTER GUY? I DUNNO... HOW?
WITH HIS NUTS IN A JAM!
HEE HEE!
AWRIGHT... THAT WAS OK, BUT NOT AS GOOD AS THE OTHER TWO...
YEAH, YOU'RE RIGHT...
ANYWAY, SLEEP TIGHT!
G'NIGHT, PLUMCAKE.
DON'T GET YOUR NOODLE BOILED!

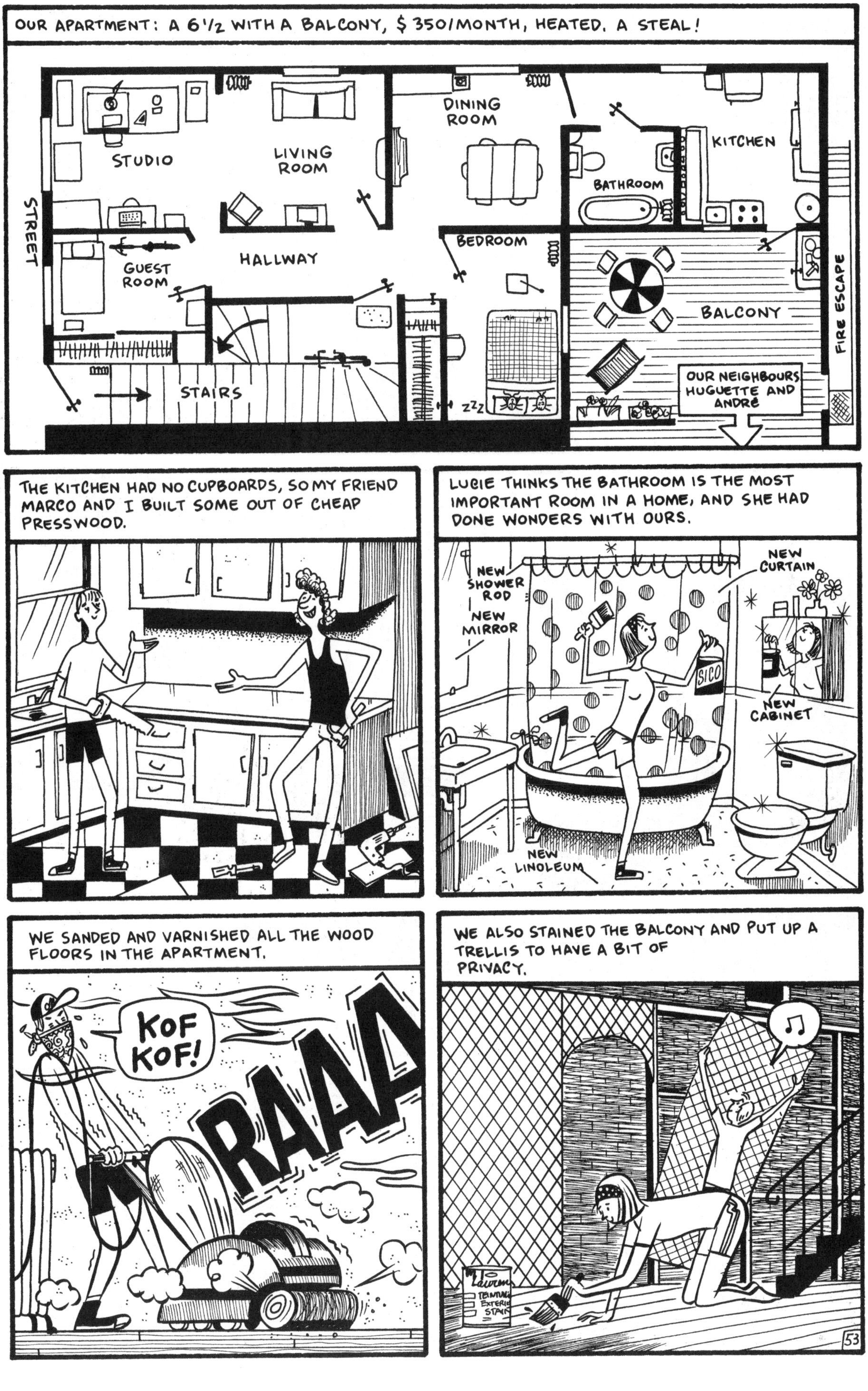
OUR APARTMENT: A 6 1/2 WITH A BALCONY, $ 350/MONTH, HEATED. A STEAL!
STREET
STUDIO
LIVING ROOM
DINING ROOM
KITCHEN
BATHROOM
BEDROOM
GUEST ROOM
HALLWAY
STAIRS
BALCONY
FIRE ESCAPE
OUR NEIGHBOURS HUGUETTE AND ANDRÉ
ZZZ
THE KITCHEN HAD NO CUPBOARDS, SO MY FRIEND MARCO AND I BUILT SOME OUT OF CHEAP PRESSWOOD.
LUCIE THINKS THE BATHROOM IS THE MOST IMPORTANT ROOM IN A HOME, AND SHE HAD DONE WONDERS WITH OURS.
NEW SHOWER ROD
NEW MIRROR
NEW CURTAIN
NEW CABINET
SICO
NEW LINOLEUM
WE SANDED AND VARNISHED ALL THE WOOD FLOORS IN THE APARTMENT.
KOF KOF!
RAAA
WE ALSO STAINED THE BALCONY AND PUT UP A TRELLIS TO HAVE A BIT OF PRIVACY.
♫

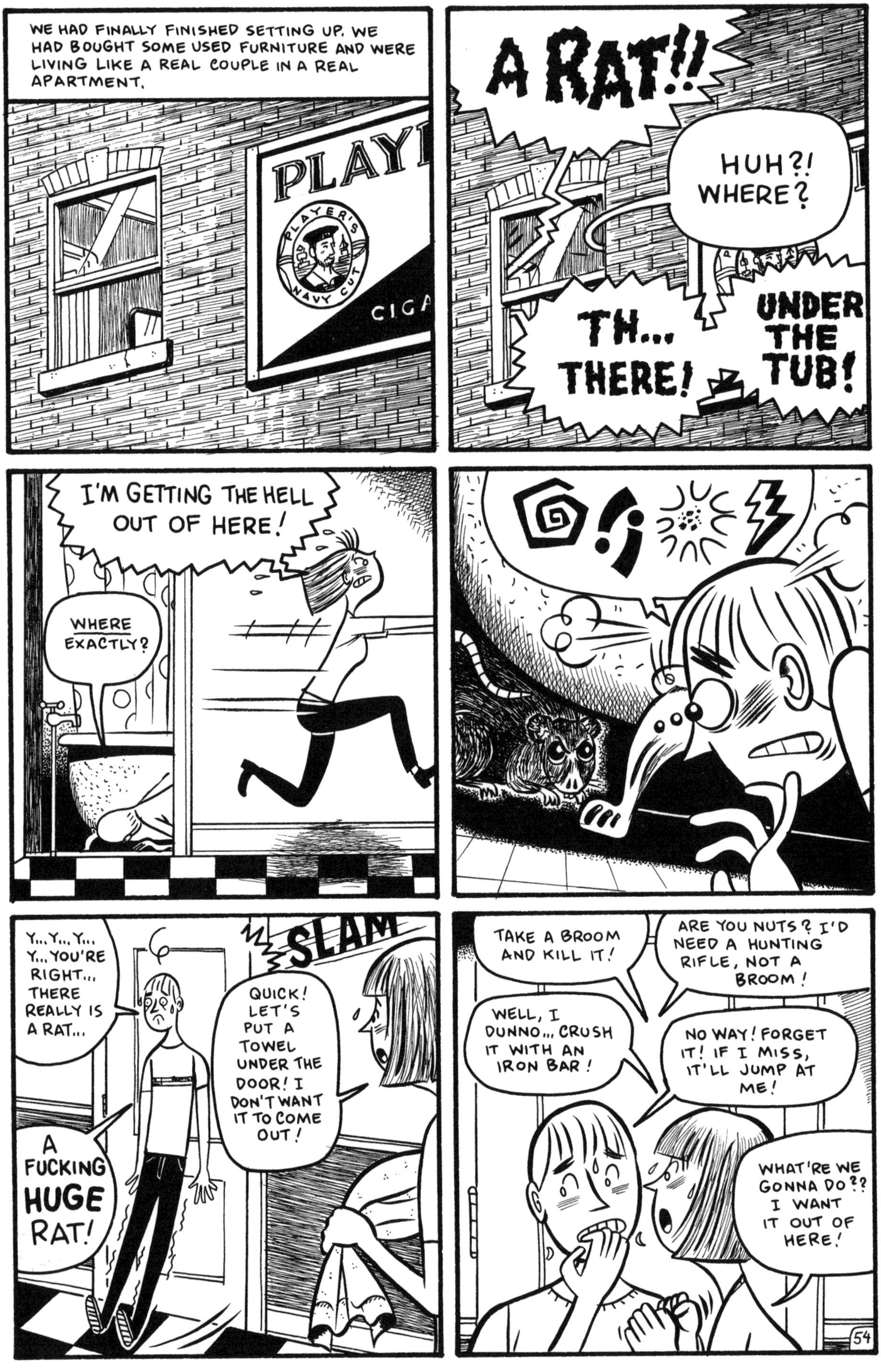
WE HAD FINALLY FINISHED SETTING UP. WE HAD BOUGHT SOME USED FURNITURE AND WERE LIVING LIKE A REAL COUPLE IN A REAL APARTMENT.
PLAY
PLAYER'S NAVY CUT
CIGA
A RAT!!
HUH?! WHERE?
TH... THERE!
UNDER THE TUB!
I'M GETTING THE HELL OUT OF HERE!
WHERE EXACTLY?
Y... Y... Y... Y... YOU'RE RIGHT... THERE REALLY IS A RAT...
A FUCKING HUGE RAT!
SLAM
QUICK! LET'S PUT A TOWEL UNDER THE DOOR! I DON'T WANT IT TO COME OUT!
TAKE A BROOM AND KILL IT!
ARE YOU NUTS? I'D NEED A HUNTING RIFLE, NOT A BROOM!
WELL, I DUNNO... CRUSH IT WITH AN IRON BAR!
NO WAY! FORGET IT! IF I MISS, IT'LL JUMP AT ME!
WHAT'RE WE GONNA DO?? I WANT IT OUT OF HERE!

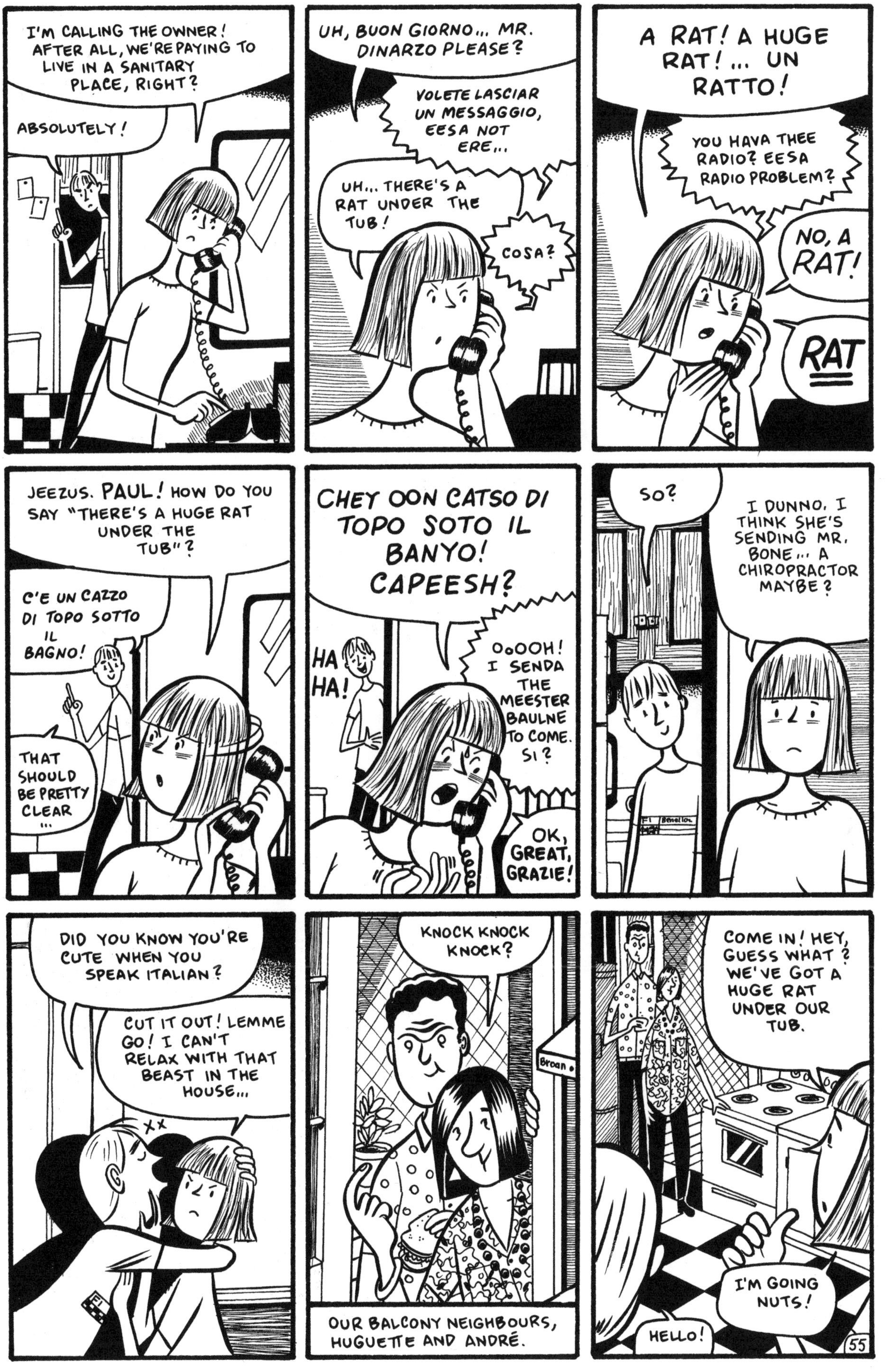
I'M CALLING THE OWNER! AFTER ALL, WE'RE PAYING TO LIVE IN A SANITARY PLACE, RIGHT?
ABSOLUTELY!
UH, BUON GIORNO... MR. DINARZO PLEASE?
VOLETE LASCIAR UN MESSAGGIO, EESA NOT ERE...
UH... THERE'S A RAT UNDER THE TUB!
COSA?
A RAT! A HUGE RAT! ... UN RATTO!
YOU HAVA THEE RADIO? EESA RADIO PROBLEM?
NO, A RAT!
RAT
JEEZUS. PAUL! HOW DO YOU SAY "THERE'S A HUGE RAT UNDER THE TUB"?
C'E UN CAZZO DI TOPO SOTTO IL BAGNO!
THAT SHOULD BE PRETTY CLEAR...
CHEY OON CATSO DI TOPO SOTO IL BANYO! CAPEESH?
HA HA!
OoOOH! I SENDA THE MEESTER BAULNE TO COME. SI?
OK, GREAT, GRAZIE!
SO?
I DUNNO. I THINK SHE'S SENDING MR. BONE... A CHIROPRACTOR MAYBE?
DID YOU KNOW YOU'RE CUTE WHEN YOU SPEAK ITALIAN?
CUT IT OUT! LEMME GO! I CAN'T RELAX WITH THAT BEAST IN THE HOUSE...
KNOCK KNOCK KNOCK?
Broan
OUR BALCONY NEIGHBOURS, HUGUETTE AND ANDRÉ.
COME IN! HEY, GUESS WHAT? WE'VE GOT A HUGE RAT UNDER OUR TUB.
I'M GOING NUTS!
HELLO!

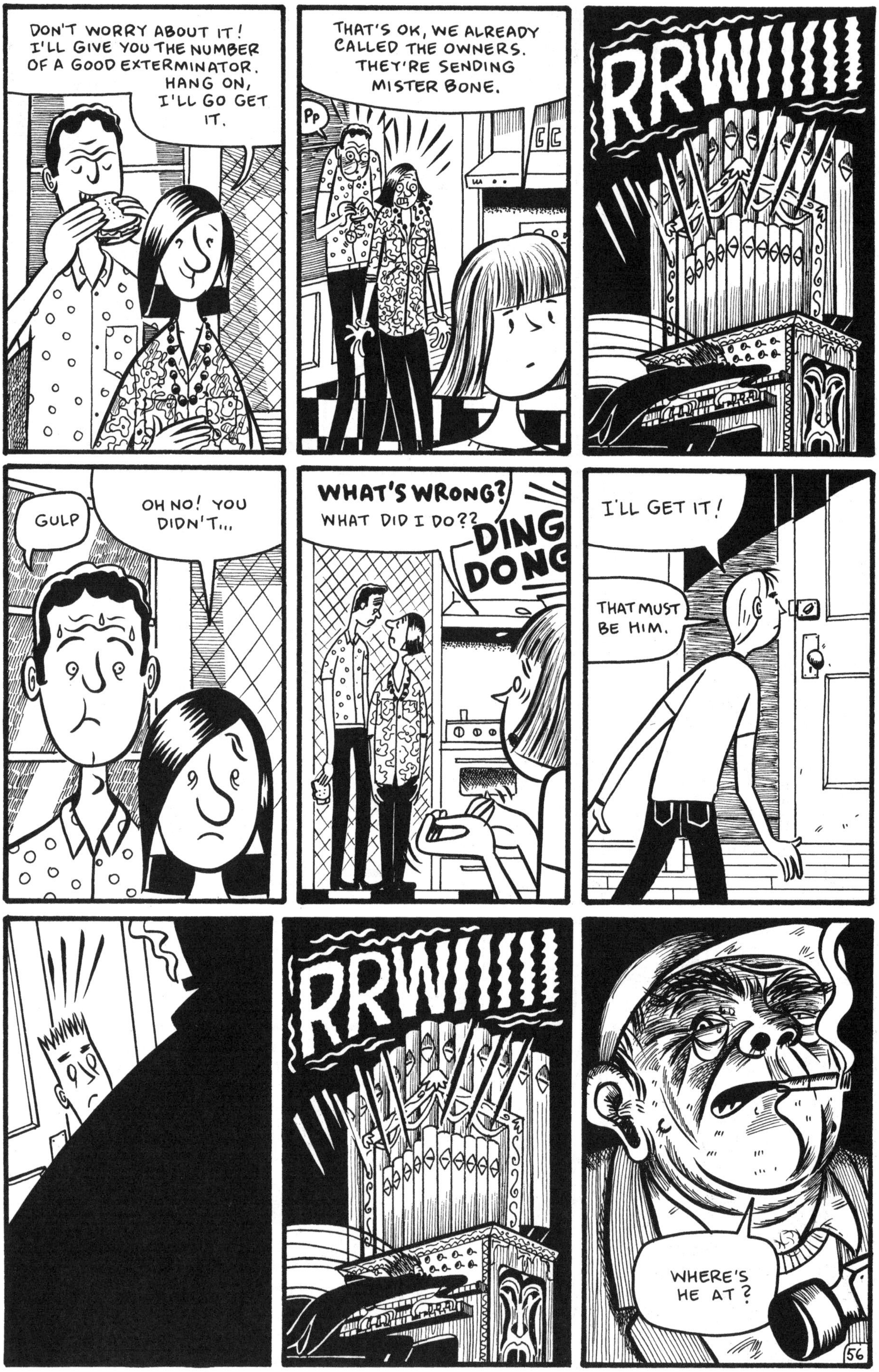
DON'T WORRY ABOUT IT! I'LL GIVE YOU THE NUMBER OF A GOOD EXTERMINATOR. HANG ON, I'LL GO GET IT.
THAT'S OK, WE ALREADY CALLED THE OWNERS. THEY'RE SENDING MISTER BONE.
PP
RRWIIIIII
GULP
OH NO! YOU DIDN'T...
WHAT'S WRONG? WHAT DID I DO??
DING DONG
I'LL GET IT!
THAT MUST BE HIM.
RRWIIIIII
WHERE'S HE AT?
56

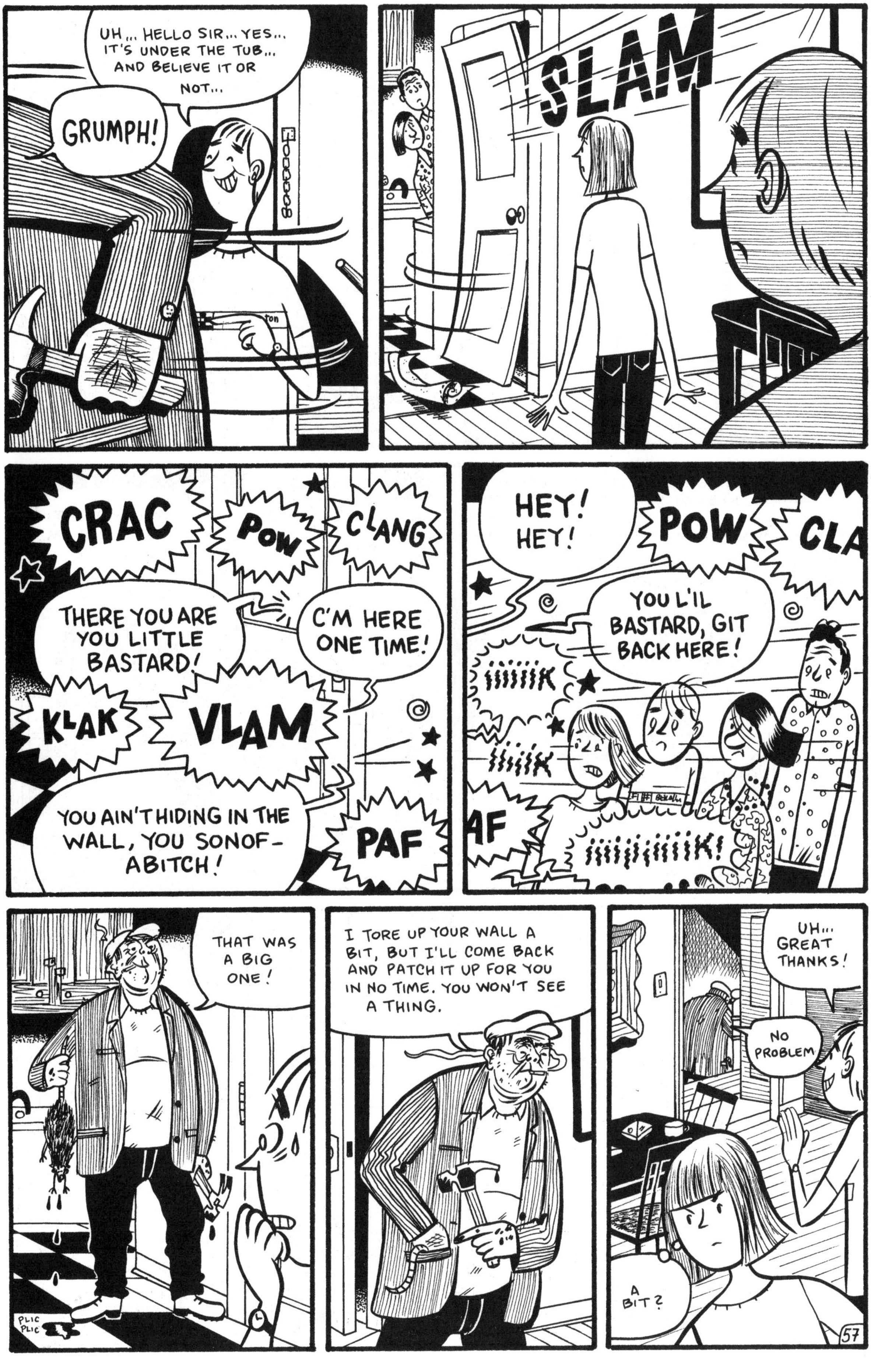

UH... HELLO SIR... YES... IT'S UNDER THE TUB... AND BELIEVE IT OR NOT...
GRUMPH!
SLAM
CRAC
POW
CLANG
THERE YOU ARE YOU LITTLE BASTARD!
C'M HERE ONE TIME!
KLAK
VLAM
YOU AIN'T HIDING IN THE WALL, YOU SONOF-ABITCH!
PAF
HEY! HEY!
POW
CLA
YOU L'IL BASTARD, GIT BACK HERE!
IIIIIIK
IIIIIK
AF
IIIIIIIIIIIIK!
THAT WAS A BIG ONE!
PLIC PLIC
I TORE UP YOUR WALL A BIT, BUT I'LL COME BACK AND PATCH IT UP FOR YOU IN NO TIME. YOU WON'T SEE A THING.
UH... GREAT THANKS!
NO PROBLEM
A BIT?

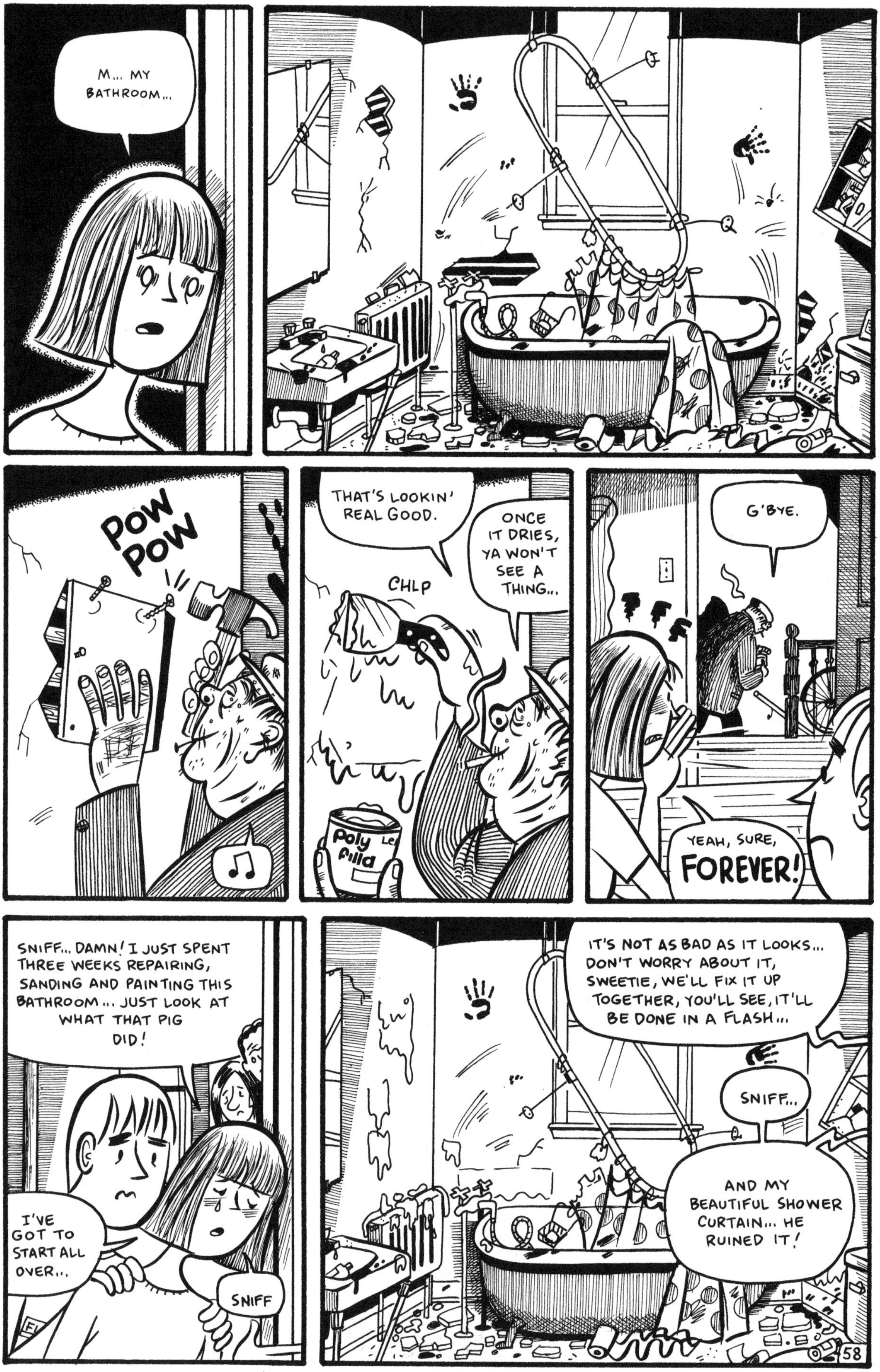
M... MY BATHROOM...
POW POW
THAT'S LOOKIN' REAL GOOD.
CHLP
ONCE IT DRIES, YA WON'T SEE A THING...
Poly Filla
G'BYE.
YEAH, SURE, FOREVER!
SNIFF... DAMN! I JUST SPENT THREE WEEKS REPAIRING, SANDING AND PAINTING THIS BATHROOM... JUST LOOK AT WHAT THAT PIG DID!
I'VE GOT TO START ALL OVER...
SNIFF
IT'S NOT AS BAD AS IT LOOKS... DON'T WORRY ABOUT IT, SWEETIE, WE'LL FIX IT UP TOGETHER, YOU'LL SEE, IT'LL BE DONE IN A FLASH...
SNIFF...
AND MY BEAUTIFUL SHOWER CURTAIN... HE RUINED IT!

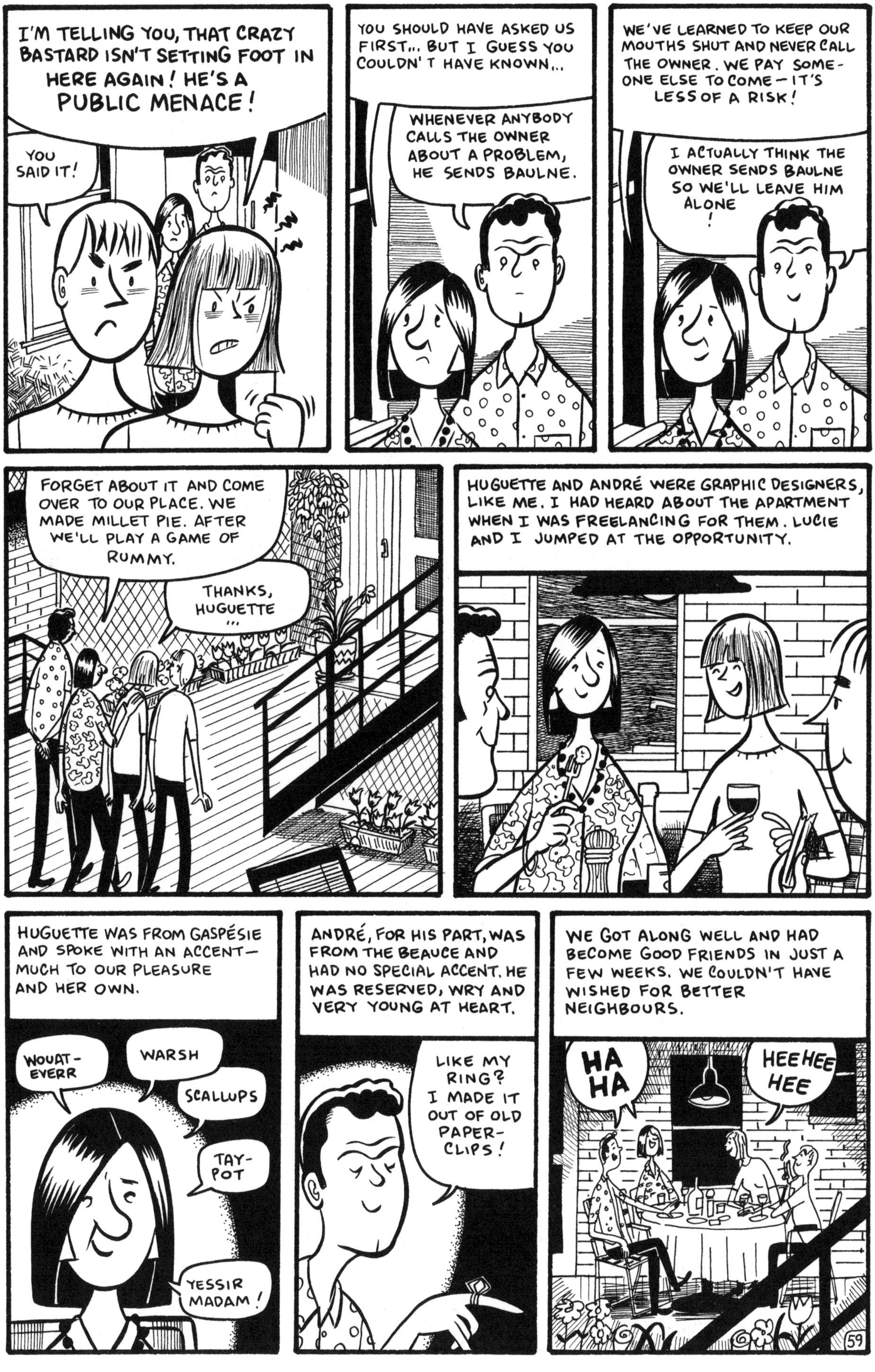
I'M TELLING YOU, THAT CRAZY BASTARD ISN'T SETTING FOOT IN HERE AGAIN! HE'S A PUBLIC MENACE!
YOU SAID IT!
YOU SHOULD HAVE ASKED US FIRST... BUT I GUESS YOU COULDN'T HAVE KNOWN...
WHENEVER ANYBODY CALLS THE OWNER ABOUT A PROBLEM, HE SENDS BAULNE.
WE'VE LEARNED TO KEEP OUR MOUTHS SHUT AND NEVER CALL THE OWNER. WE PAY SOMEONE ELSE TO COME — IT'S LESS OF A RISK!
I ACTUALLY THINK THE OWNER SENDS BAULNE SO WE'LL LEAVE HIM ALONE!
FORGET ABOUT IT AND COME OVER TO OUR PLACE. WE MADE MILLET PIE. AFTER WE'LL PLAY A GAME OF RUMMY.
THANKS, HUGUETTE...
HUGUETTE AND ANDRÉ WERE GRAPHIC DESIGNERS, LIKE ME. I HAD HEARD ABOUT THE APARTMENT WHEN I WAS FREELANCING FOR THEM. LUCIE AND I JUMPED AT THE OPPORTUNITY.
HUGUETTE WAS FROM GASPÉSIE AND SPOKE WITH AN ACCENT— MUCH TO OUR PLEASURE AND HER OWN.
WOUAT-EVERR
WARSH
SCALLUPS
TAY-POT
YESSIR MADAM!
ANDRÉ, FOR HIS PART, WAS FROM THE BEAUCE AND HAD NO SPECIAL ACCENT. HE WAS RESERVED, WRY AND VERY YOUNG AT HEART.
LIKE MY RING? I MADE IT OUT OF OLD PAPER-CLIPS!
WE GOT ALONG WELL AND HAD BECOME GOOD FRIENDS IN JUST A FEW WEEKS. WE COULDN'T HAVE WISHED FOR BETTER NEIGHBOURS.
HA HA
HEE HEE HEE

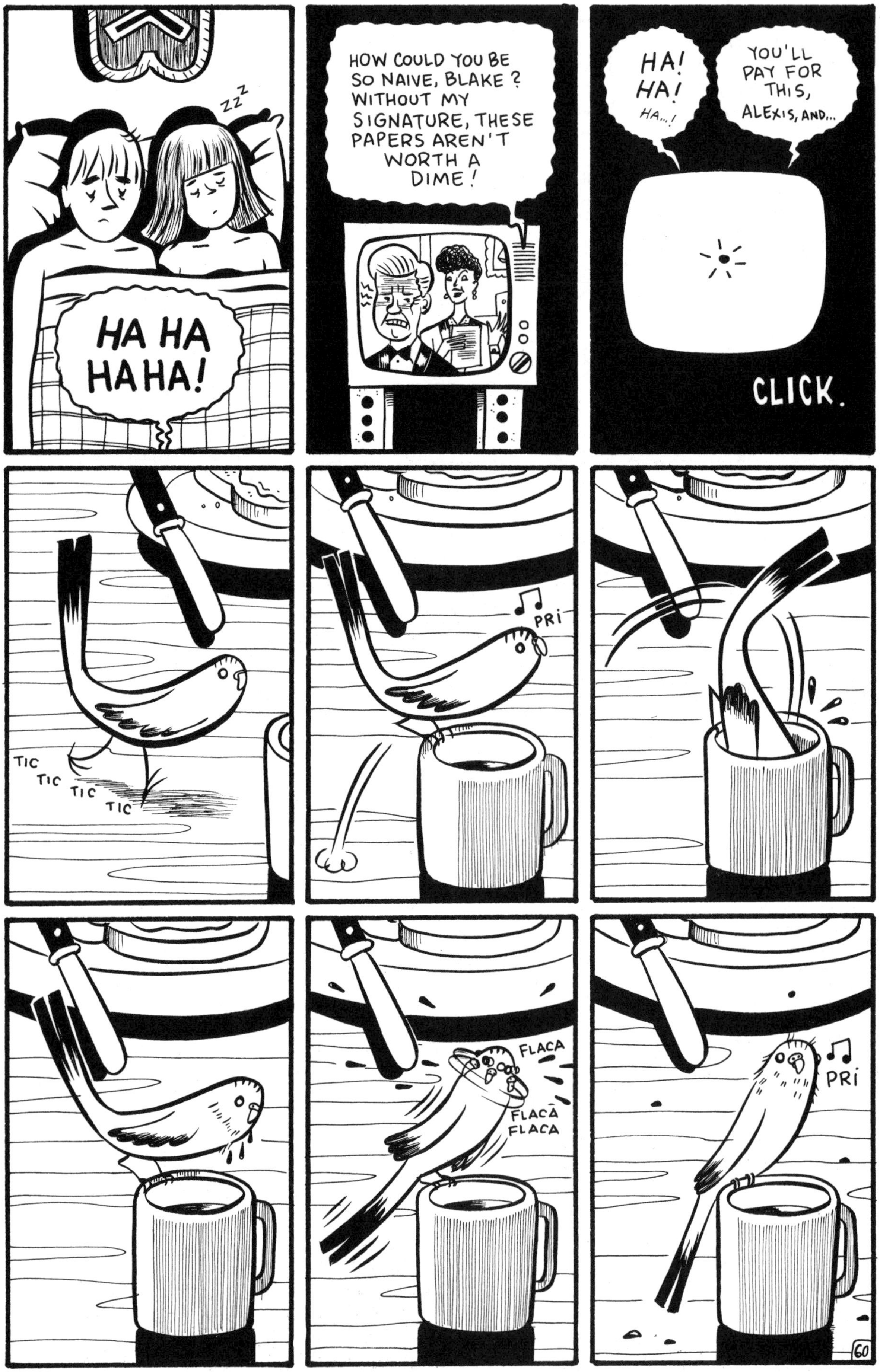
ZZZ
HA HA HAHA!
HOW COULD YOU BE SO NAIVE, BLAKE ? WITHOUT MY SIGNATURE, THESE PAPERS AREN'T WORTH A DIME!
HA! HA! HA...!
YOU'LL PAY FOR THIS, ALEXIS, AND...
CLICK.
TIC TIC TIC TIC
PRI
FLACA
FLACA FLACA
PRI

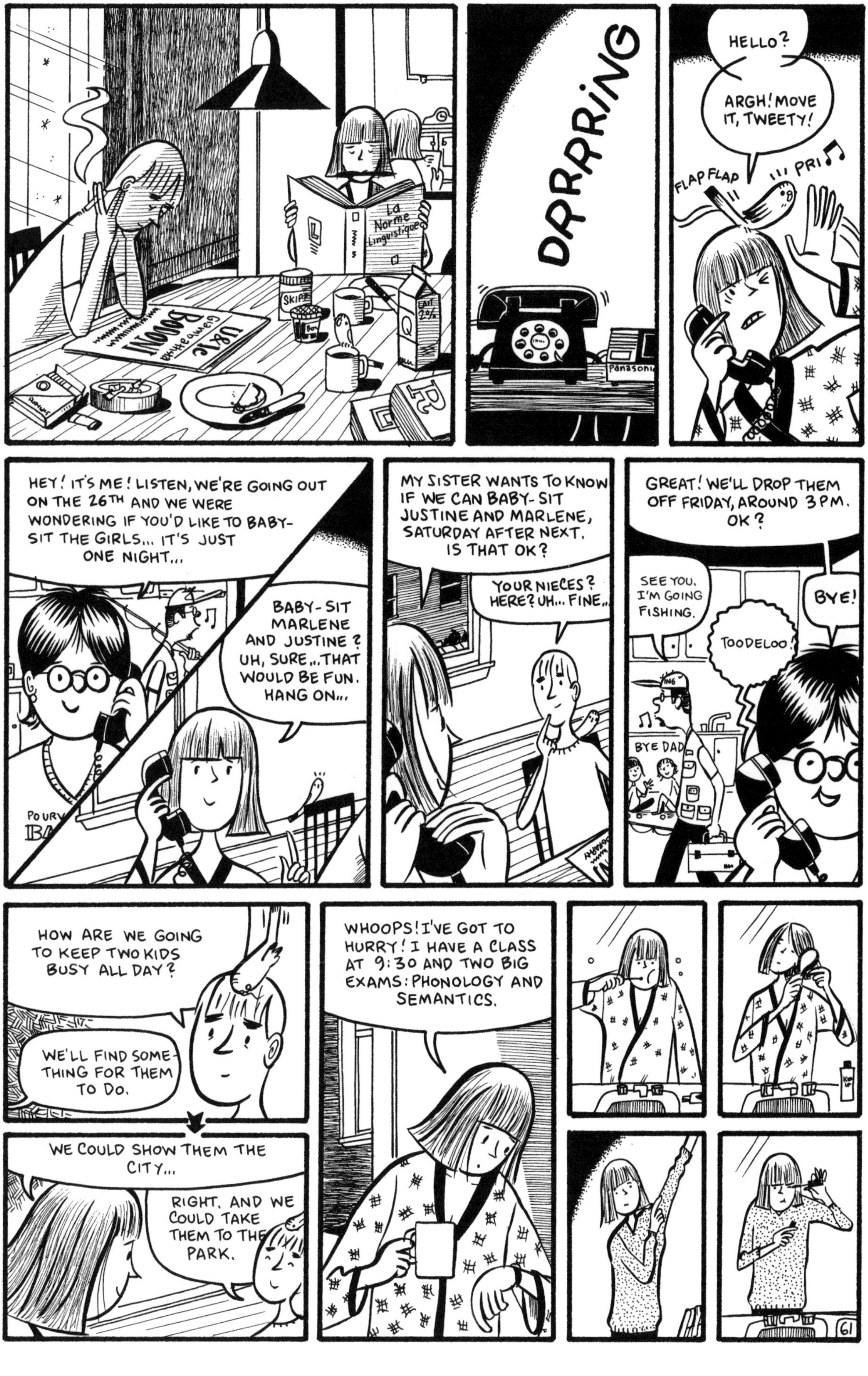
Le Bodoni
La Norme linguistique
DRRRING
Panasonic
HELLO?
ARGH! MOVE IT, TWEETY!
FLAP FLAP
PRI ♫
HEY! IT'S ME! LISTEN, WE'RE GOING OUT ON THE 26TH AND WE WERE WONDERING IF YOU'D LIKE TO BABY-SIT THE GIRLS... IT'S JUST ONE NIGHT...
BABY-SIT MARLENE AND JUSTINE? UH, SURE... THAT WOULD BE FUN. HANG ON...
MY SISTER WANTS TO KNOW IF WE CAN BABY-SIT JUSTINE AND MARLENE, SATURDAY AFTER NEXT. IS THAT OK?
YOUR NIECES? HERE? UH... FINE...
GREAT! WE'LL DROP THEM OFF FRIDAY, AROUND 3 PM. OK?
SEE YOU. I'M GOING FISHING.
TOODELOO!
BYE!
BYE DAD
HOW ARE WE GOING TO KEEP TWO KIDS BUSY ALL DAY?
WE'LL FIND SOMETHING FOR THEM TO DO.
WE COULD SHOW THEM THE CITY...
RIGHT. AND WE COULD TAKE THEM TO THE PARK.
WHOOPS! I'VE GOT TO HURRY! I HAVE A CLASS AT 9:30 AND TWO BIG EXAMS: PHONOLOGY AND SEMANTICS.

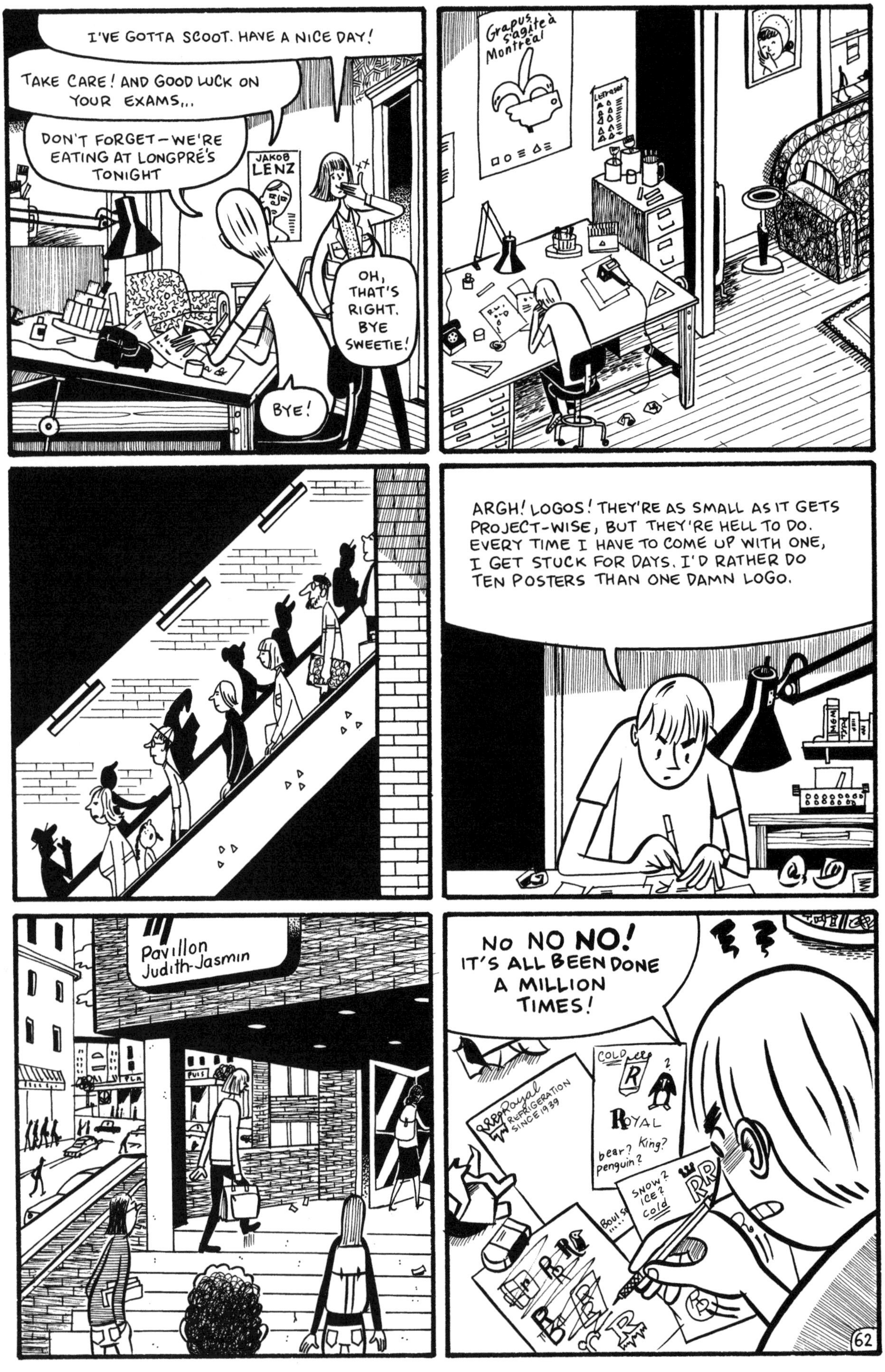
I'VE GOTTA SCOOT. HAVE A NICE DAY!
TAKE CARE! AND GOOD LUCK ON YOUR EXAMS...
DON'T FORGET—WE'RE EATING AT LONGPRÉ'S TONIGHT
JAKOB LENZ
OH, THAT'S RIGHT. BYE SWEETIE!
BYE!
Grapus s'agite à Montréal
Letraset
ARGH! LOGOS! THEY'RE AS SMALL AS IT GETS PROJECT-WISE, BUT THEY'RE HELL TO DO. EVERY TIME I HAVE TO COME UP WITH ONE, I GET STUCK FOR DAYS. I'D RATHER DO TEN POSTERS THAN ONE DAMN LOGO.
Pavillon Judith-Jasmin
No NO NO! IT'S ALL BEEN DONE A MILLION TIMES!
Royal REFRIGERATION SINCE 1939
COLD
ROYAL
bear? King? penguin?
SNOW? ICE? cold

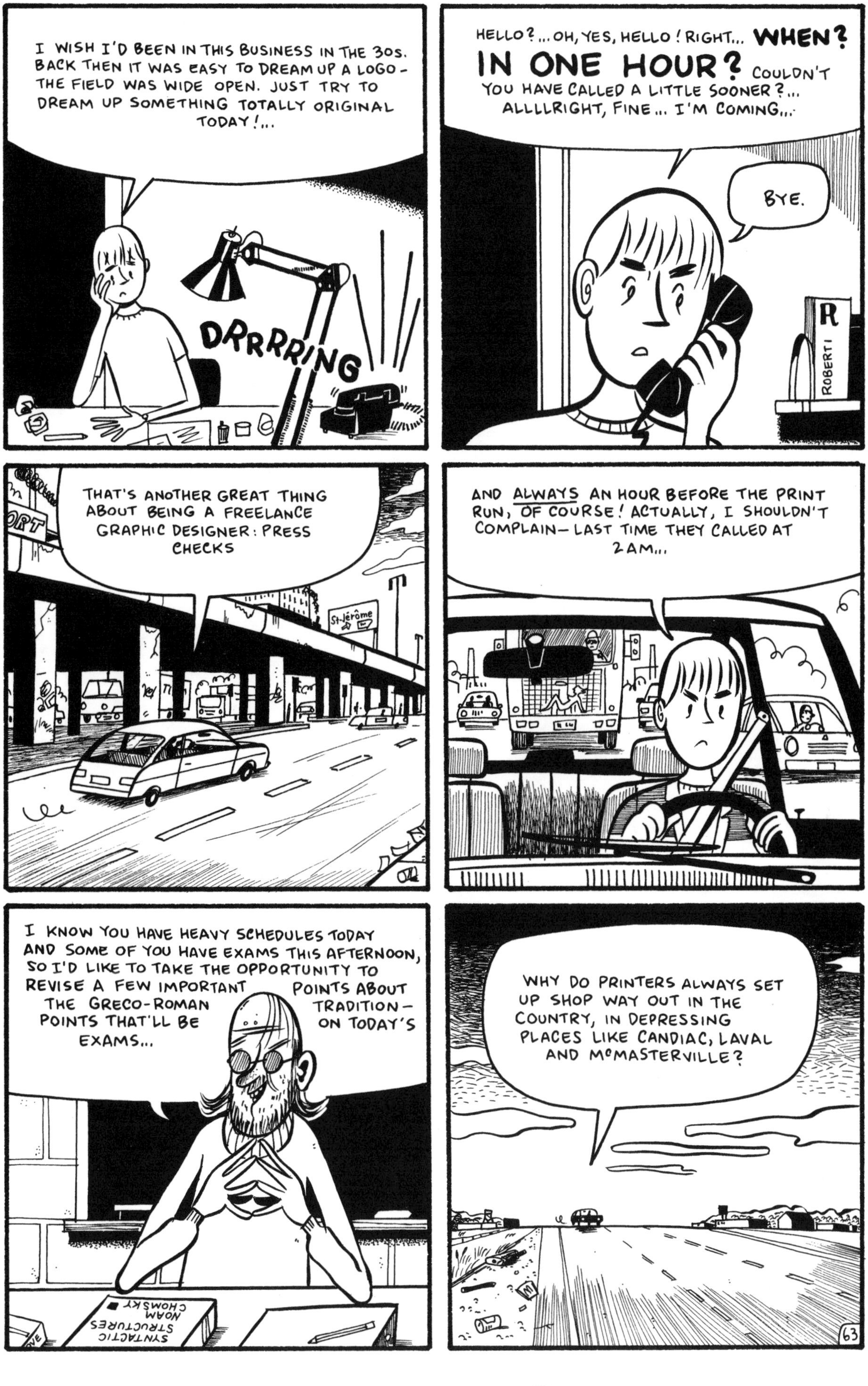
I WISH I'D BEEN IN THIS BUSINESS IN THE 30S. BACK THEN IT WAS EASY TO DREAM UP A LOGO - THE FIELD WAS WIDE OPEN. JUST TRY TO DREAM UP SOMETHING TOTALLY ORIGINAL TODAY!...
DRRRRRING
HELLO?... OH, YES, HELLO! RIGHT... WHEN? IN ONE HOUR? COULDN'T YOU HAVE CALLED A LITTLE SOONER?... ALLLLRIGHT, FINE... I'M COMING...
BYE.
R
ROBERTI
THAT'S ANOTHER GREAT THING ABOUT BEING A FREELANCE GRAPHIC DESIGNER: PRESS CHECKS
St-Jérôme
AND ALWAYS AN HOUR BEFORE THE PRINT RUN, OF COURSE! ACTUALLY, I SHOULDN'T COMPLAIN— LAST TIME THEY CALLED AT 2AM...
I KNOW YOU HAVE HEAVY SCHEDULES TODAY AND SOME OF YOU HAVE EXAMS THIS AFTERNOON, SO I'D LIKE TO TAKE THE OPPORTUNITY TO REVISE A FEW IMPORTANT POINTS ABOUT THE GRECO-ROMAN TRADITION— POINTS THAT'LL BE ON TODAY'S EXAMS...
SYNTACTIC STRUCTURES NOAM CHOMSKY
WHY DO PRINTERS ALWAYS SET UP SHOP WAY OUT IN THE COUNTRY, IN DEPRESSING PLACES LIKE CANDIAC, LAVAL AND McMASTERVILLE?
63

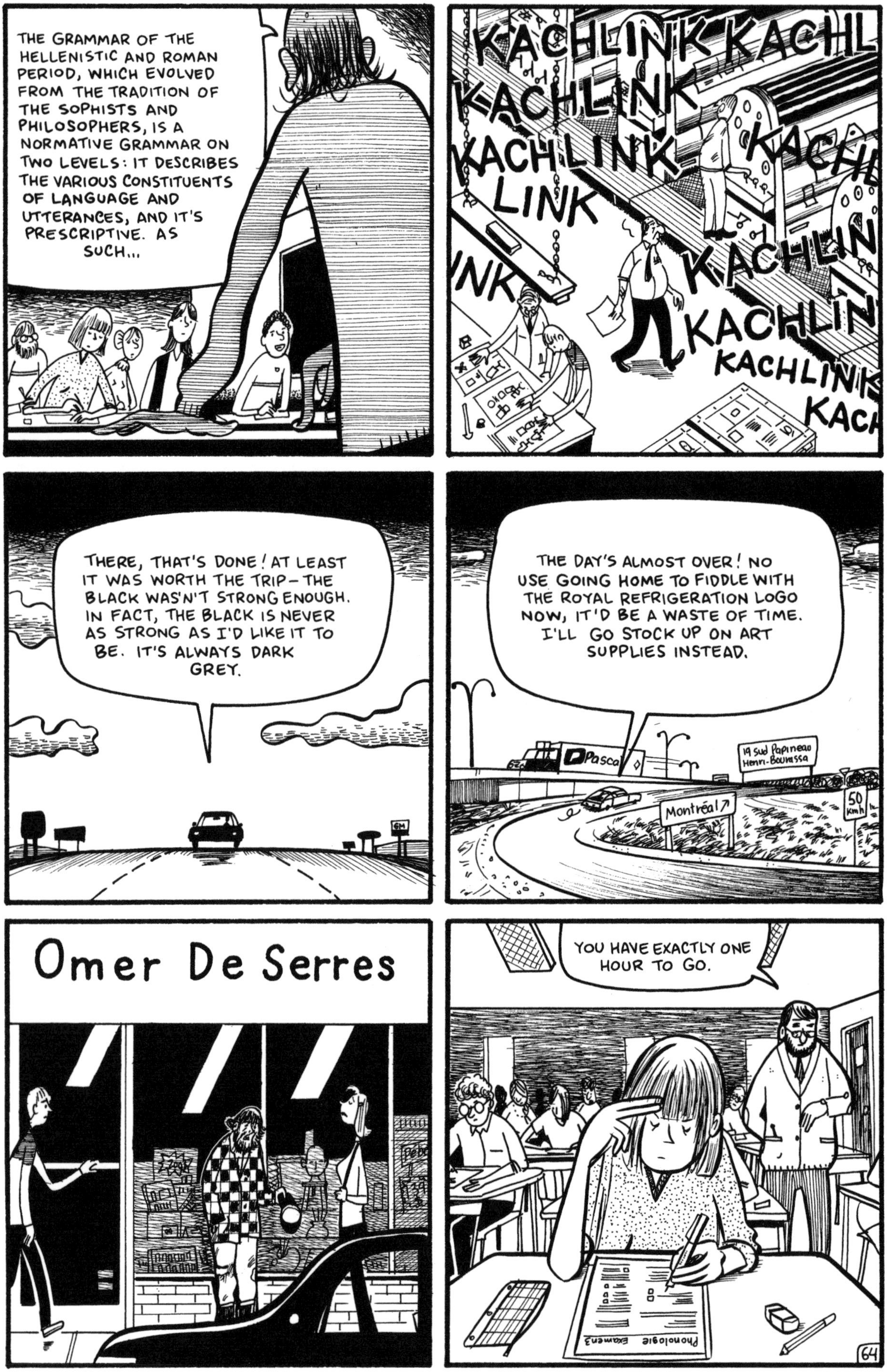
THE GRAMMAR OF THE HELLENISTIC AND ROMAN PERIOD, WHICH EVOLVED FROM THE TRADITION OF THE SOPHISTS AND PHILOSOPHERS, IS A NORMATIVE GRAMMAR ON TWO LEVELS: IT DESCRIBES THE VARIOUS CONSTITUENTS OF LANGUAGE AND UTTERANCES, AND IT'S PRESCRIPTIVE. AS SUCH...
KACHLINK KACHL
KACHLINK
KACHLINK
LINK
KACH
NK
KACHLIN
KACHLIN
KACHLINK
KACH
THERE, THAT'S DONE! AT LEAST IT WAS WORTH THE TRIP– THE BLACK WAS'N'T STRONG ENOUGH. IN FACT, THE BLACK IS NEVER AS STRONG AS I'D LIKE IT TO BE. IT'S ALWAYS DARK GREY.
THE DAY'S ALMOST OVER! NO USE GOING HOME TO FIDDLE WITH THE ROYAL REFRIGERATION LOGO NOW, IT'D BE A WASTE OF TIME. I'LL GO STOCK UP ON ART SUPPLIES INSTEAD.
19 Sud Papineau
Henri-Bourassa
Montréal
50 km/h
Omer De Serres
YOU HAVE EXACTLY ONE HOUR TO GO.
Phonologie Examens
64

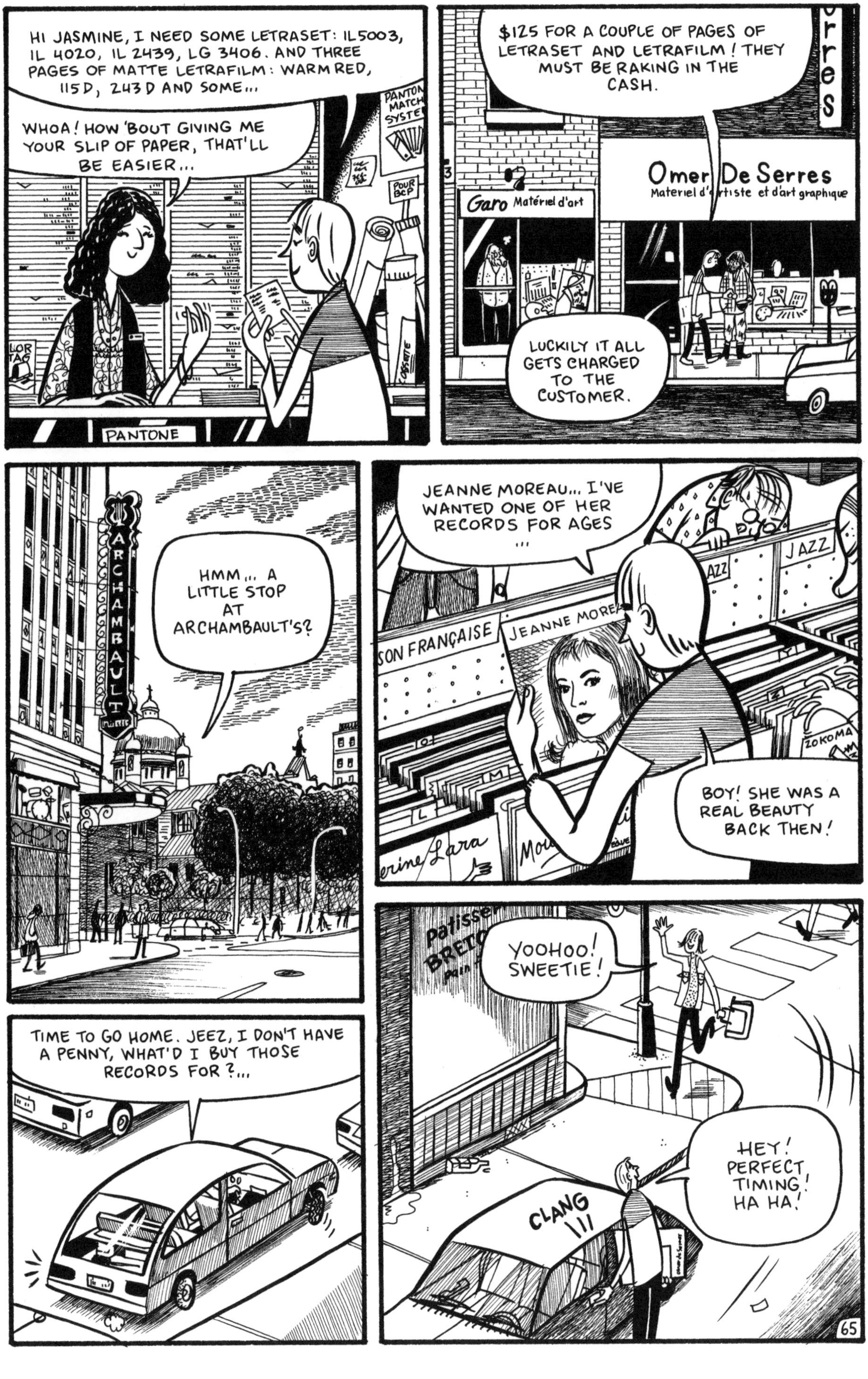
HI JASMINE, I NEED SOME LETRASET: IL5003, IL 4020, IL 2439, LG 3406. AND THREE PAGES OF MATTE LETRAFILM: WARM RED, 115D, 243D AND SOME...
WHOA! HOW 'BOUT GIVING ME YOUR SLIP OF PAPER, THAT'LL BE EASIER...
PANTONE MATCH SYSTE
POUR BCP
PANTONE
$125 FOR A COUPLE OF PAGES OF LETRASET AND LETRAFILM! THEY MUST BE RAKING IN THE CASH.
Garo Matériel d'art
Omer De Serres
Materiel d'artiste et d'art graphique
LUCKILY IT ALL GETS CHARGED TO THE CUSTOMER.
ARCHAMBAULT
HMM... A LITTLE STOP AT ARCHAMBAULT'S?
JEANNE MOREAU... I'VE WANTED ONE OF HER RECORDS FOR AGES...
JAZZ
JEANNE MORE
SON FRANÇAISE
BOY! SHE WAS A REAL BEAUTY BACK THEN!
TIME TO GO HOME. JEEZ, I DON'T HAVE A PENNY, WHAT'D I BUY THOSE RECORDS FOR?...
YOOHOO! SWEETIE!
HEY! PERFECT TIMING! HA HA!
CLANG

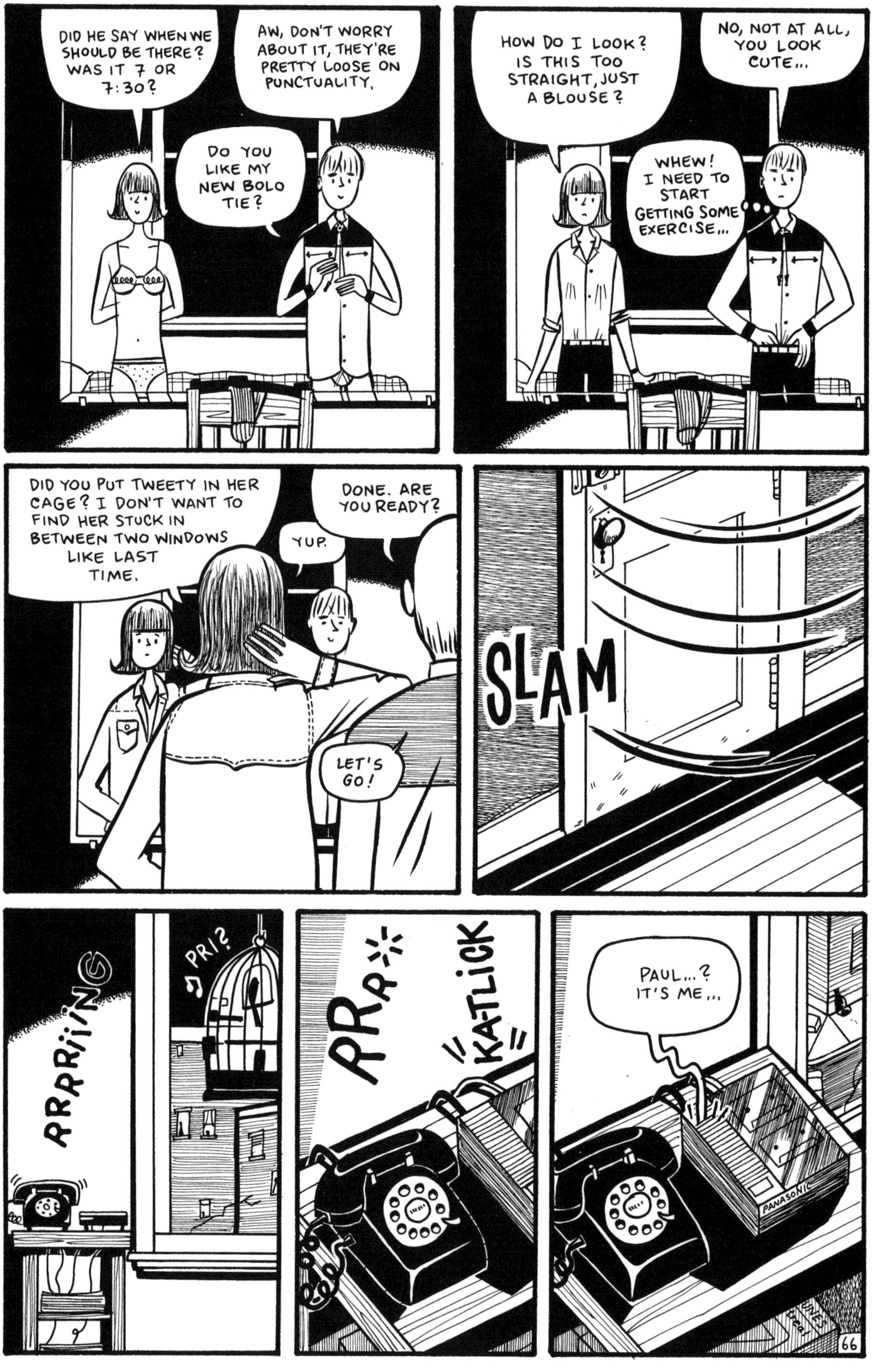
DID HE SAY WHEN WE SHOULD BE THERE? WAS IT 7 OR 7:30?
AW, DON'T WORRY ABOUT IT, THEY'RE PRETTY LOOSE ON PUNCTUALITY.
DO YOU LIKE MY NEW BOLO TIE?
HOW DO I LOOK? IS THIS TOO STRAIGHT, JUST A BLOUSE?
NO, NOT AT ALL, YOU LOOK CUTE...
WHEW! I NEED TO START GETTING SOME EXERCISE...
DID YOU PUT TWEETY IN HER CAGE? I DON'T WANT TO FIND HER STUCK IN BETWEEN TWO WINDOWS LIKE LAST TIME.
YUP.
DONE. ARE YOU READY?
LET'S GO!
SLAM
RRRRiiiiNG
PRI?
RRR
KA-TLICK
PAUL...? IT'S ME...
PANASONIC

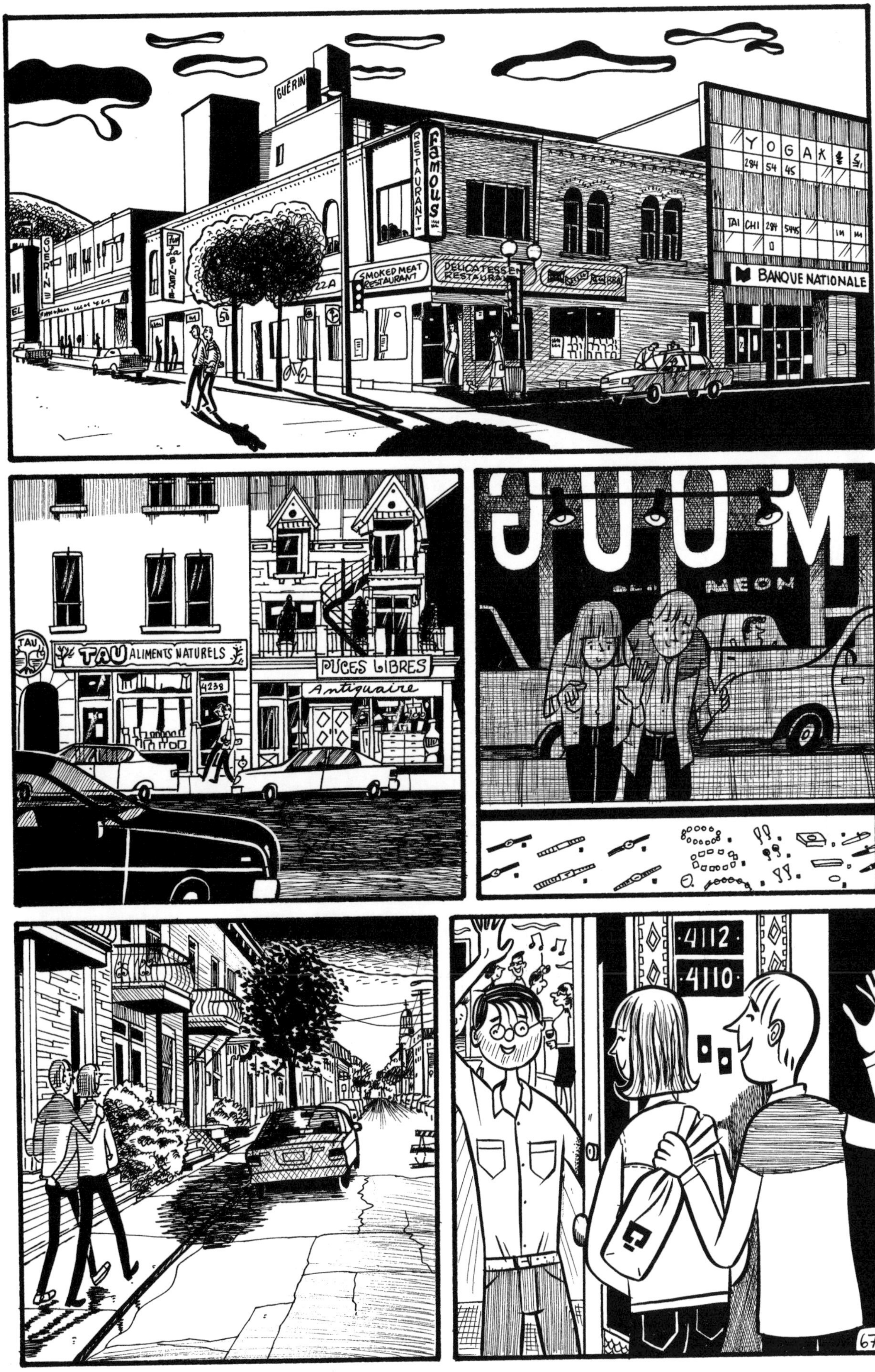
GUÉRIN
RESTAURANT
Famous
GUÉRIN
La Binerie
SMOKED MEAT RESTAURANT
DELICATESSEN RESTAURANT
YOGA
TAI CHI
BANQUE NATIONALE
TAU
TAU ALIMENTS NATURELS
4238
PUCES LIBRES
Antiquaire
4112
4110

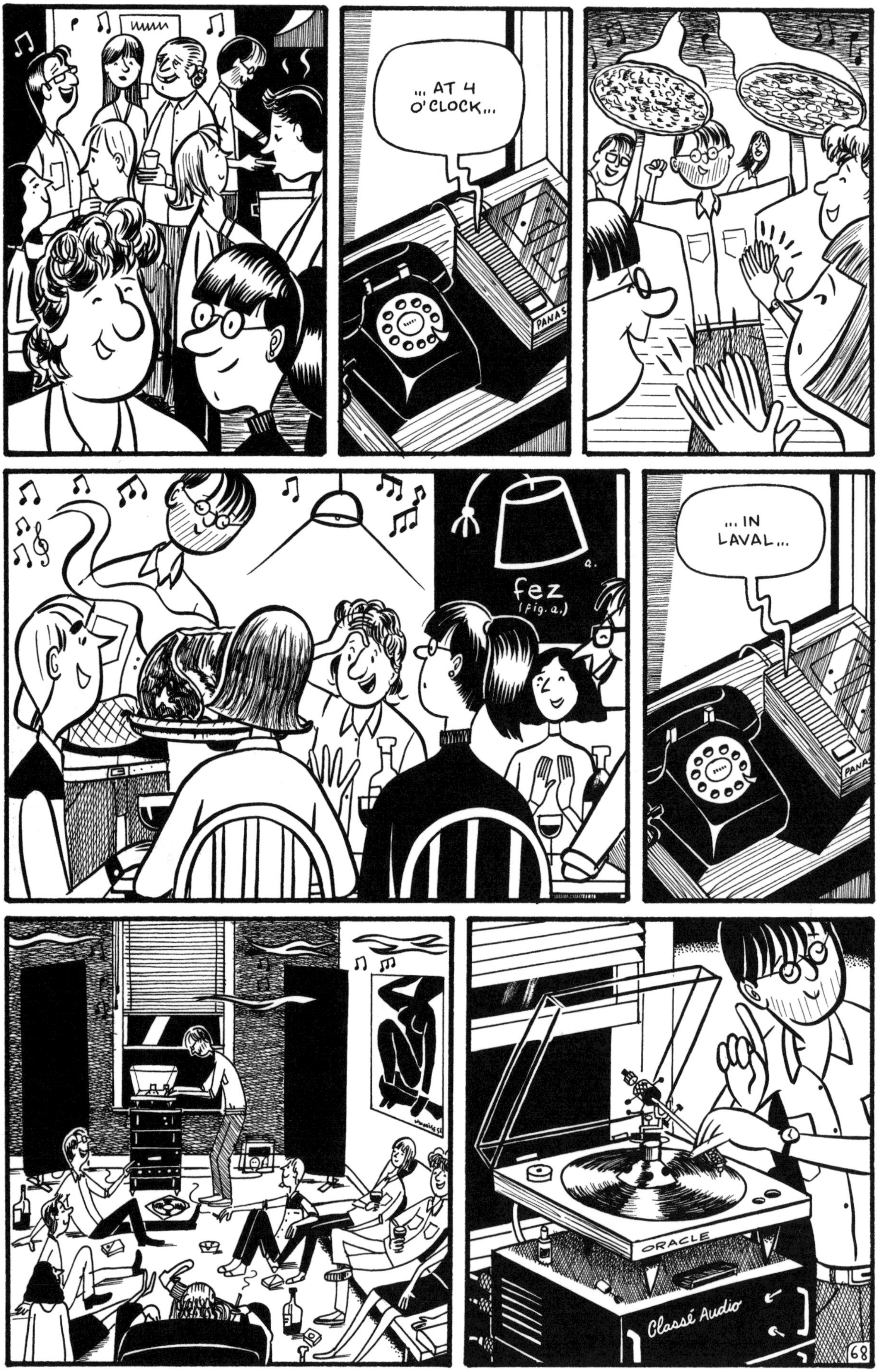
... AT 4 O'CLOCK...
PANAS
a.
fez
(fig. a.)
... IN LAVAL...
PANAS
ORACLE
Classé Audio

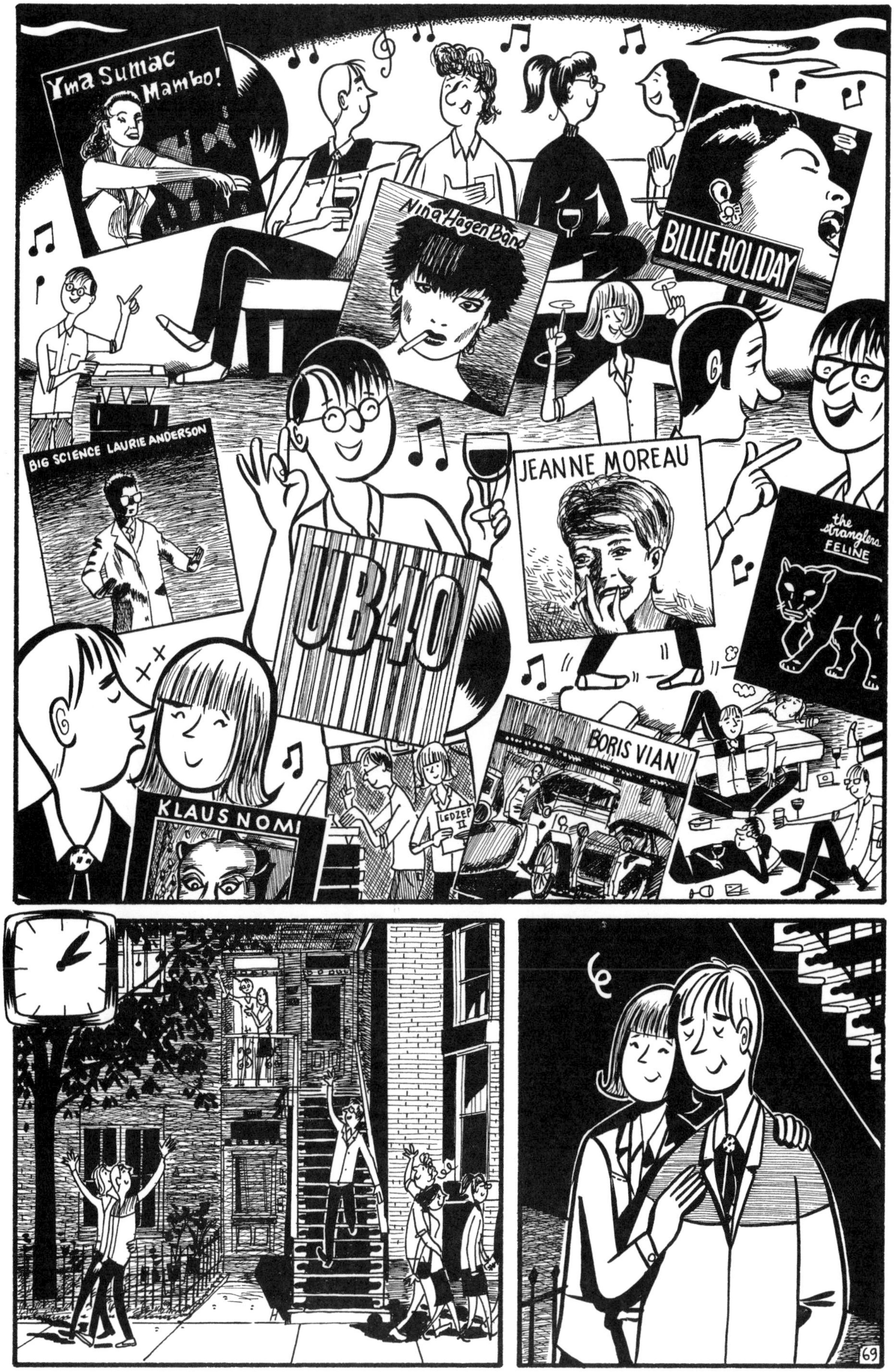
Yma Sumac
Mambo!
Nina Hagen Band
BILLIE HOLIDAY
BIG SCIENCE LAURIE ANDERSON
JEANNE MOREAU
UB40
the stranglers
FELINE
BORIS VIAN
LEDZEP II
KLAUS NOMI

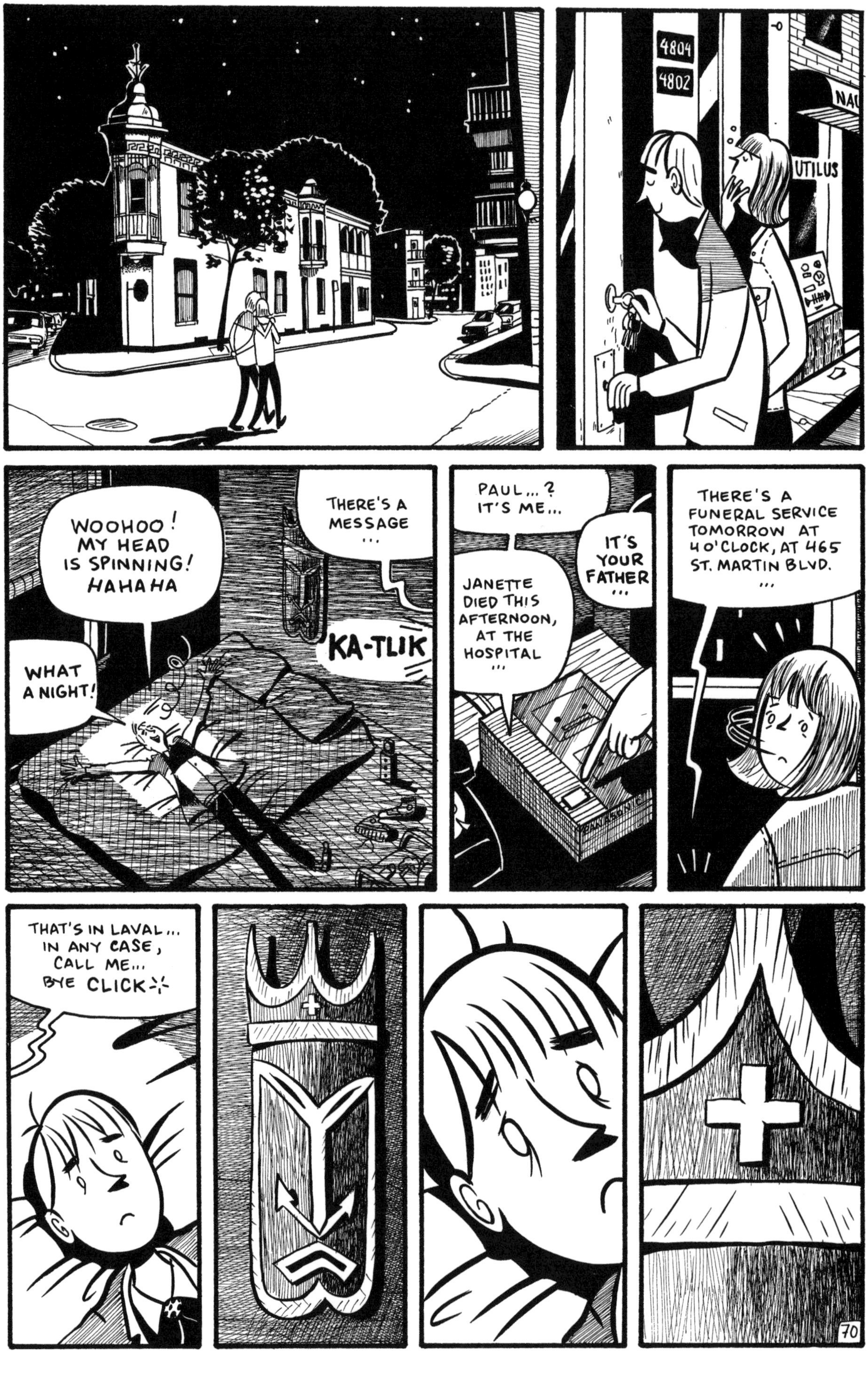
4804
4802
NAU
UTILUS
WOOHOO! MY HEAD IS SPINNING! HAHAHA
WHAT A NIGHT!
THERE'S A MESSAGE ...
KA-TLIK
PAUL...? IT'S ME...
IT'S YOUR FATHER ...
JANETTE DIED THIS AFTERNOON, AT THE HOSPITAL ...
THERE'S A FUNERAL SERVICE TOMORROW AT 4 O'CLOCK, AT 465 ST. MARTIN BLVD. ...
THAT'S IN LAVAL... IN ANY CASE, CALL ME... BYE CLICK

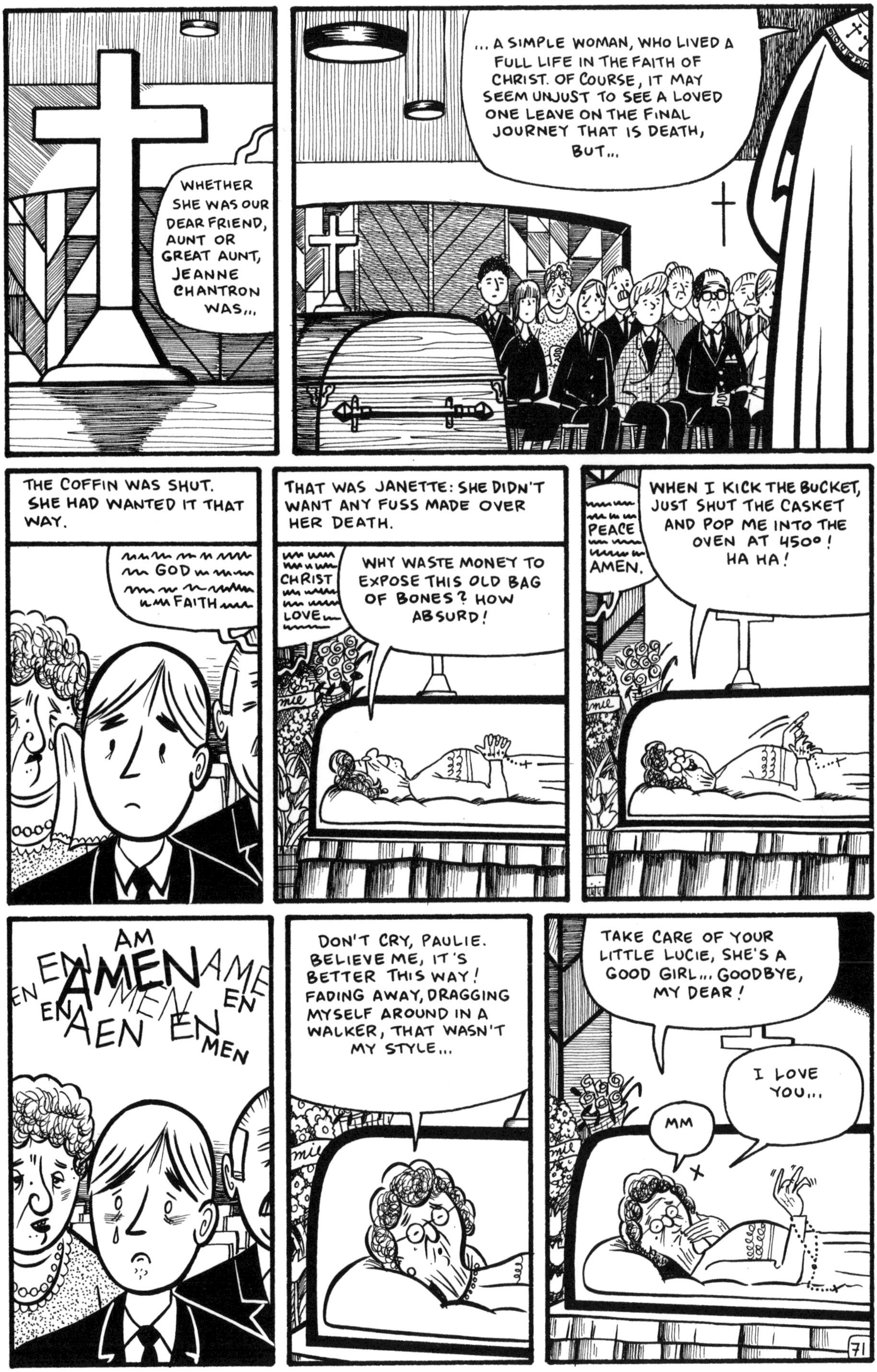
WHETHER SHE WAS OUR DEAR FRIEND, AUNT OR GREAT AUNT, JEANNE CHANTRON WAS...
... A SIMPLE WOMAN, WHO LIVED A FULL LIFE IN THE FAITH OF CHRIST. OF COURSE, IT MAY SEEM UNJUST TO SEE A LOVED ONE LEAVE ON THE FINAL JOURNEY THAT IS DEATH, BUT...
THE COFFIN WAS SHUT. SHE HAD WANTED IT THAT WAY.
GOD
FAITH
THAT WAS JANETTE: SHE DIDN'T WANT ANY FUSS MADE OVER HER DEATH.
CHRIST
LOVE
WHY WASTE MONEY TO EXPOSE THIS OLD BAG OF BONES? HOW ABSURD!
PEACE
AMEN.
WHEN I KICK THE BUCKET, JUST SHUT THE CASKET AND POP ME INTO THE OVEN AT 450°! HA HA!
AM AMEN AME EN EN EN MEN EN AEN EN MEN
DON'T CRY, PAULIE. BELIEVE ME, IT'S BETTER THIS WAY! FADING AWAY, DRAGGING MYSELF AROUND IN A WALKER, THAT WASN'T MY STYLE...
TAKE CARE OF YOUR LITTLE LUCIE, SHE'S A GOOD GIRL... GOODBYE, MY DEAR!
I LOVE YOU...
MM

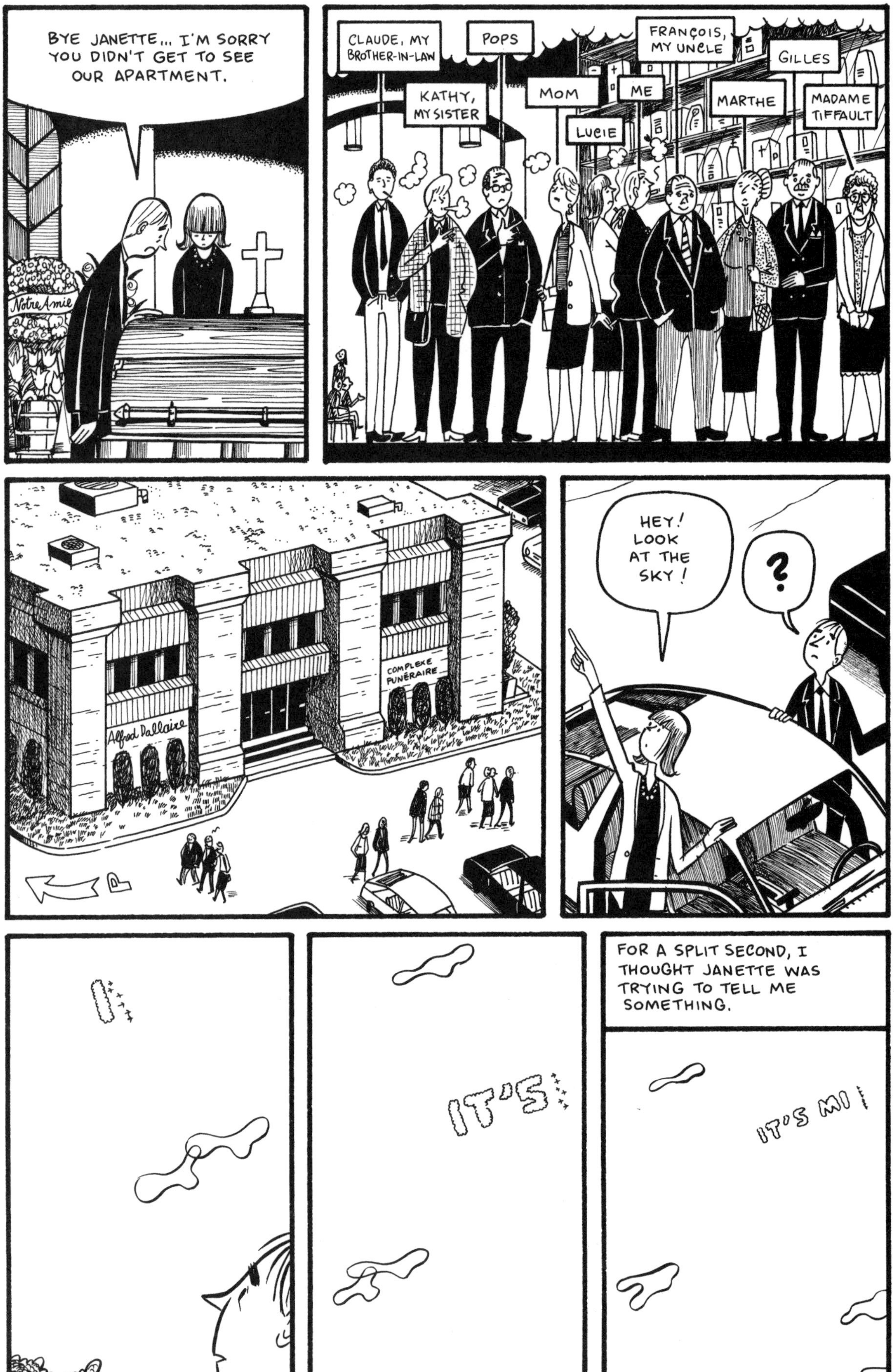

BYE JANETTE... I'M SORRY YOU DIDN'T GET TO SEE OUR APARTMENT.
Notre Amie
CLAUDE, MY BROTHER-IN-LAW
KATHY, MY SISTER
POPS
MOM
LUCIE
FRANÇOIS, MY UNCLE
ME
MARTHE
GILLES
MADAME TIFFAULT
Alfred Dallaire
COMPLEXE FUNÉRAIRE
HEY! LOOK AT THE SKY!
?
IT'S
FOR A SPLIT SECOND, I THOUGHT JANETTE WAS TRYING TO TELL ME SOMETHING.
IT'S MI

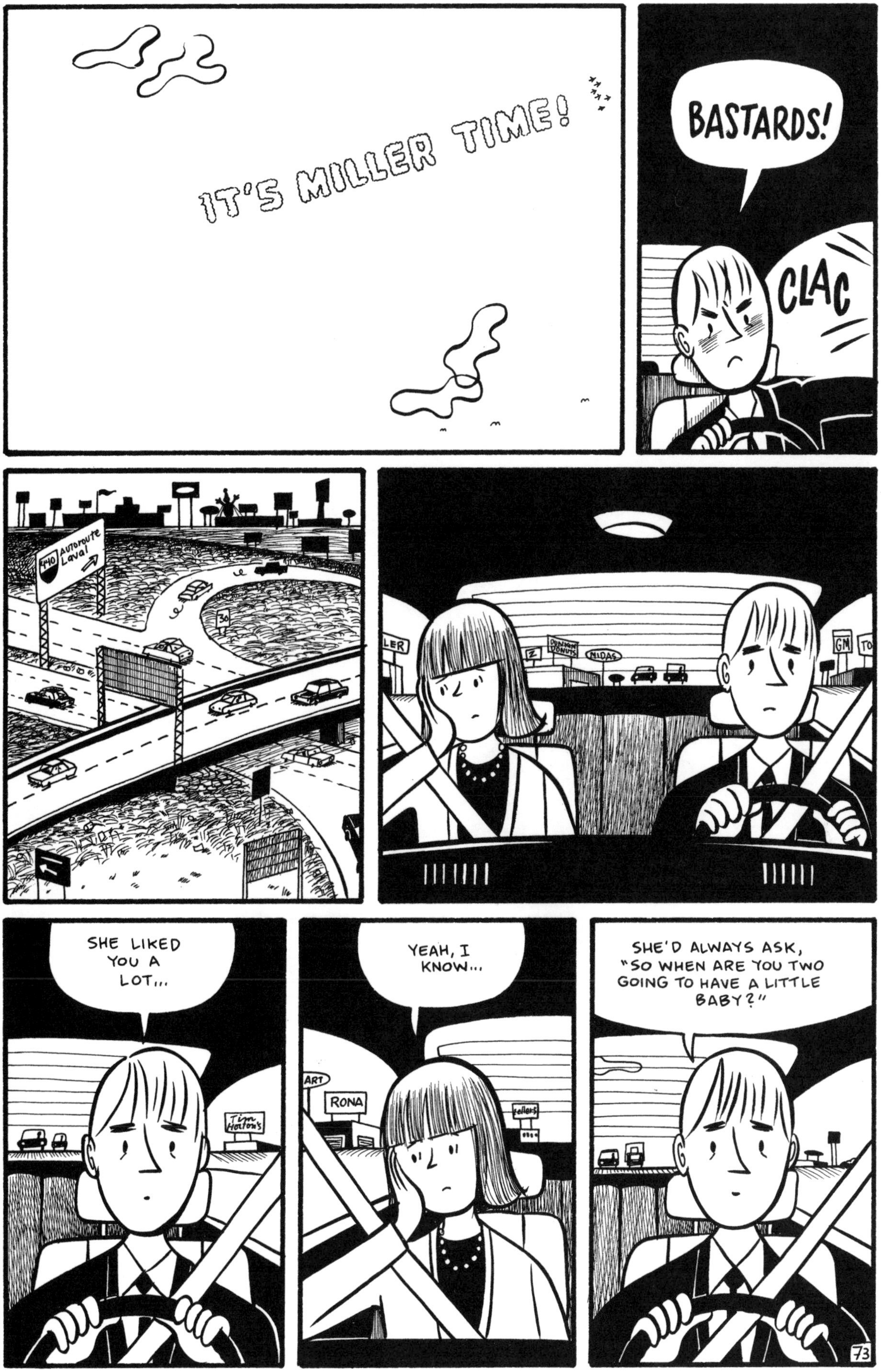
IT'S MILLER TIME!
BASTARDS!
CLAC
440
Autoroute Laval
MIDAS
GM
SHE LIKED YOU A LOT...
YEAH, I KNOW...
RONA
SHE'D ALWAYS ASK, "SO WHEN ARE YOU TWO GOING TO HAVE A LITTLE BABY?"

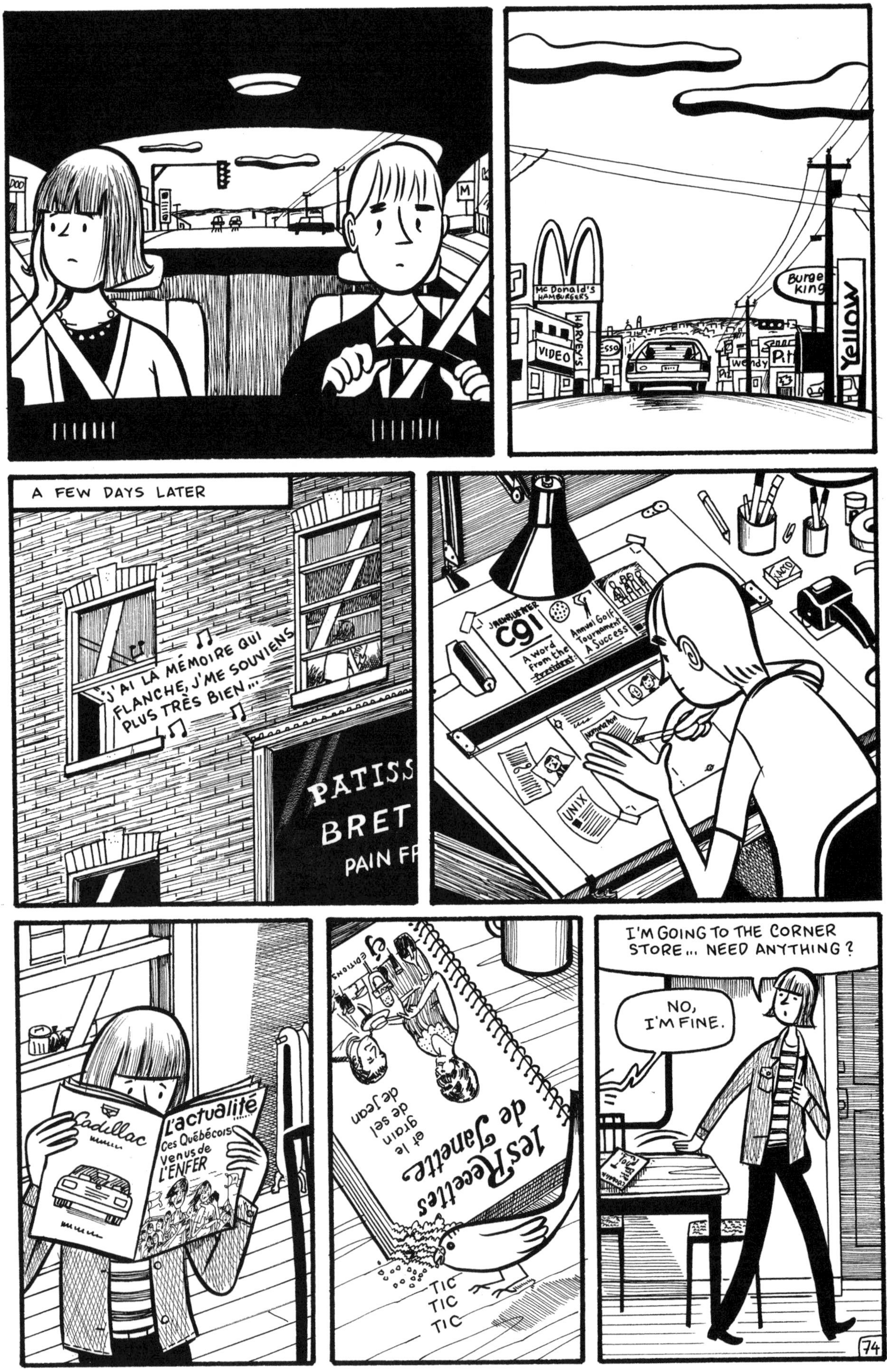
McDonald's HAMBURGERS
VIDEO
HARVEY'S
wendy
Yellow
A FEW DAYS LATER
J'AI LA MÉMOIRE QUI FLANCHE, J'ME SOUVIENS PLUS TRÈS BIEN...
PATISS
BRET
PAIN F
cgi
A word from the President
Annual Golf Tournament A Success
UNIX
Cadillac
L'actualité
Ces Québécors Venus de L'ENFER
les Recettes de Janette
et le grain de sel de Jean
TIC
TIC
TIC
I'M GOING TO THE CORNER STORE... NEED ANYTHING?
NO, I'M FINE.

*JEANNE MOREAU SINGING CYRUS BASSIAK

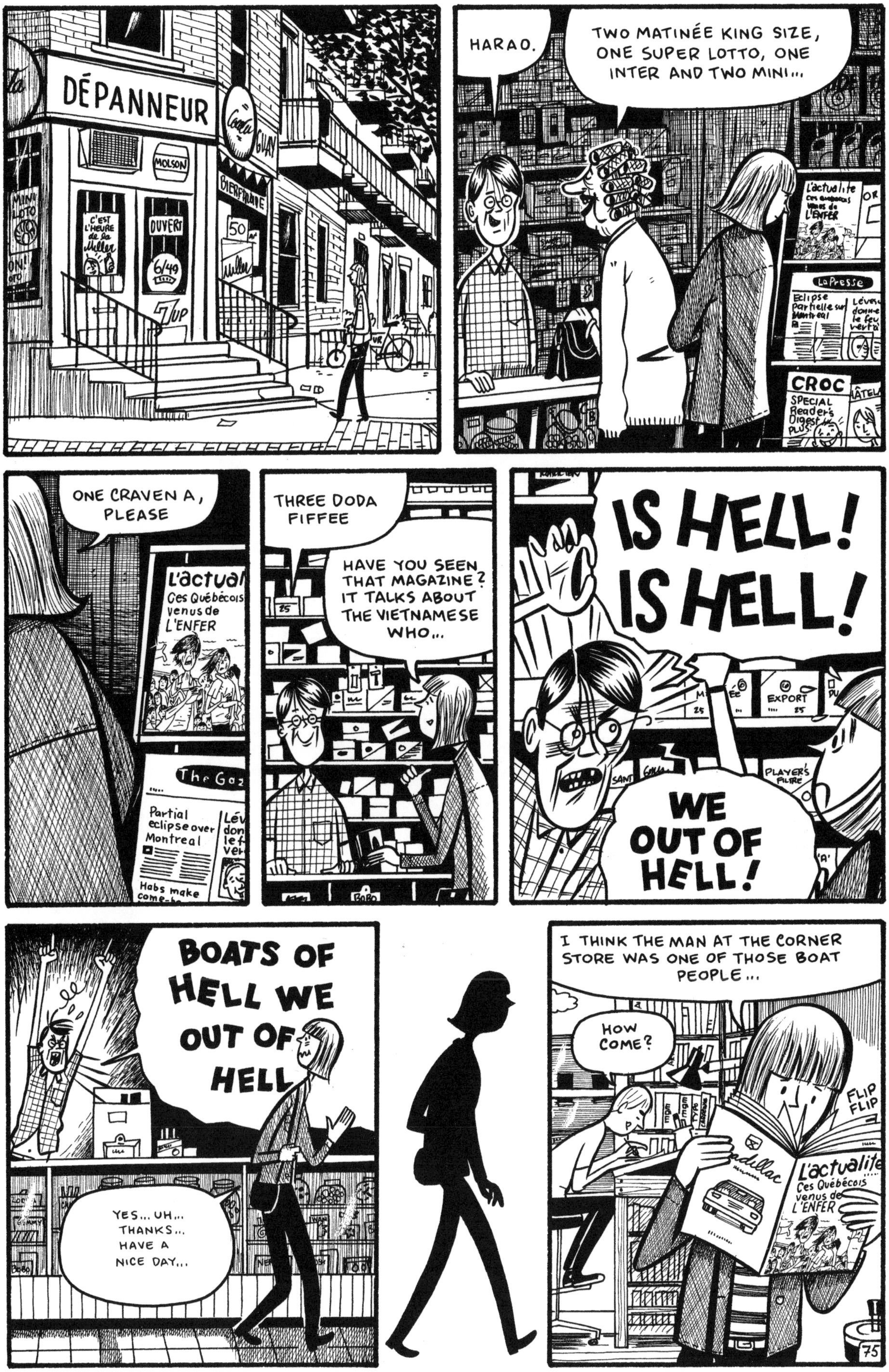
DÉPANNEUR
MOLSON
OUVERT
6/49
HARAO.
TWO MATINÉE KING SIZE, ONE SUPER LOTTO, ONE INTER AND TWO MINI...
CROC
ONE CRAVEN A, PLEASE
L'actual
Ces Québécois venus de L'ENFER
Partial eclipse over Montreal
Habs make
THREE DODA FIFFEE
HAVE YOU SEEN THAT MAGAZINE? IT TALKS ABOUT THE VIETNAMESE WHO...
IS HELL! IS HELL!
WE OUT OF HELL!
EXPORT
PLAYER'S FILTRE
BOATS OF HELL WE OUT OF HELL
YES... UH... THANKS... HAVE A NICE DAY...
I THINK THE MAN AT THE CORNER STORE WAS ONE OF THOSE BOAT PEOPLE...
HOW COME?
FLIP FLIP
L'actualite
Ces Québécois venus de L'ENFER

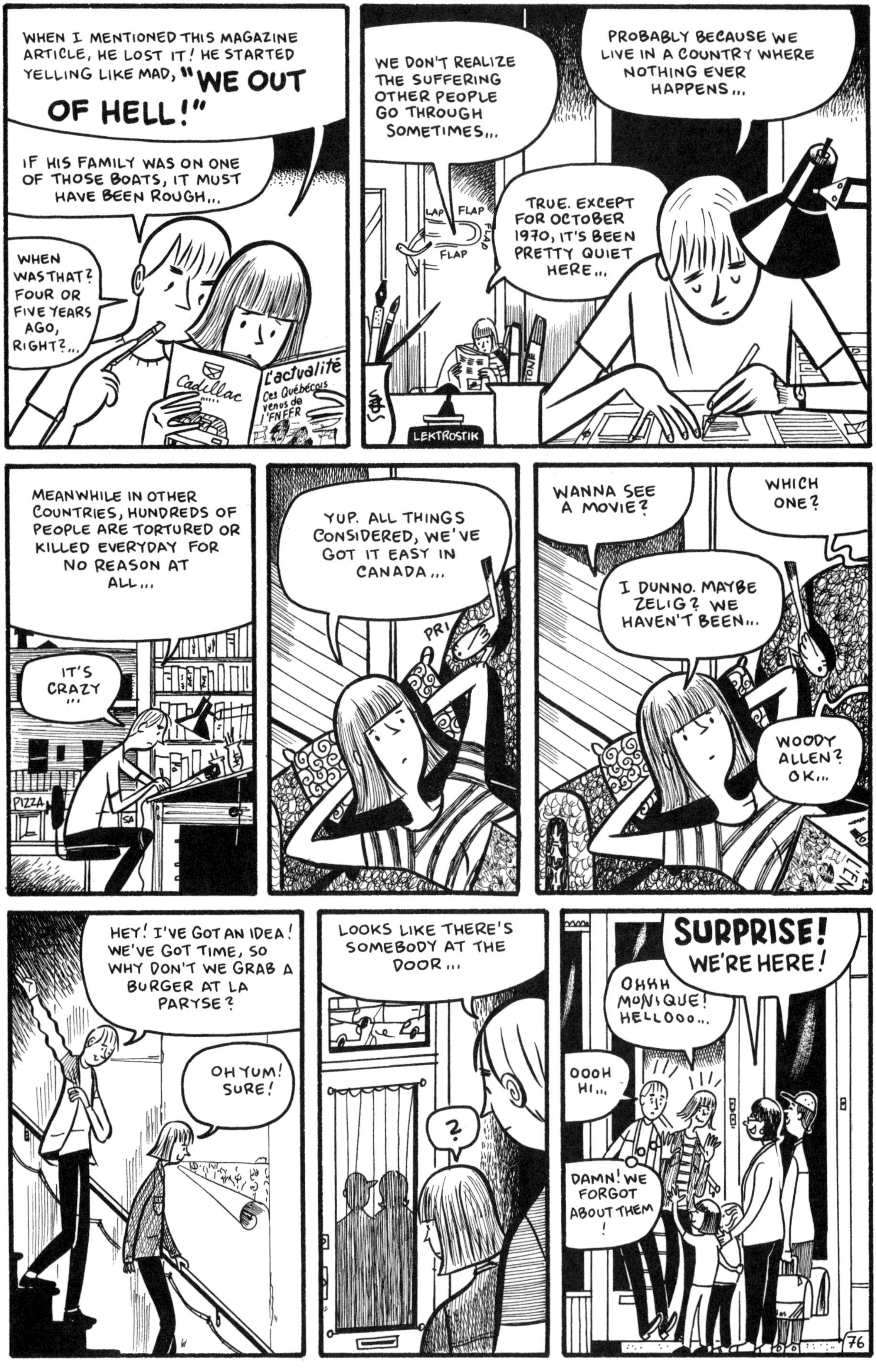
WHEN I MENTIONED THIS MAGAZINE ARTICLE, HE LOST IT! HE STARTED YELLING LIKE MAD, "WE OUT OF HELL!"
IF HIS FAMILY WAS ON ONE OF THOSE BOATS, IT MUST HAVE BEEN ROUGH...
WHEN WAS THAT? FOUR OR FIVE YEARS AGO, RIGHT?...
Cadillac
L'actualité
Ces Québécois venus de l'ENFER
WE DON'T REALIZE THE SUFFERING OTHER PEOPLE GO THROUGH SOMETIMES...
PROBABLY BECAUSE WE LIVE IN A COUNTRY WHERE NOTHING EVER HAPPENS...
LAP FLAP
FLAP
FLAP
TRUE. EXCEPT FOR OCTOBER 1970, IT'S BEEN PRETTY QUIET HERE...
LEKTROSTIK
MEANWHILE IN OTHER COUNTRIES, HUNDREDS OF PEOPLE ARE TORTURED OR KILLED EVERYDAY FOR NO REASON AT ALL...
IT'S CRAZY...
PIZZA
YUP. ALL THINGS CONSIDERED, WE'VE GOT IT EASY IN CANADA...
PRI
WANNA SEE A MOVIE?
WHICH ONE?
I DUNNO. MAYBE ZELIG? WE HAVEN'T BEEN...
WOODY ALLEN? OK...
HEY! I'VE GOT AN IDEA! WE'VE GOT TIME, SO WHY DON'T WE GRAB A BURGER AT LA PARYSE?
OH YUM! SURE!
LOOKS LIKE THERE'S SOMEBODY AT THE DOOR...
?
SURPRISE! WE'RE HERE!
OHHH MONIQUE! HELLOOO...
OOOH HI...
DAMN! WE FORGOT ABOUT THEM!

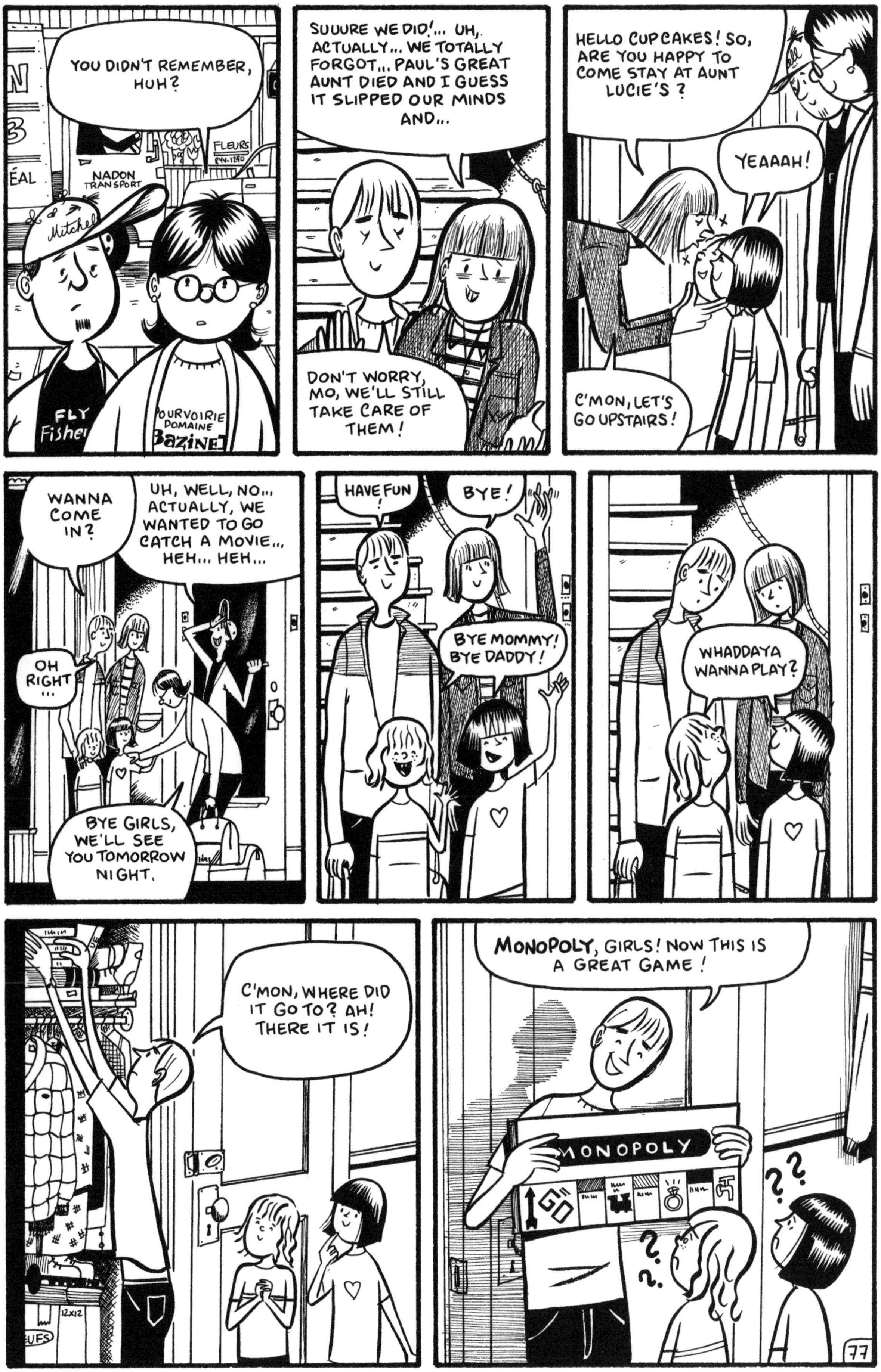

ÉAL
NADON TRANSPORT
FLEURS
YOU DIDN'T REMEMBER, HUH?
Mitchell
FLY Fisher
POURVOIRIE DOMAINE BAZINET
SUUURE WE DID!... UH, ACTUALLY... WE TOTALLY FORGOT... PAUL'S GREAT AUNT DIED AND I GUESS IT SLIPPED OUR MINDS AND...
DON'T WORRY, MO, WE'LL STILL TAKE CARE OF THEM!
HELLO CUPCAKES! SO, ARE YOU HAPPY TO COME STAY AT AUNT LUCIE'S?
YEAAAH!
C'MON, LET'S GO UPSTAIRS!
WANNA COME IN?
UH, WELL, NO... ACTUALLY, WE WANTED TO GO CATCH A MOVIE... HEH... HEH...
OH RIGHT...
BYE GIRLS, WE'LL SEE YOU TOMORROW NIGHT.
HAVE FUN!
BYE!
BYE MOMMY! BYE DADDY!
WHADDAYA WANNA PLAY?
C'MON, WHERE DID IT GO TO? AH! THERE IT IS!
12X12
MONOPOLY, GIRLS! NOW THIS IS A GREAT GAME!
MONOPOLY
GO

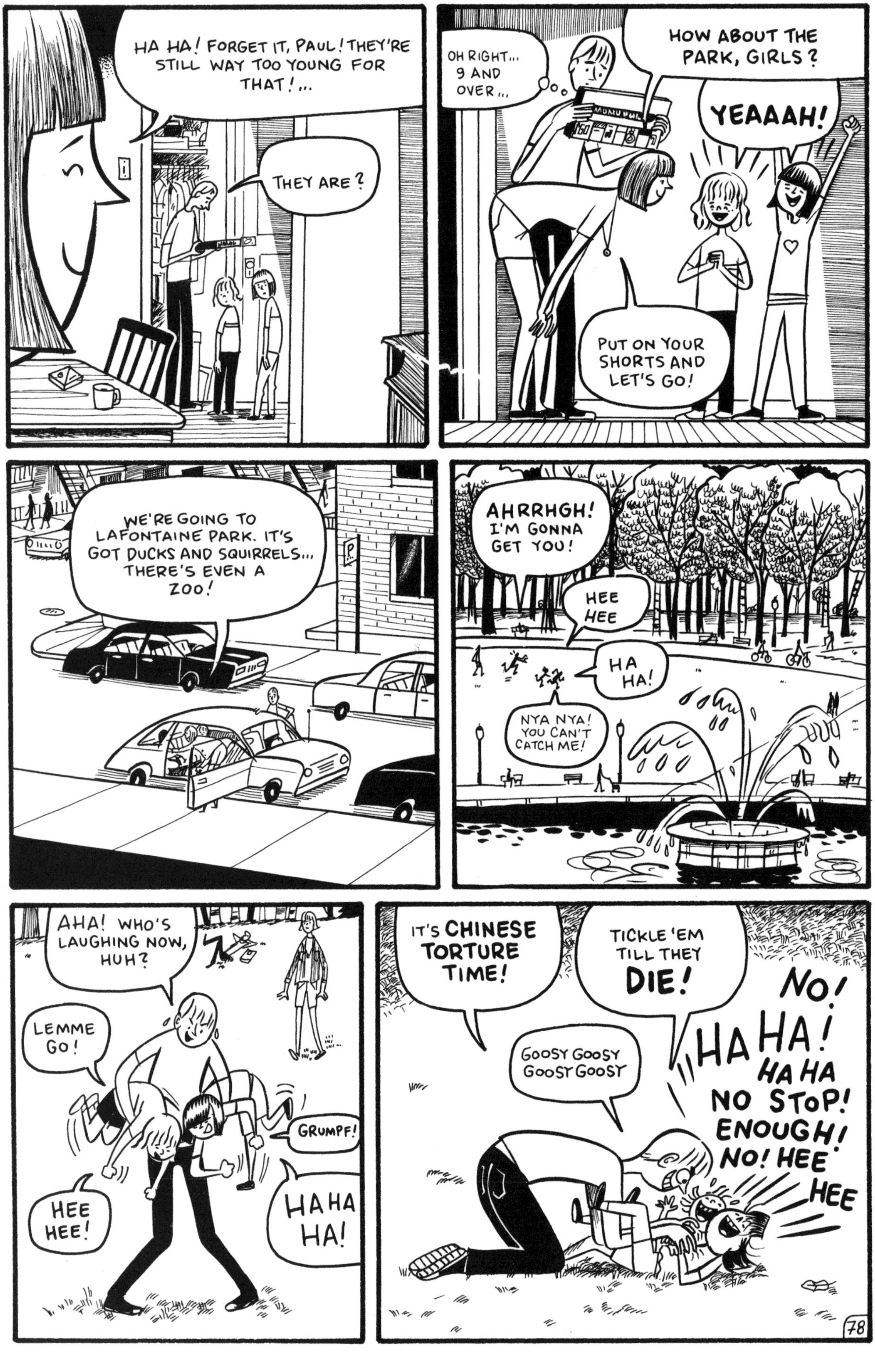
HA HA! FORGET IT, PAUL! THEY'RE STILL WAY TOO YOUNG FOR THAT!...
THEY ARE?
OH RIGHT... 9 AND OVER...
HOW ABOUT THE PARK, GIRLS?
YEAAAH!
PUT ON YOUR SHORTS AND LET'S GO!
WE'RE GOING TO LAFONTAINE PARK. IT'S GOT DUCKS AND SQUIRRELS... THERE'S EVEN A ZOO!
AHRRHGH! I'M GONNA GET YOU!
HEE HEE
HA HA!
NYA NYA! YOU CAN'T CATCH ME!
AHA! WHO'S LAUGHING NOW, HUH?
LEMME GO!
GRUMPF!
HEE HEE!
HA HA HA!
IT'S CHINESE TORTURE TIME!
TICKLE 'EM TILL THEY DIE!
GOOSY GOOSY GOOSY GOOSY
NO! HA HA! HA HA NO STOP! ENOUGH! NO! HEE HEE
78

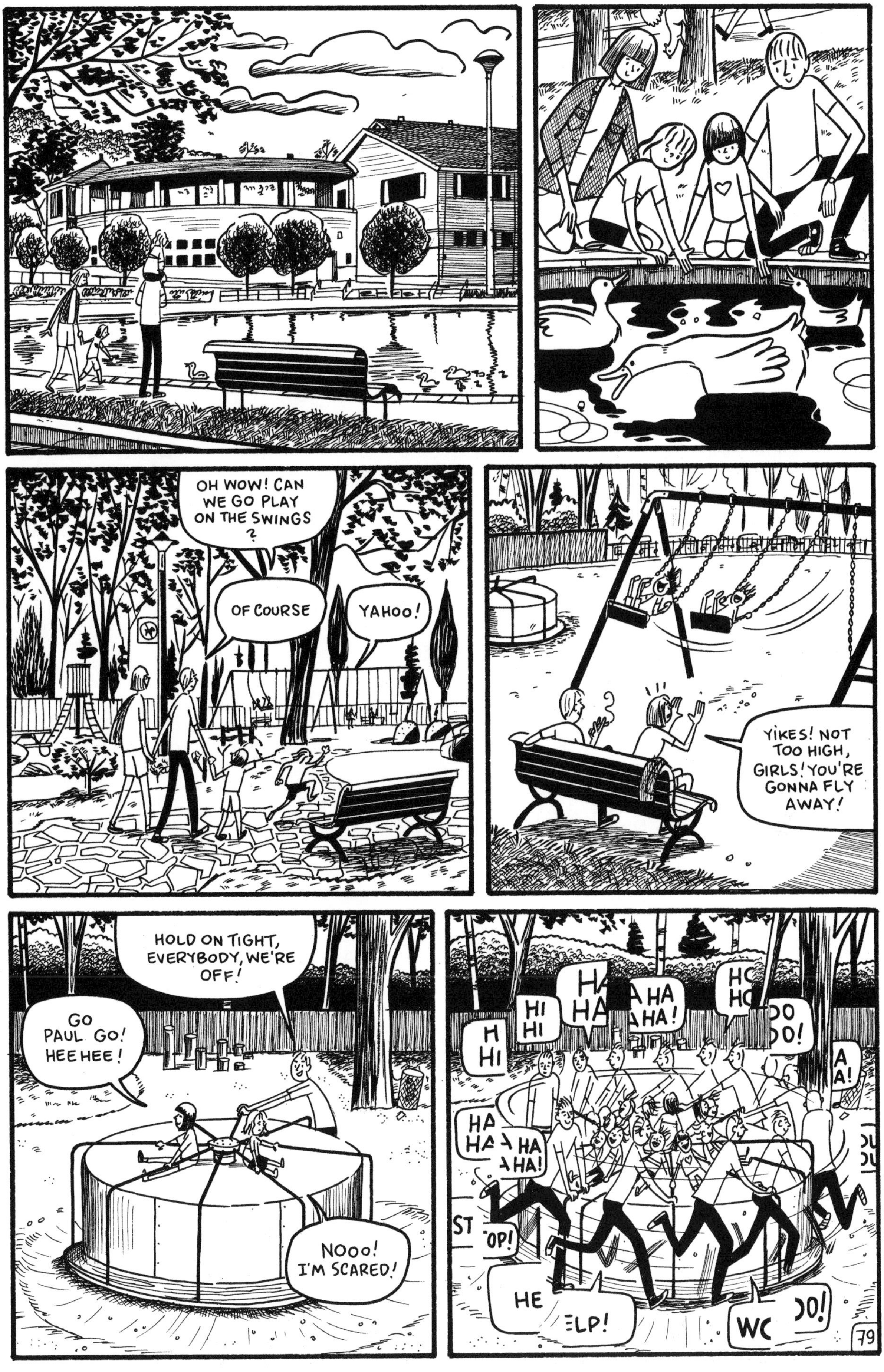
OH WOW! CAN WE GO PLAY ON THE SWINGS ?
OF COURSE
YAHOO!
YIKES! NOT TOO HIGH, GIRLS! YOU'RE GONNA FLY AWAY!
HOLD ON TIGHT, EVERYBODY, WE'RE OFF!
GO PAUL GO! HEE HEE!
NOoo! I'M SCARED!
HI HI
HA HA
HA HA!
HE
ELP!
ST
OP!

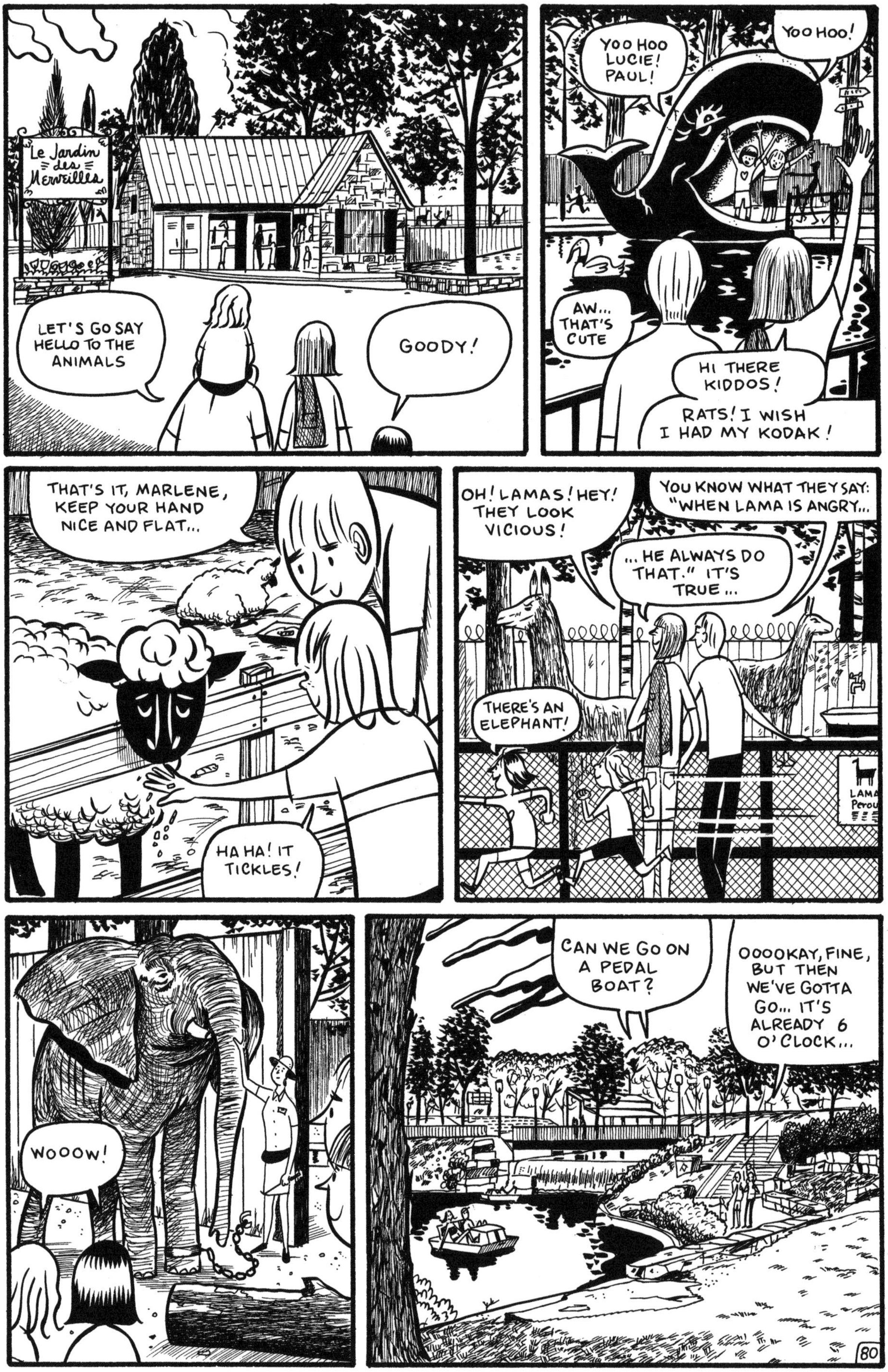
Le Jardin des Merveilles
LET'S GO SAY HELLO TO THE ANIMALS
GOODY!
YOO HOO LUCIE! PAUL!
YOO HOO!
AW... THAT'S CUTE
HI THERE KIDDOS!
RATS! I WISH I HAD MY KODAK!
THAT'S IT, MARLENE, KEEP YOUR HAND NICE AND FLAT...
HA HA! IT TICKLES!
OH! LAMAS! HEY! THEY LOOK VICIOUS!
YOU KNOW WHAT THEY SAY: "WHEN LAMA IS ANGRY...
... HE ALWAYS DO THAT." IT'S TRUE...
THERE'S AN ELEPHANT!
LAMA Perou
WOOOW!
CAN WE GO ON A PEDAL BOAT?
OOOOKAY, FINE, BUT THEN WE'VE GOTTA GO... IT'S ALREADY 6 O'CLOCK...

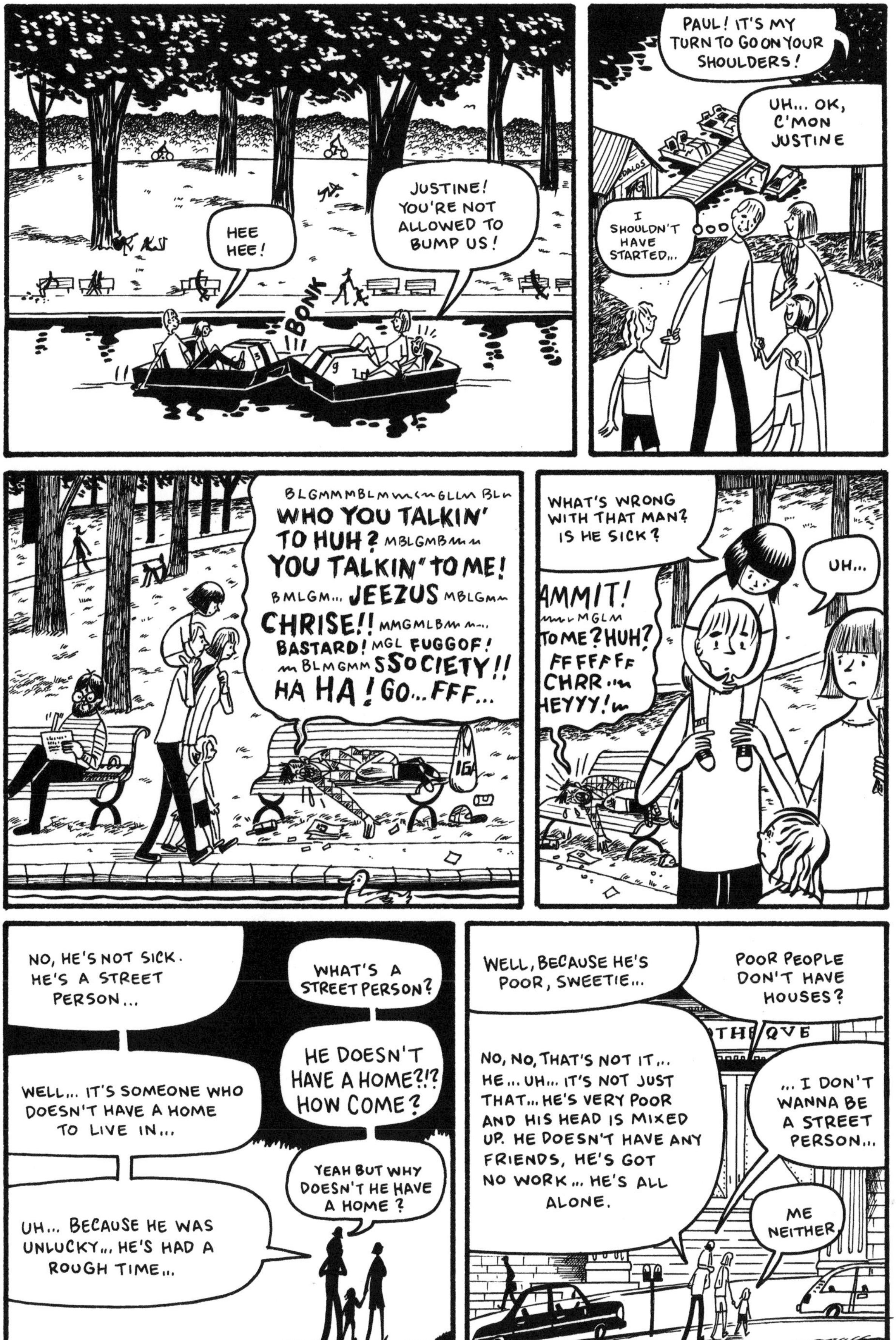
HEE HEE!
JUSTINE! YOU'RE NOT ALLOWED TO BUMP US!
BONK
PAUL! IT'S MY TURN TO GO ON YOUR SHOULDERS!
UH... OK, C'MON JUSTINE
I SHOULDN'T HAVE STARTED...
BLGMMBLM
WHO YOU TALKIN' TO HUH? MBLGMB
YOU TALKIN' TO ME!
BMLGM... JEEZUS MBLGM
CHRISE!! MMGMLBM
BASTARD! MGL FUGGOF!
BLGMM SSOCIETY!!
HA HA! GO... FFF...
WHAT'S WRONG WITH THAT MAN? IS HE SICK?
AMMIT!
MGLM
TO ME? HUH?
FFFFFFF
CHRR
HEYYY!
UH...
NO, HE'S NOT SICK. HE'S A STREET PERSON...
WHAT'S A STREET PERSON?
WELL... IT'S SOMEONE WHO DOESN'T HAVE A HOME TO LIVE IN...
HE DOESN'T HAVE A HOME?!? HOW COME?
UH... BECAUSE HE WAS UNLUCKY... HE'S HAD A ROUGH TIME...
YEAH BUT WHY DOESN'T HE HAVE A HOME?
WELL, BECAUSE HE'S POOR, SWEETIE...
POOR PEOPLE DON'T HAVE HOUSES?
NO, NO, THAT'S NOT IT... HE... UH... IT'S NOT JUST THAT... HE'S VERY POOR AND HIS HEAD IS MIXED UP. HE DOESN'T HAVE ANY FRIENDS, HE'S GOT NO WORK... HE'S ALL ALONE.
... I DON'T WANNA BE A STREET PERSON...
ME NEITHER

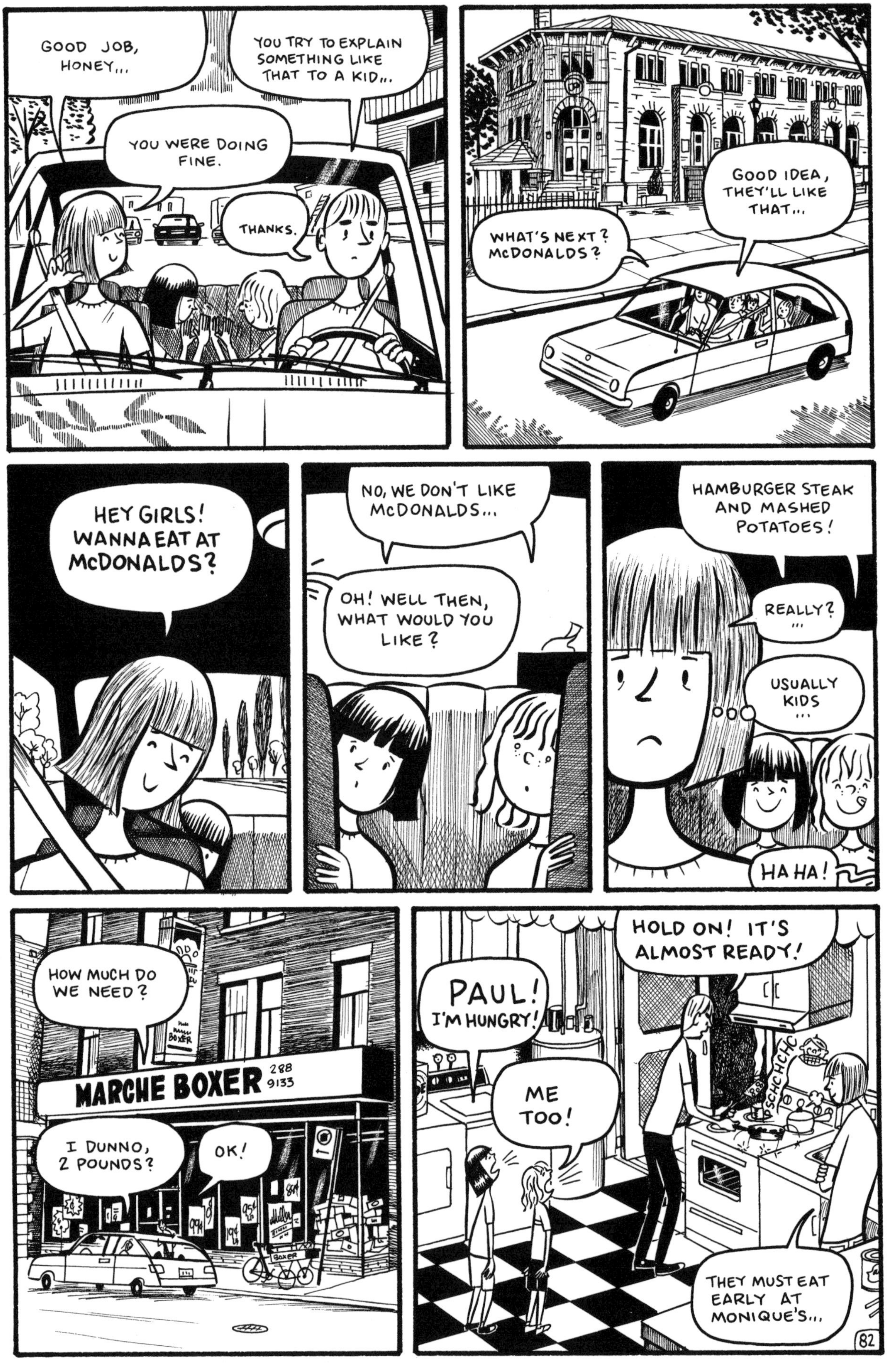
GOOD JOB, HONEY...
YOU TRY TO EXPLAIN SOMETHING LIKE THAT TO A KID...
YOU WERE DOING FINE.
THANKS.
WHAT'S NEXT? McDONALDS?
GOOD IDEA, THEY'LL LIKE THAT...
HEY GIRLS! WANNA EAT AT McDONALDS?
NO, WE DON'T LIKE McDONALDS...
OH! WELL THEN, WHAT WOULD YOU LIKE?
HAMBURGER STEAK AND MASHED POTATOES!
REALLY? ...
USUALLY KIDS ...
HA HA!
HOW MUCH DO WE NEED?
MARCHE BOXER 288 9133
I DUNNO, 2 POUNDS?
OK!
HOLD ON! IT'S ALMOST READY!
PAUL! I'M HUNGRY!
ME TOO!
THEY MUST EAT EARLY AT MONIQUE'S...

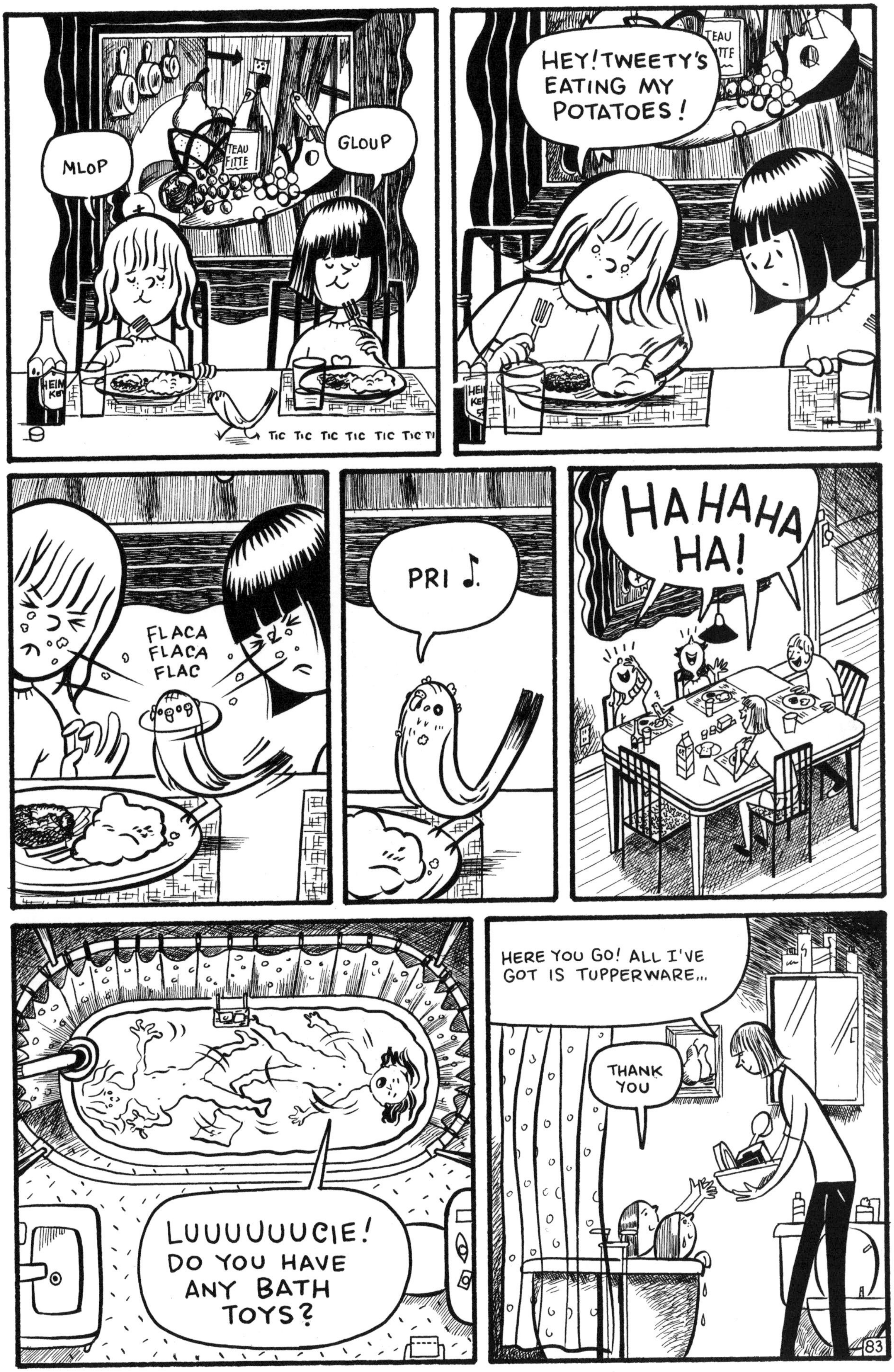

MLOP
GLOUP
TEAU FITTE
HEIN KEN
TIC TIC TIC TIC TIC TIC TI
HEY! TWEETY'S EATING MY POTATOES!
FLACA FLACA FLAC
PRI ♩.
HAHAHA HA!
HERE YOU GO! ALL I'VE GOT IS TUPPERWARE...
THANK YOU
LUUUUUUCIE! DO YOU HAVE ANY BATH TOYS?

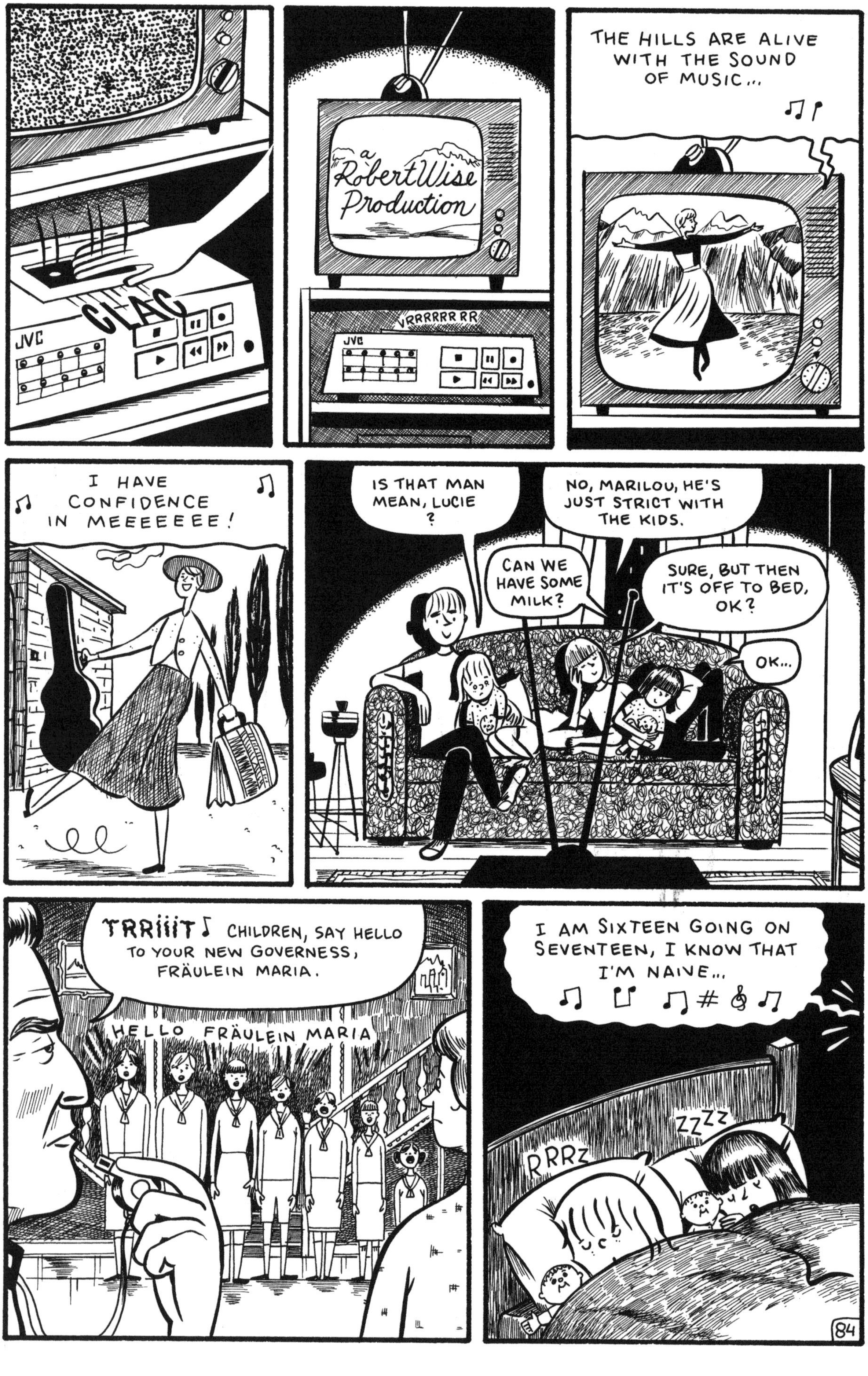
CLAC
JVC
VRRRRRR RR
JVC
a Robert Wise Production
THE HILLS ARE ALIVE WITH THE SOUND OF MUSIC...
I HAVE CONFIDENCE IN MEEEEEEE!
IS THAT MAN MEAN, LUCIE ?
NO, MARILOU, HE'S JUST STRICT WITH THE KIDS.
CAN WE HAVE SOME MILK?
SURE, BUT THEN IT'S OFF TO BED, OK?
OK...
TRRiiiT CHILDREN, SAY HELLO TO YOUR NEW GOVERNESS, FRÄULEIN MARIA.
HELLO FRÄULEIN MARIA
I AM SIXTEEN GOING ON SEVENTEEN, I KNOW THAT I'M NAIVE...
ZZZZ
RRRZ

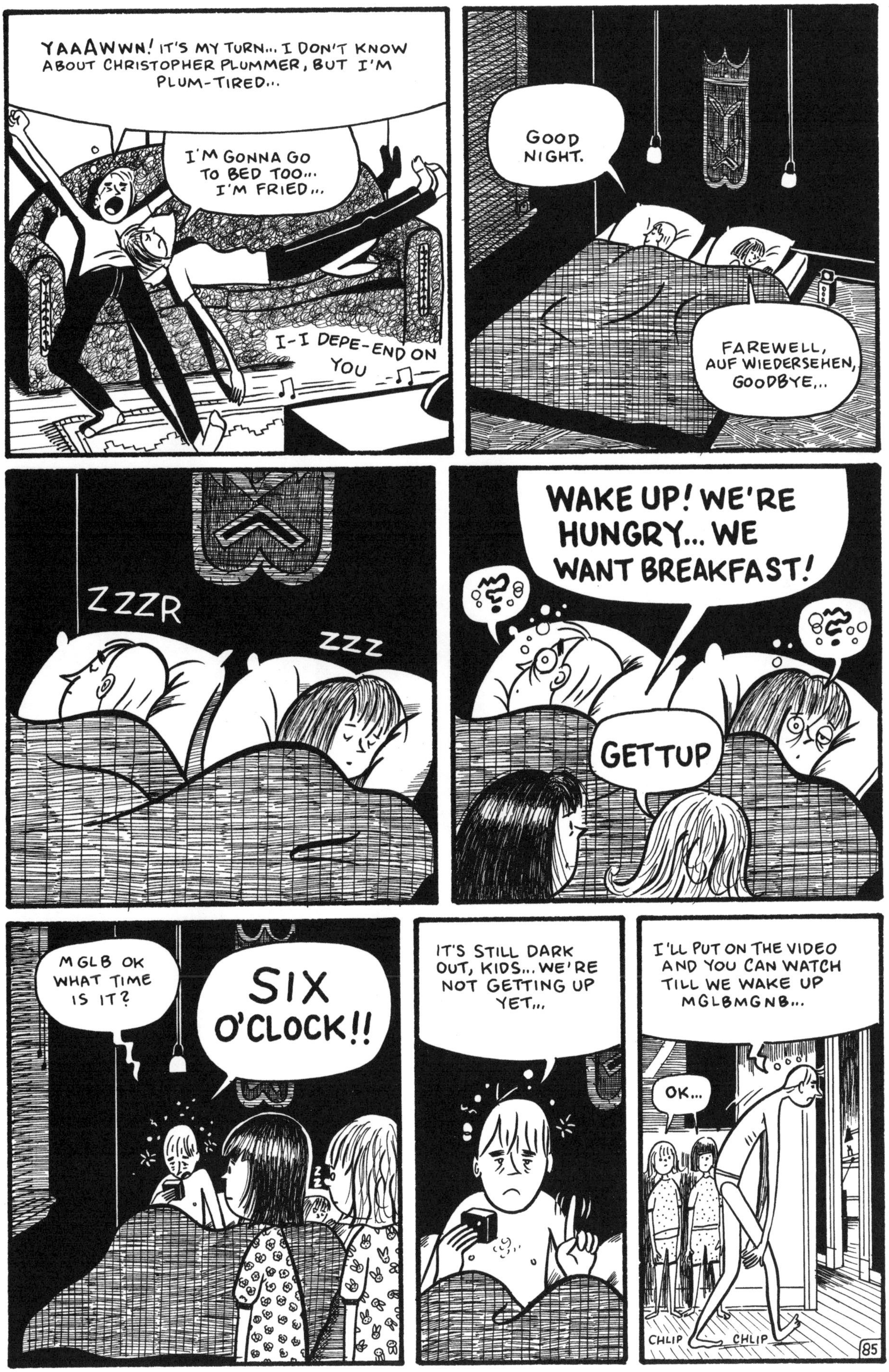
YAAAWWN! IT'S MY TURN... I DON'T KNOW ABOUT CHRISTOPHER PLUMMER, BUT I'M PLUM-TIRED...
I'M GONNA GO TO BED TOO... I'M FRIED...
I-I DEPE-END ON YOU
GOOD NIGHT.
FAREWELL, AUF WIEDERSEHEN, GOODBYE,..
ZZZR
ZZZ
WAKE UP! WE'RE HUNGRY... WE WANT BREAKFAST!
GETTUP
MGLB OK WHAT TIME IS IT?
SIX O'CLOCK!!
IT'S STILL DARK OUT, KIDS... WE'RE NOT GETTING UP YET...
I'LL PUT ON THE VIDEO AND YOU CAN WATCH TILL WE WAKE UP MGLBMGNB...
OK...
CHLIP
CHLIP

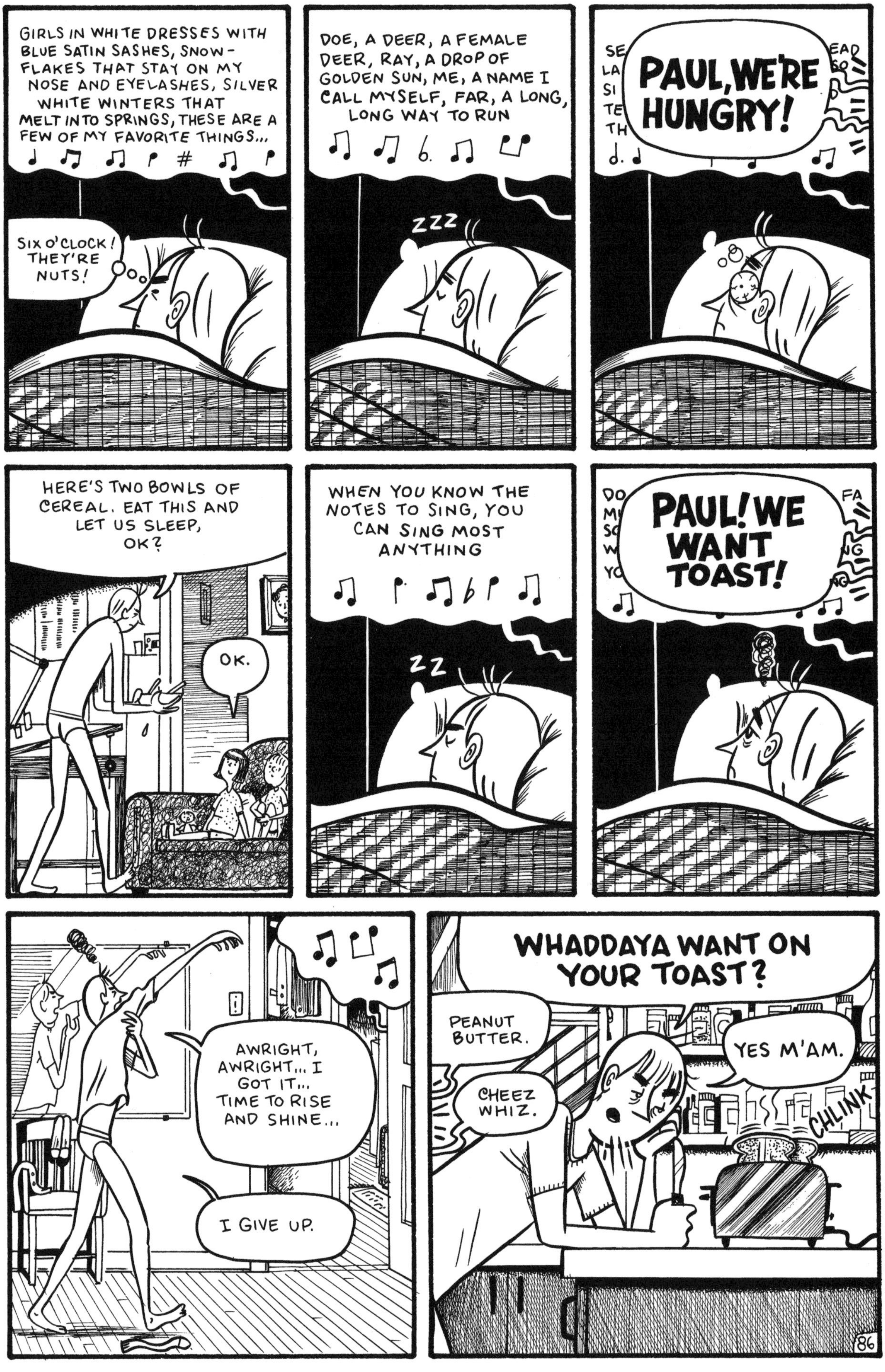
GIRLS IN WHITE DRESSES WITH BLUE SATIN SASHES, SNOW-FLAKES THAT STAY ON MY NOSE AND EYELASHES, SILVER WHITE WINTERS THAT MELT INTO SPRINGS, THESE ARE A FEW OF MY FAVORITE THINGS...
SIX O'CLOCK! THEY'RE NUTS!
DOE, A DEER, A FEMALE DEER, RAY, A DROP OF GOLDEN SUN, ME, A NAME I CALL MYSELF, FAR, A LONG, LONG WAY TO RUN
ZZZ
PAUL, WE'RE HUNGRY!
HERE'S TWO BOWLS OF CEREAL. EAT THIS AND LET US SLEEP, OK?
OK.
WHEN YOU KNOW THE NOTES TO SING, YOU CAN SING MOST ANYTHING
ZZ
PAUL! WE WANT TOAST!
AWRIGHT, AWRIGHT... I GOT IT... TIME TO RISE AND SHINE...
I GIVE UP.
WHADDAYA WANT ON YOUR TOAST?
PEANUT BUTTER.
CHEEZ WHIZ.
YES M'AM.
CHLINK

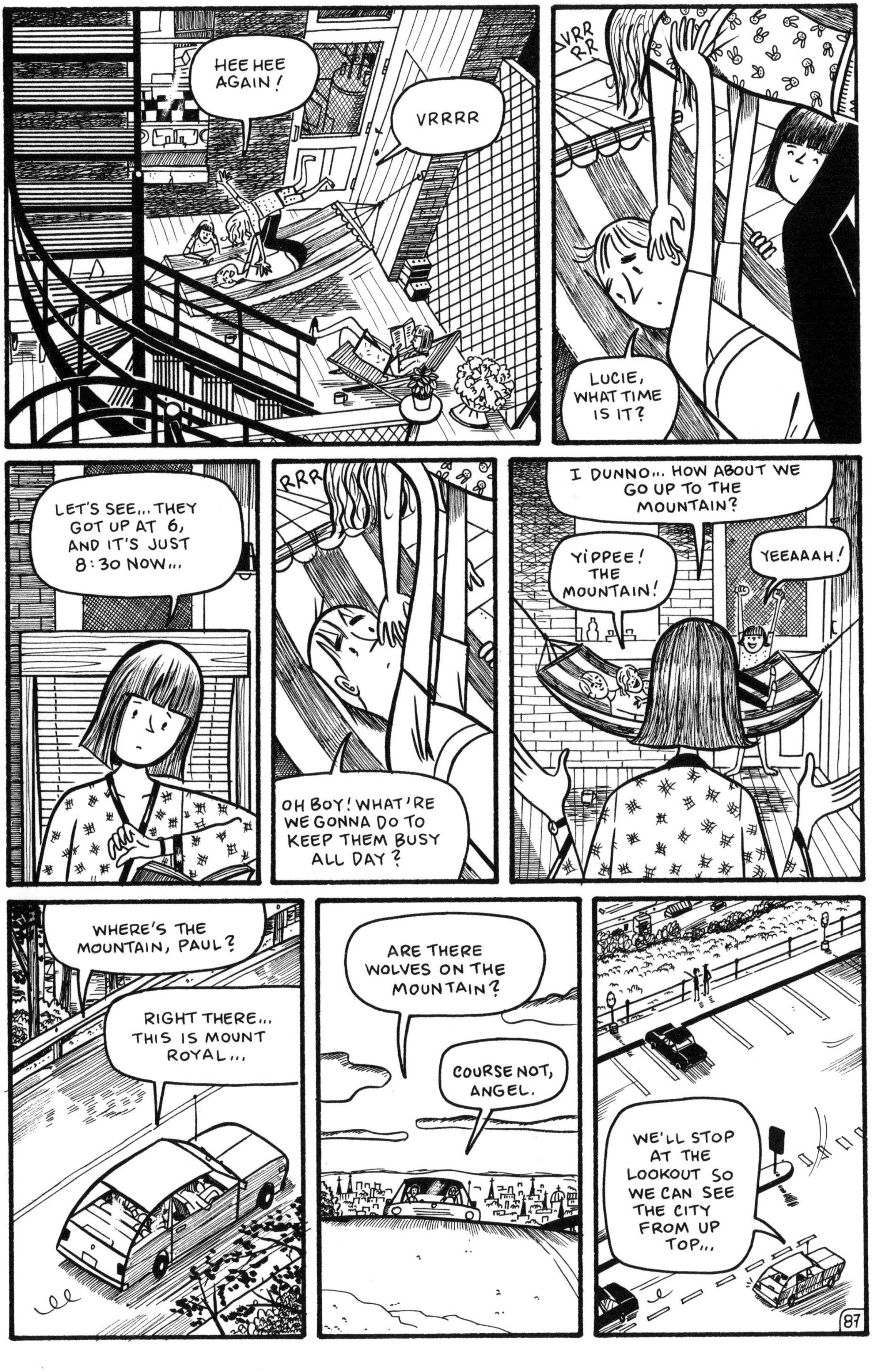
HEE HEE AGAIN!
VRRRR
VRR RR
LUCIE, WHAT TIME IS IT?
LET'S SEE... THEY GOT UP AT 6, AND IT'S JUST 8:30 NOW...
RRR
OH BOY! WHAT'RE WE GONNA DO TO KEEP THEM BUSY ALL DAY?
I DUNNO... HOW ABOUT WE GO UP TO THE MOUNTAIN?
YIPPEE! THE MOUNTAIN!
YEEAAAH!
WHERE'S THE MOUNTAIN, PAUL?
RIGHT THERE... THIS IS MOUNT ROYAL...
ARE THERE WOLVES ON THE MOUNTAIN?
COURSE NOT, ANGEL.
WE'LL STOP AT THE LOOKOUT SO WE CAN SEE THE CITY FROM UP TOP...

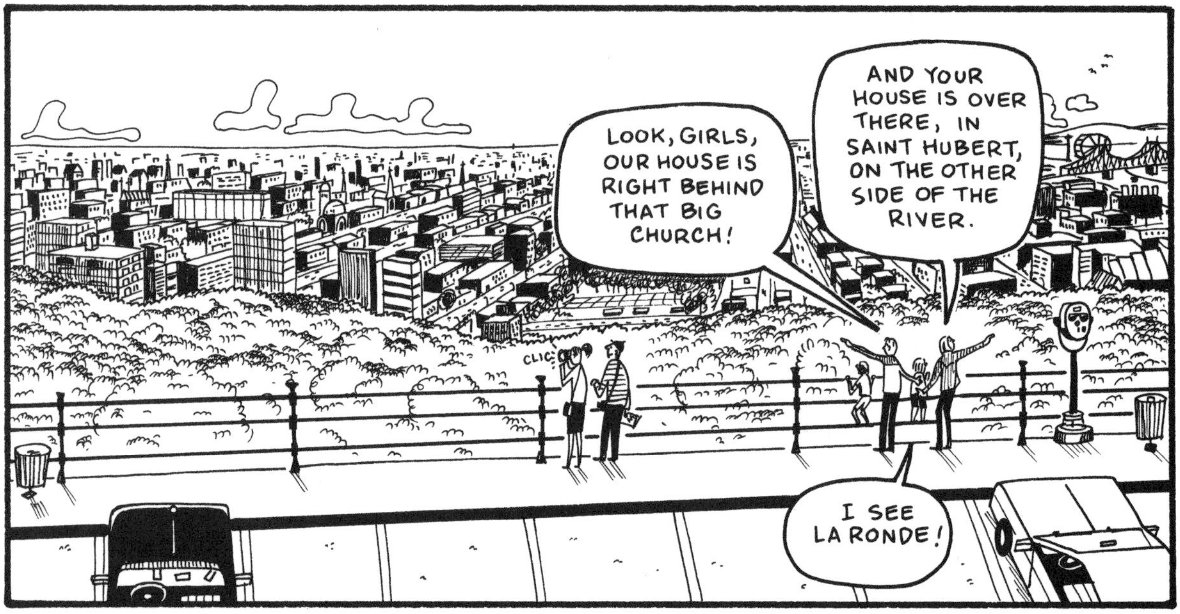
CLIC
LOOK, GIRLS, OUR HOUSE IS RIGHT BEHIND THAT BIG CHURCH!
AND YOUR HOUSE IS OVER THERE, IN SAINT HUBERT, ON THE OTHER SIDE OF THE RIVER.
I SEE LA RONDE!

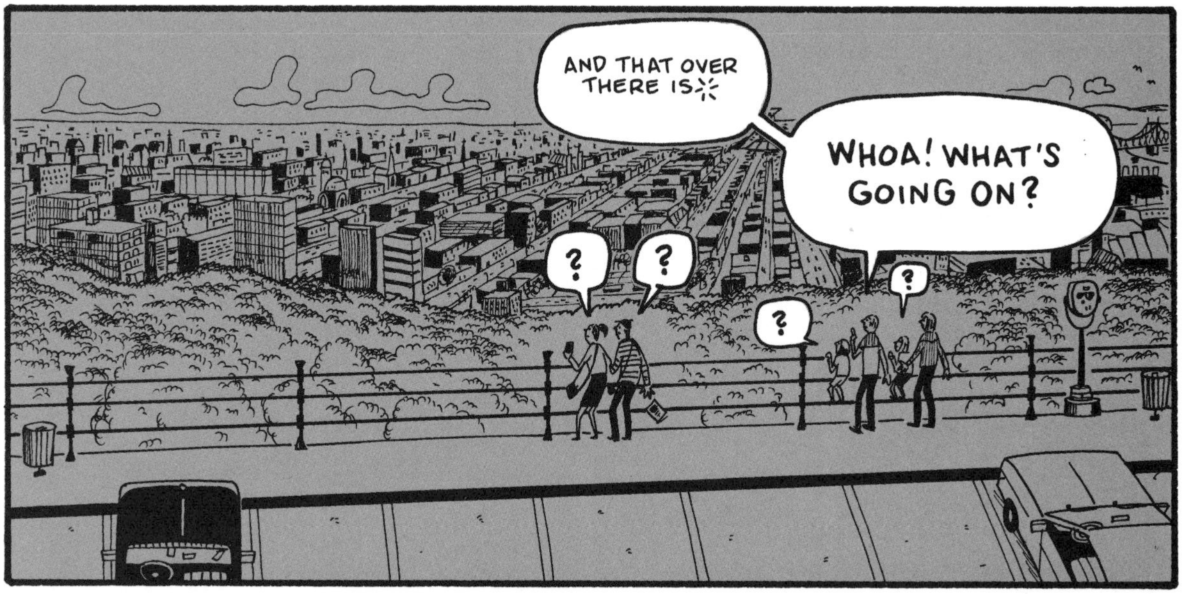
AND THAT OVER THERE IS
WHOA! WHAT'S GOING ON?
?
?
?
?

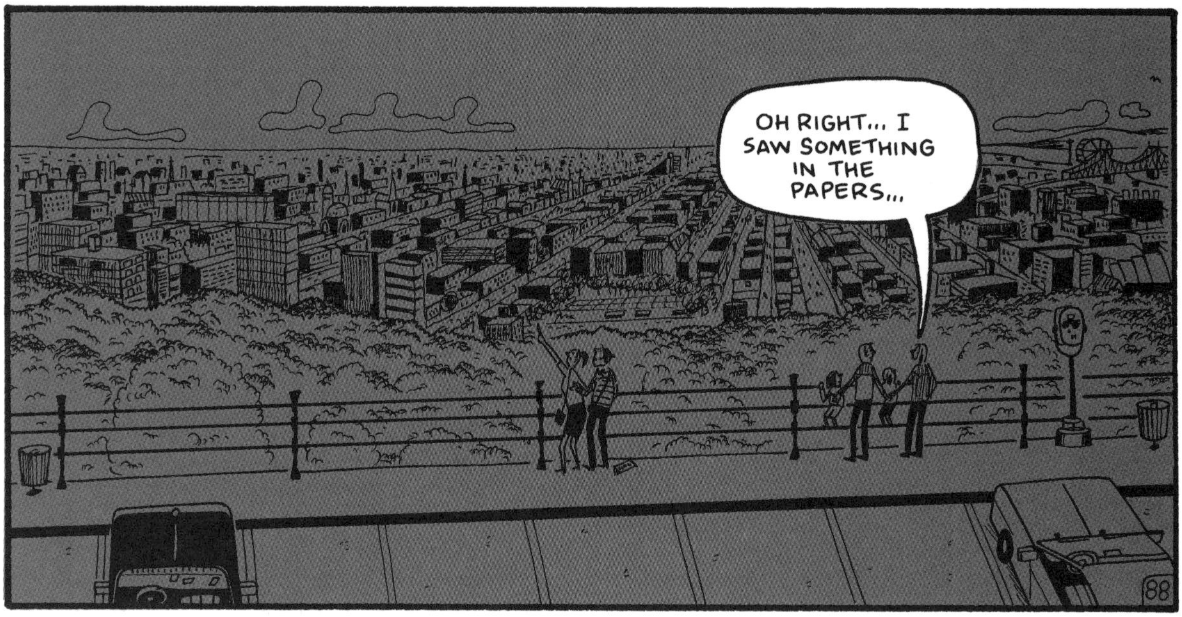
OH RIGHT... I SAW SOMETHING IN THE PAPERS...

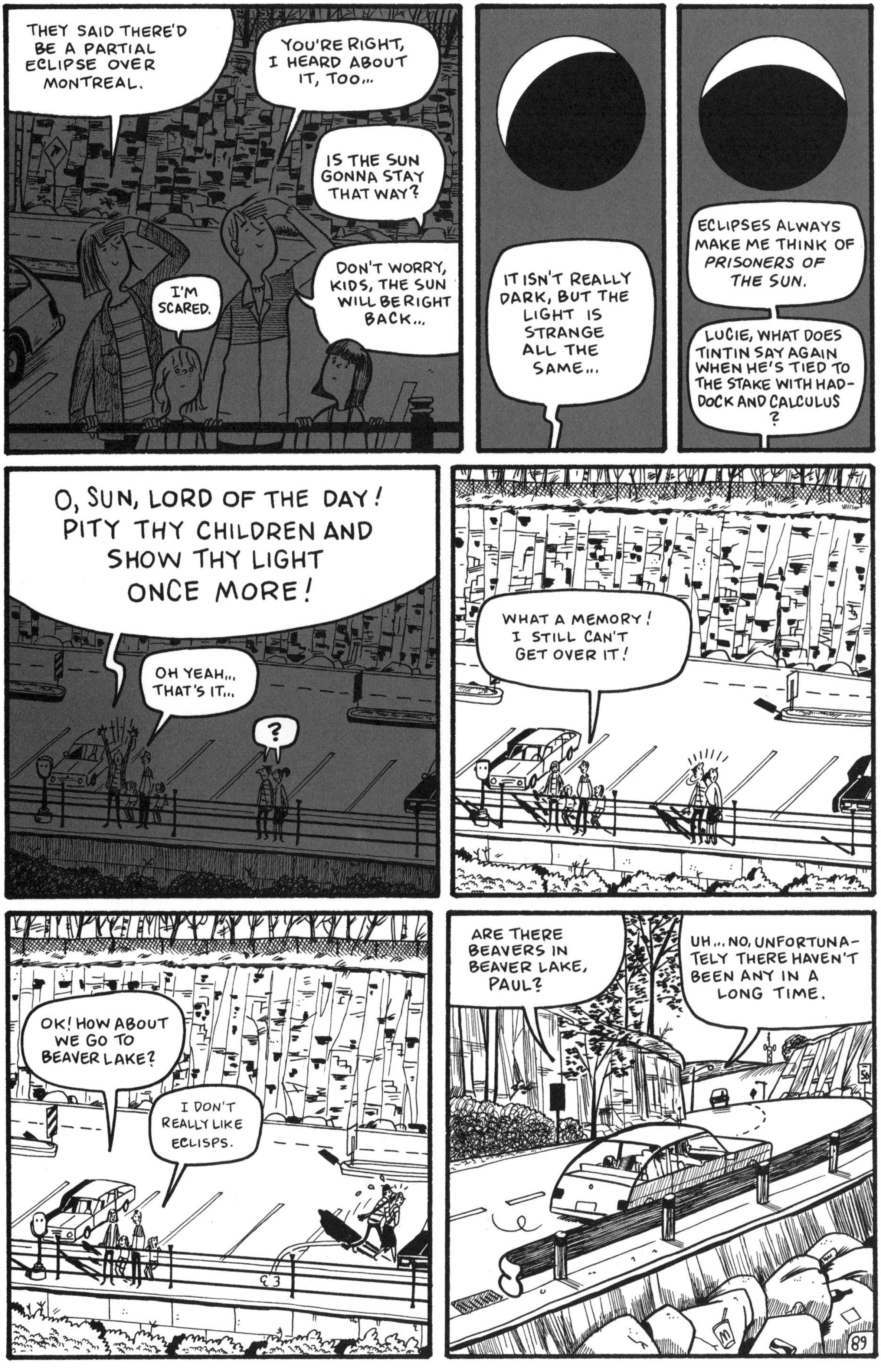
THEY SAID THERE'D BE A PARTIAL ECLIPSE OVER MONTREAL.
YOU'RE RIGHT, I HEARD ABOUT IT, TOO...
IS THE SUN GONNA STAY THAT WAY?
I'M SCARED.
DON'T WORRY, KIDS, THE SUN WILL BE RIGHT BACK...
IT ISN'T REALLY DARK, BUT THE LIGHT IS STRANGE ALL THE SAME...
ECLIPSES ALWAYS MAKE ME THINK OF *PRISONERS OF THE SUN*.
LUCIE, WHAT DOES TINTIN SAY AGAIN WHEN HE'S TIED TO THE STAKE WITH HADDOCK AND CALCULUS?
O, SUN, LORD OF THE DAY! PITY THY CHILDREN AND SHOW THY LIGHT ONCE MORE!
OH YEAH... THAT'S IT...
?
WHAT A MEMORY! I STILL CAN'T GET OVER IT!
OK! HOW ABOUT WE GO TO BEAVER LAKE?
I DON'T REALLY LIKE ECLISPS.
ARE THERE BEAVERS IN BEAVER LAKE, PAUL?
UH... NO, UNFORTUNATELY THERE HAVEN'T BEEN ANY IN A LONG TIME.

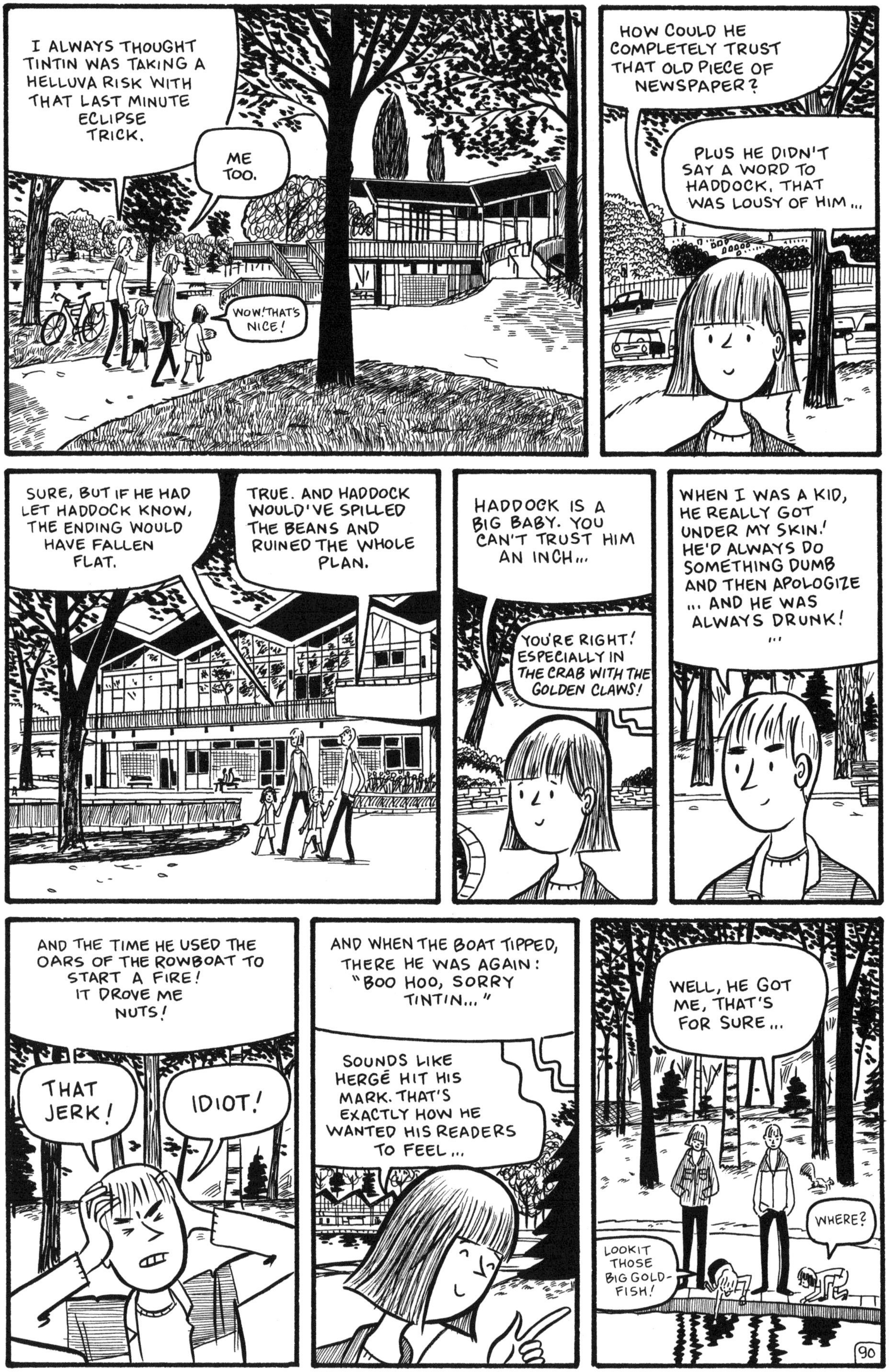
I ALWAYS THOUGHT TINTIN WAS TAKING A HELLUVA RISK WITH THAT LAST MINUTE ECLIPSE TRICK.
ME TOO.
WOW! THAT'S NICE!
HOW COULD HE COMPLETELY TRUST THAT OLD PIECE OF NEWSPAPER?
PLUS HE DIDN'T SAY A WORD TO HADDOCK, THAT WAS LOUSY OF HIM...
SURE, BUT IF HE HAD LET HADDOCK KNOW, THE ENDING WOULD HAVE FALLEN FLAT.
TRUE. AND HADDOCK WOULD'VE SPILLED THE BEANS AND RUINED THE WHOLE PLAN.
HADDOCK IS A BIG BABY. YOU CAN'T TRUST HIM AN INCH...
YOU'RE RIGHT! ESPECIALLY IN THE CRAB WITH THE GOLDEN CLAWS!
WHEN I WAS A KID, HE REALLY GOT UNDER MY SKIN! HE'D ALWAYS DO SOMETHING DUMB AND THEN APOLOGIZE ... AND HE WAS ALWAYS DRUNK! ...
AND THE TIME HE USED THE OARS OF THE ROWBOAT TO START A FIRE! IT DROVE ME NUTS!
THAT JERK!
IDIOT!
AND WHEN THE BOAT TIPPED, THERE HE WAS AGAIN: "BOO HOO, SORRY TINTIN..."
SOUNDS LIKE HERGÉ HIT HIS MARK. THAT'S EXACTLY HOW HE WANTED HIS READERS TO FEEL...
WELL, HE GOT ME, THAT'S FOR SURE...
LOOKIT THOSE BIG GOLD-FISH!
WHERE?

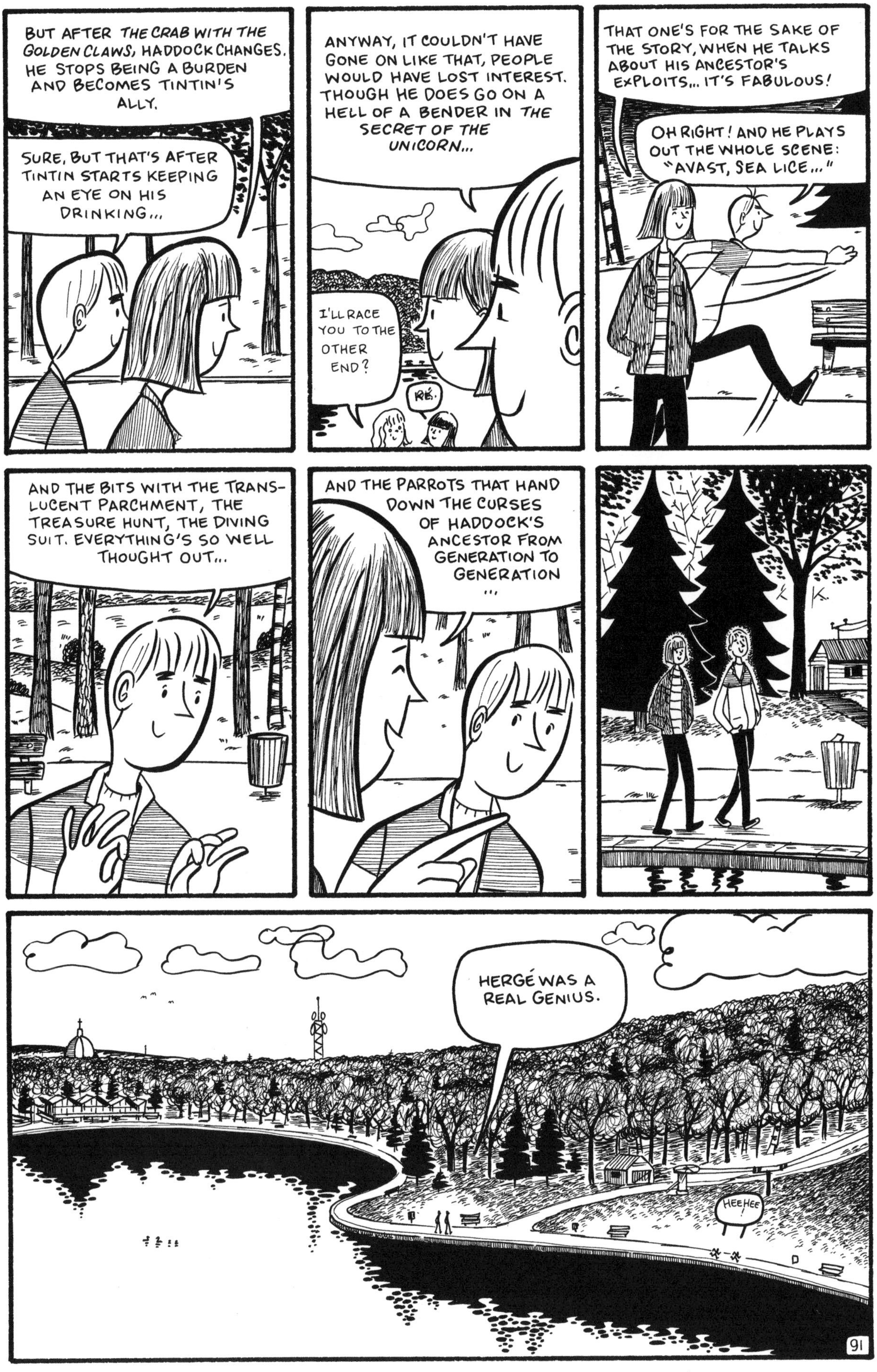
BUT AFTER *THE CRAB WITH THE GOLDEN CLAWS*, HADDOCK CHANGES. HE STOPS BEING A BURDEN AND BECOMES TINTIN'S ALLY.
SURE, BUT THAT'S AFTER TINTIN STARTS KEEPING AN EYE ON HIS DRINKING...
ANYWAY, IT COULDN'T HAVE GONE ON LIKE THAT, PEOPLE WOULD HAVE LOST INTEREST. THOUGH HE DOES GO ON A HELL OF A BENDER IN *THE SECRET OF THE UNICORN*...
I'LL RACE YOU TO THE OTHER END?
THAT ONE'S FOR THE SAKE OF THE STORY, WHEN HE TALKS ABOUT HIS ANCESTOR'S EXPLOITS... IT'S FABULOUS!
OH RIGHT! AND HE PLAYS OUT THE WHOLE SCENE: "AVAST, SEA LICE..."
AND THE BITS WITH THE TRANSLUCENT PARCHMENT, THE TREASURE HUNT, THE DIVING SUIT. EVERYTHING'S SO WELL THOUGHT OUT...
AND THE PARROTS THAT HAND DOWN THE CURSES OF HADDOCK'S ANCESTOR FROM GENERATION TO GENERATION ...
HERGÉ WAS A REAL GENIUS.
HEE HEE

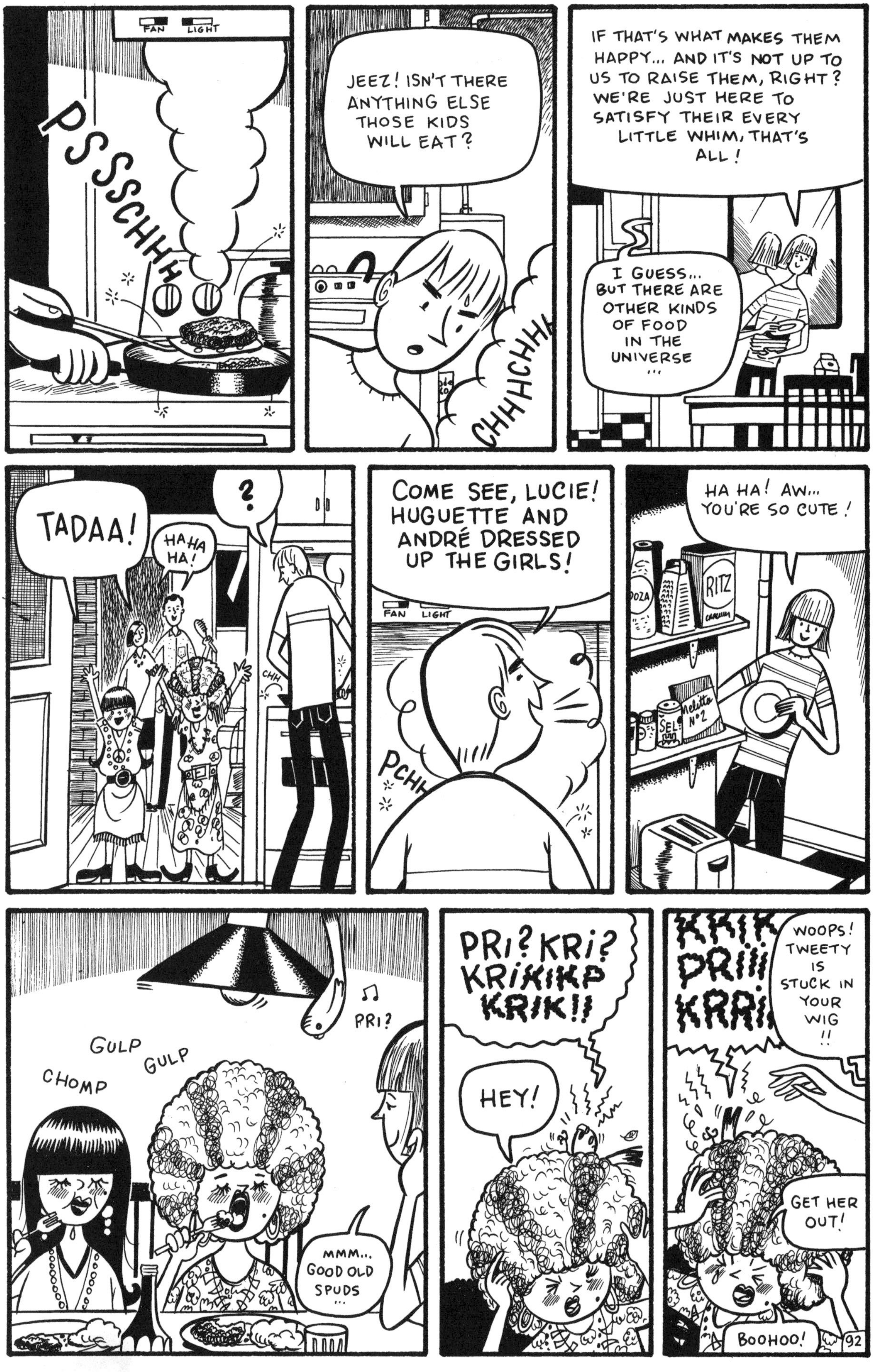
FAN LIGHT
PSSSCHHHH
JEEZ! ISN'T THERE ANYTHING ELSE THOSE KIDS WILL EAT?
CHHHCHHH
IF THAT'S WHAT MAKES THEM HAPPY... AND IT'S NOT UP TO US TO RAISE THEM, RIGHT? WE'RE JUST HERE TO SATISFY THEIR EVERY LITTLE WHIM, THAT'S ALL!
I GUESS... BUT THERE ARE OTHER KINDS OF FOOD IN THE UNIVERSE ...
TADAA!
HA HA HA!
?
CHH
COME SEE, LUCIE! HUGUETTE AND ANDRÉ DRESSED UP THE GIRLS!
FAN LIGHT
PCHH
HA HA! AW... YOU'RE SO CUTE!
RITZ
SEL
Melitta N°2
♫ PRI?
GULP GULP
CHOMP
MMM... GOOD OLD SPUDS ...
PRI? KRI? KRIKIKP KRIK!!
HEY!
KRIK PRIIII KRRI
WOOPS! TWEETY IS STUCK IN YOUR WIG !!
GET HER OUT!
BOOHOO!

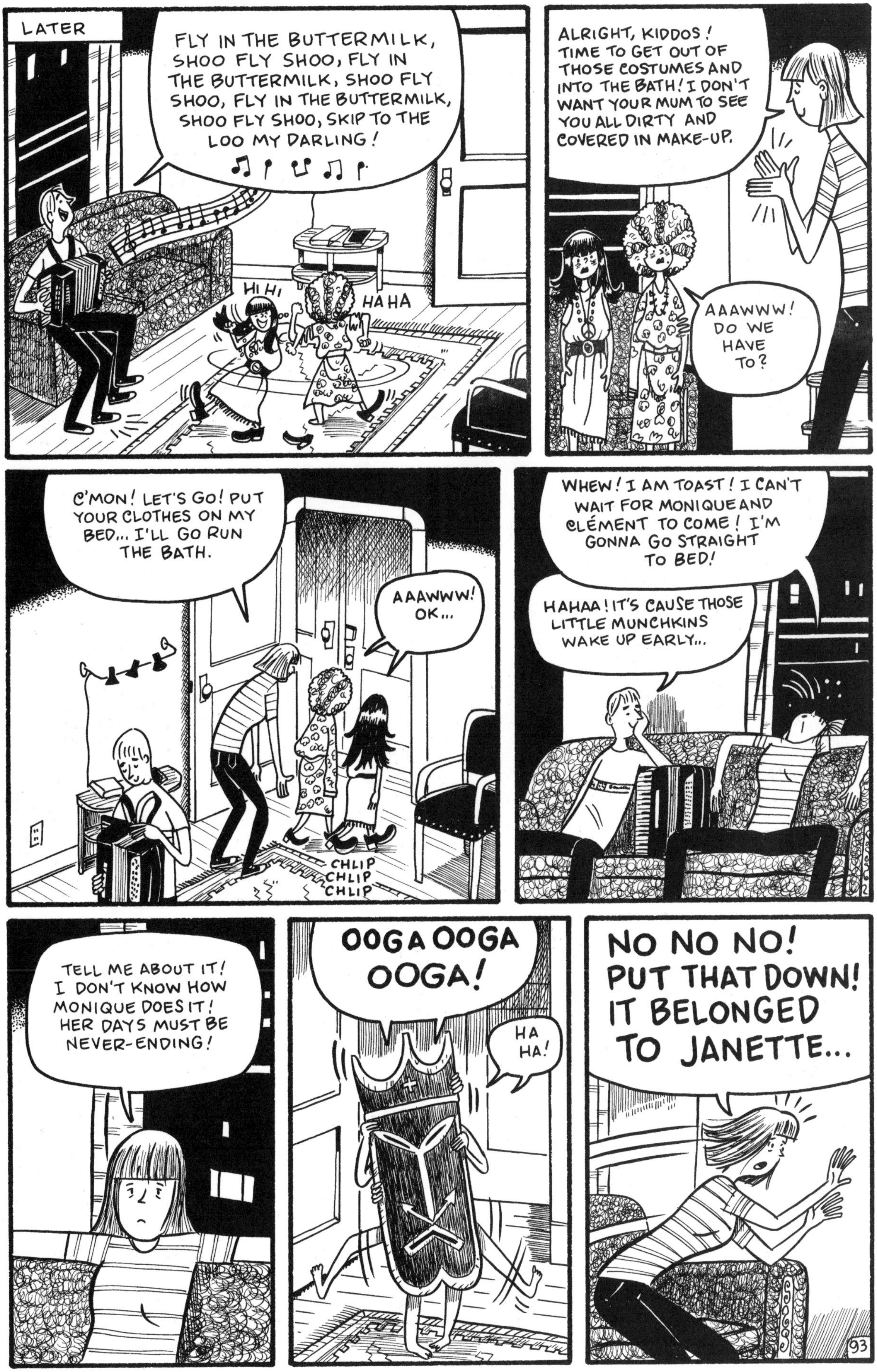
LATER
FLY IN THE BUTTERMILK, SHOO FLY SHOO, FLY IN THE BUTTERMILK, SHOO FLY SHOO, FLY IN THE BUTTERMILK, SHOO FLY SHOO, SKIP TO THE LOO MY DARLING!
HI HI
HA HA
ALRIGHT, KIDDOS! TIME TO GET OUT OF THOSE COSTUMES AND INTO THE BATH! I DON'T WANT YOUR MUM TO SEE YOU ALL DIRTY AND COVERED IN MAKE-UP.
AAAWWW! DO WE HAVE TO?
C'MON! LET'S GO! PUT YOUR CLOTHES ON MY BED... I'LL GO RUN THE BATH.
AAAWWW! OK...
CHLIP CHLIP CHLIP
WHEW! I AM TOAST! I CAN'T WAIT FOR MONIQUE AND CLÉMENT TO COME! I'M GONNA GO STRAIGHT TO BED!
HAHAA! IT'S CAUSE THOSE LITTLE MUNCHKINS WAKE UP EARLY...
TELL ME ABOUT IT! I DON'T KNOW HOW MONIQUE DOES IT! HER DAYS MUST BE NEVER-ENDING!
OOGA OOGA OOGA!
HA HA!
NO NO NO! PUT THAT DOWN! IT BELONGED TO JANETTE...

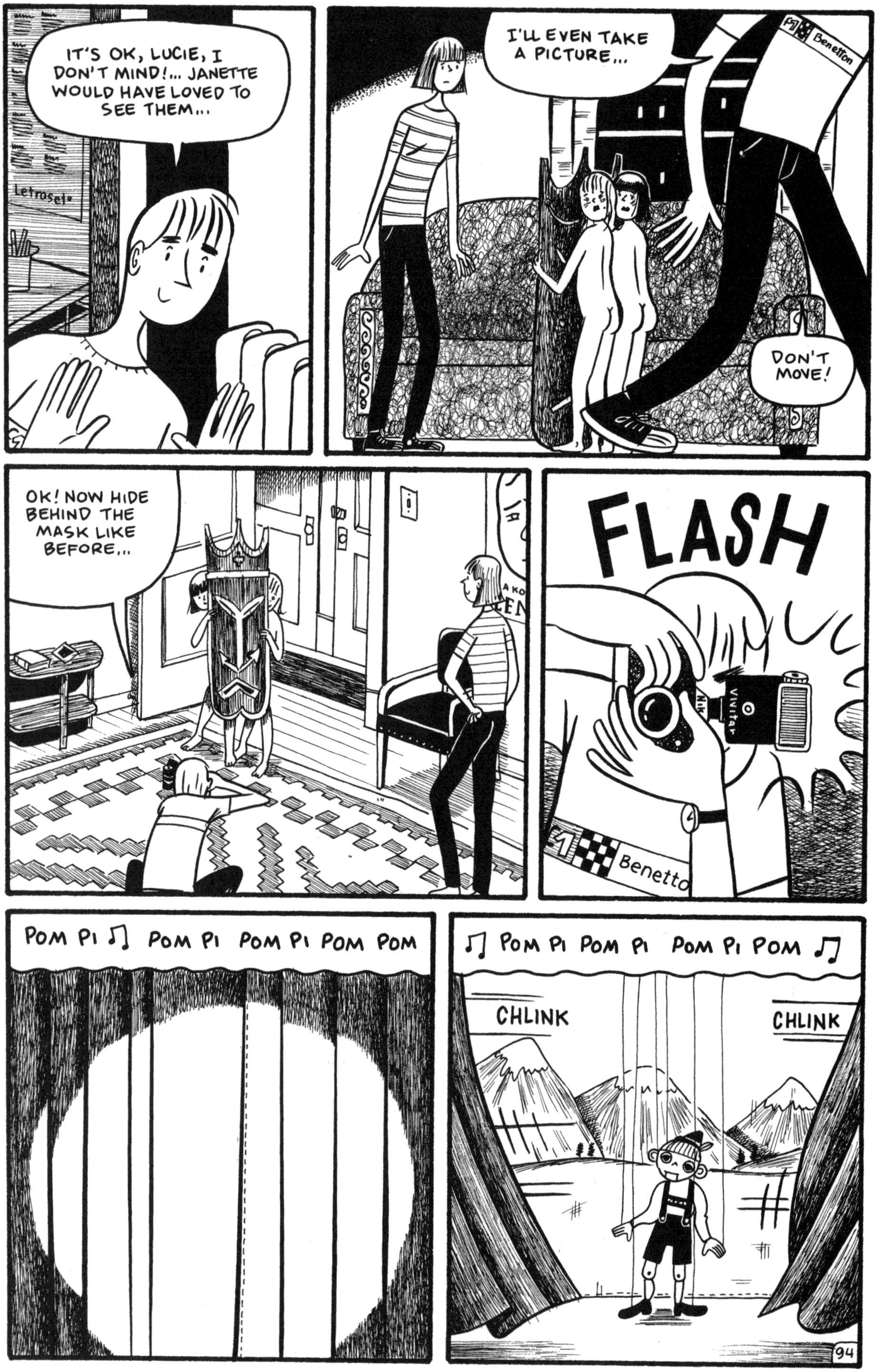
IT'S OK, LUCIE, I DON'T MIND!... JANETTE WOULD HAVE LOVED TO SEE THEM...
Letrasel
I'LL EVEN TAKE A PICTURE...
Benetton
DON'T MOVE!
OK! NOW HIDE BEHIND THE MASK LIKE BEFORE...
FLASH
Vivitar
Benetto
POM PI ♫ POM PI POM PI POM POM
♫ POM PI POM PI POM PI POM ♫
CHLINK
CHLINK

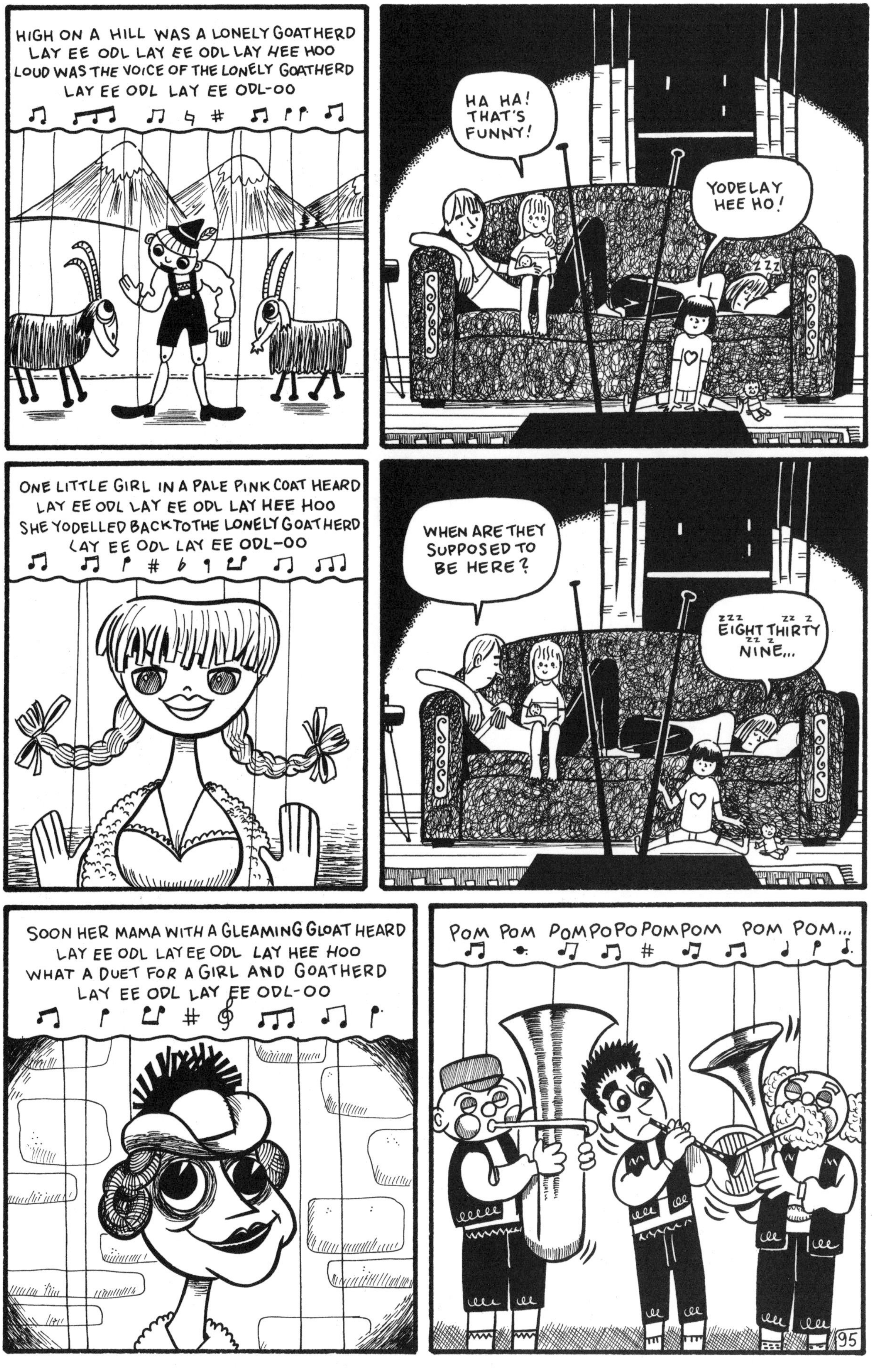
HIGH ON A HILL WAS A LONELY GOATHERD
LAY EE ODL LAY EE ODL LAY HEE HOO
LOUD WAS THE VOICE OF THE LONELY GOATHERD
LAY EE ODL LAY EE ODL-OO
HA HA! THAT'S FUNNY!
YODELAY HEE HO!
ZZZ
ONE LITTLE GIRL IN A PALE PINK COAT HEARD
LAY EE ODL LAY EE ODL LAY HEE HOO
SHE YODELLED BACK TO THE LONELY GOATHERD
LAY EE ODL LAY EE ODL-OO
WHEN ARE THEY SUPPOSED TO BE HERE?
ZZZ EIGHT THIRTY ZZ Z NINE...
SOON HER MAMA WITH A GLEAMING GLOAT HEARD
LAY EE ODL LAY EE ODL LAY HEE HOO
WHAT A DUET FOR A GIRL AND GOATHERD
LAY EE ODL LAY EE ODL-OO
POM POM POMPOPOPOMPOM POM POM...

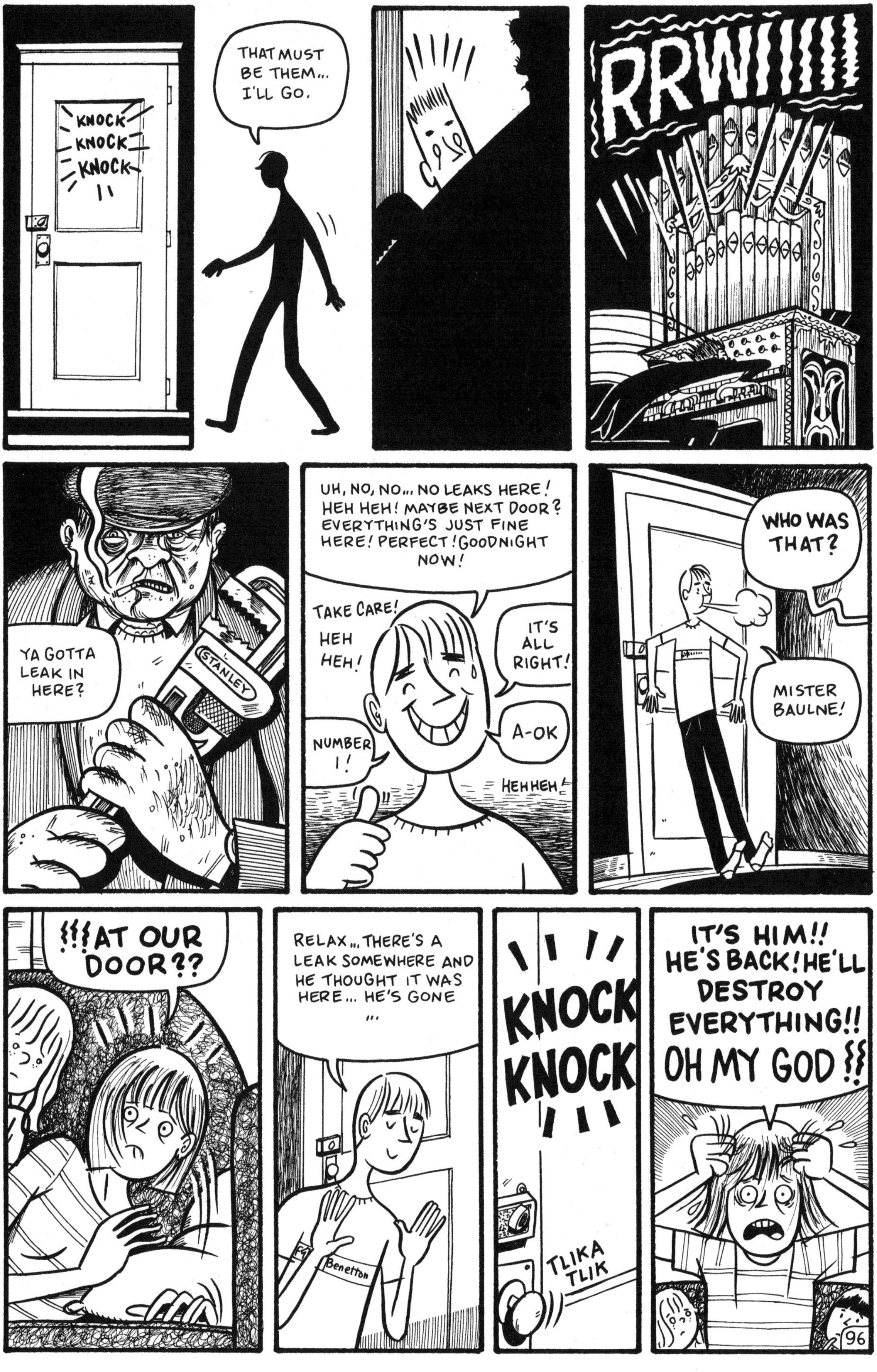
KNOCK KNOCK KNOCK
THAT MUST BE THEM... I'LL GO.
RRWIIIIII
YA GOTTA LEAK IN HERE?
STANLEY
UH, NO, NO... NO LEAKS HERE! HEH HEH! MAYBE NEXT DOOR? EVERYTHING'S JUST FINE HERE! PERFECT! GOODNIGHT NOW!
TAKE CARE!
HEH HEH!
IT'S ALL RIGHT!
A-OK
NUMBER 1!
HEH HEH!
WHO WAS THAT?
MISTER BAULNE!
?!?AT OUR DOOR??
RELAX... THERE'S A LEAK SOMEWHERE AND HE THOUGHT IT WAS HERE... HE'S GONE ...
Benetton
KNOCK KNOCK
TLIKA TLIK
IT'S HIM!! HE'S BACK! HE'LL DESTROY EVERYTHING!! OH MY GOD ?!

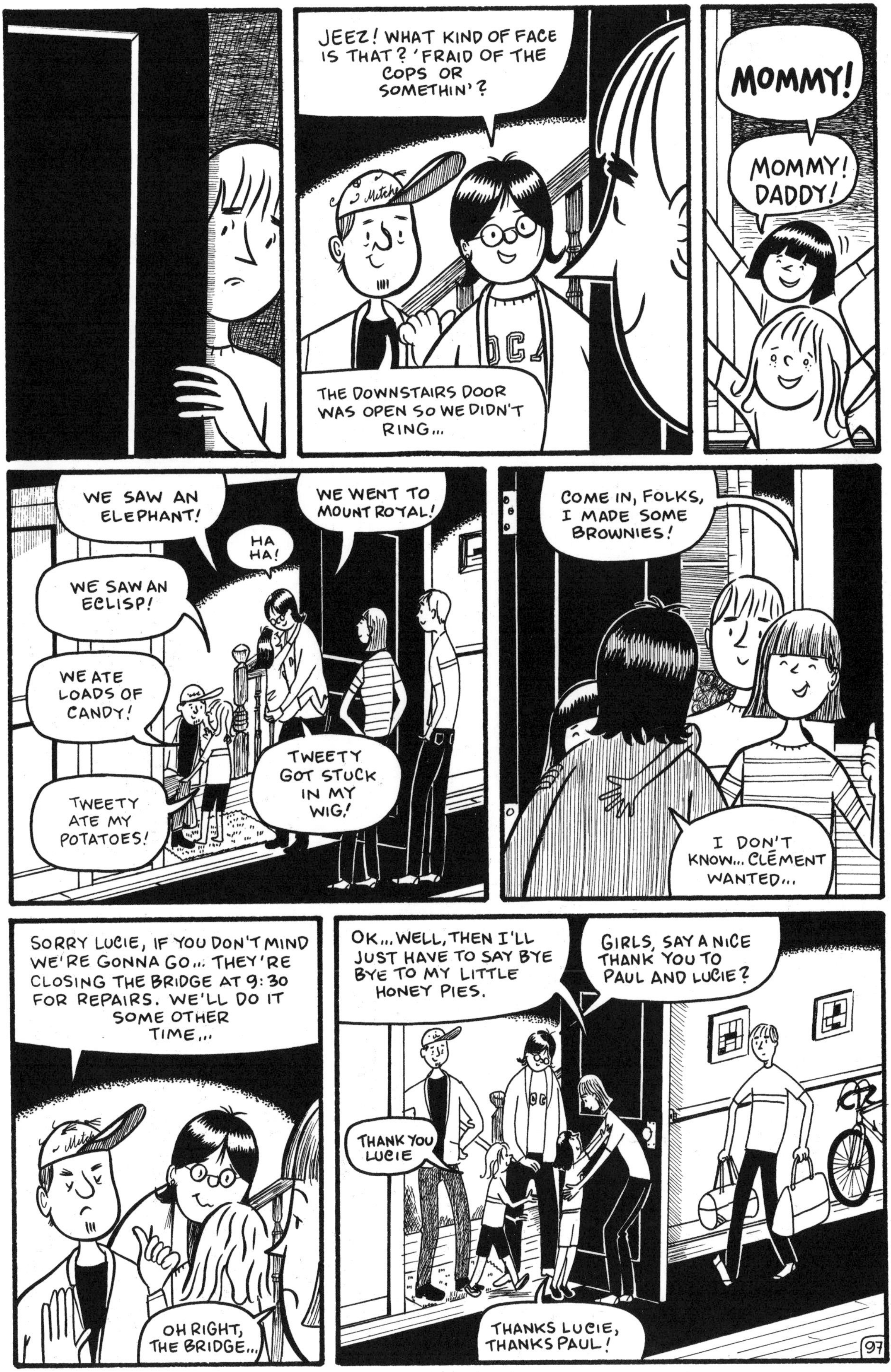
JEEZ! WHAT KIND OF FACE IS THAT? 'FRAID OF THE COPS OR SOMETHIN'?
THE DOWNSTAIRS DOOR WAS OPEN SO WE DIDN'T RING...
MOMMY!
MOMMY! DADDY!
WE SAW AN ELEPHANT!
WE WENT TO MOUNT ROYAL!
HA HA!
WE SAW AN ECLISP!
WE ATE LOADS OF CANDY!
TWEETY ATE MY POTATOES!
TWEETY GOT STUCK IN MY WIG!
COME IN, FOLKS, I MADE SOME BROWNIES!
I DON'T KNOW... CLÉMENT WANTED...
SORRY LUCIE, IF YOU DON'T MIND WE'RE GONNA GO... THEY'RE CLOSING THE BRIDGE AT 9:30 FOR REPAIRS. WE'LL DO IT SOME OTHER TIME...
OH RIGHT, THE BRIDGE...
OK... WELL, THEN I'LL JUST HAVE TO SAY BYE BYE TO MY LITTLE HONEY PIES.
GIRLS, SAY A NICE THANK YOU TO PAUL AND LUCIE?
THANK YOU LUCIE
THANKS LUCIE, THANKS PAUL!

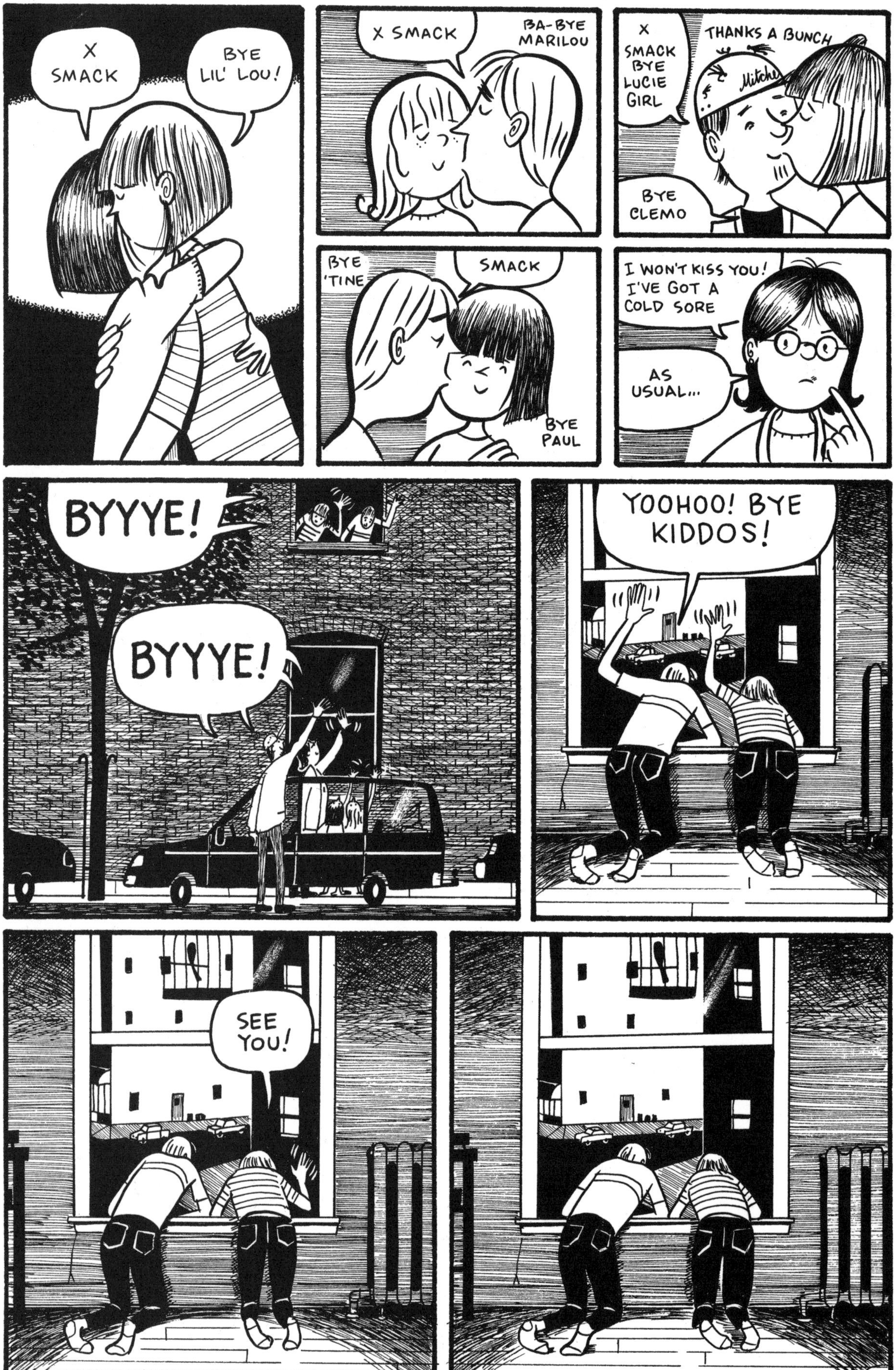

X SMACK
BYE LIL' LOU!
X SMACK
BA-BYE MARILOU
X SMACK BYE LUCIE GIRL
THANKS A BUNCH
BYE CLEMO
BYE 'TINE
SMACK
BYE PAUL
I WON'T KISS YOU! I'VE GOT A COLD SORE
AS USUAL...
BYYYE!
BYYYE!
YOOHOO! BYE KIDDOS!
SEE YOU!

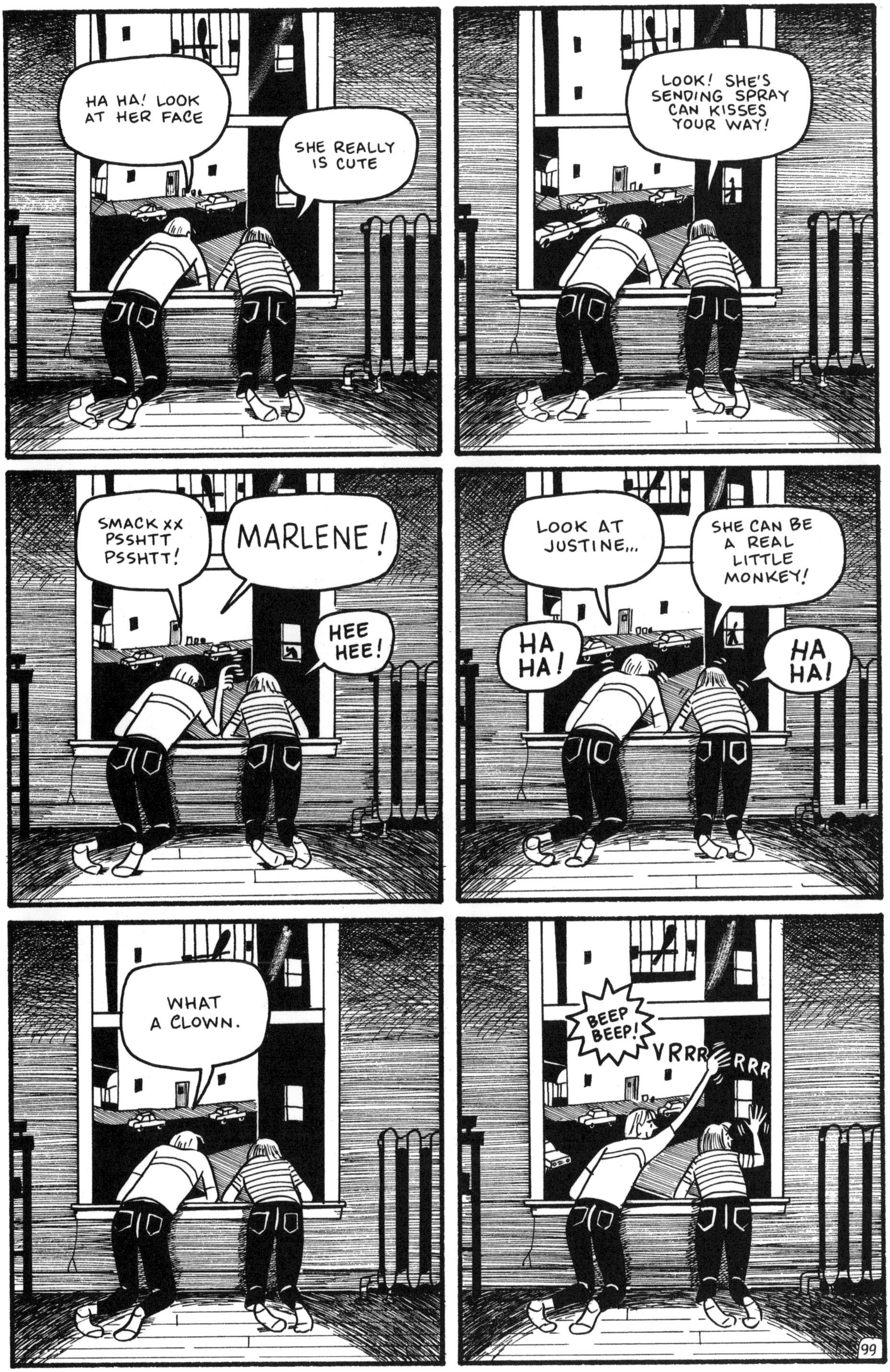

HA HA! LOOK AT HER FACE
SHE REALLY IS CUTE
LOOK! SHE'S SENDING SPRAY CAN KISSES YOUR WAY!
SMACK XX PSSHTT PSSHTT!
MARLENE!
HEE HEE!
LOOK AT JUSTINE...
SHE CAN BE A REAL LITTLE MONKEY!
HA HA!
HA HA!
WHAT A CLOWN.
BEEP BEEP!
VRRR RRR

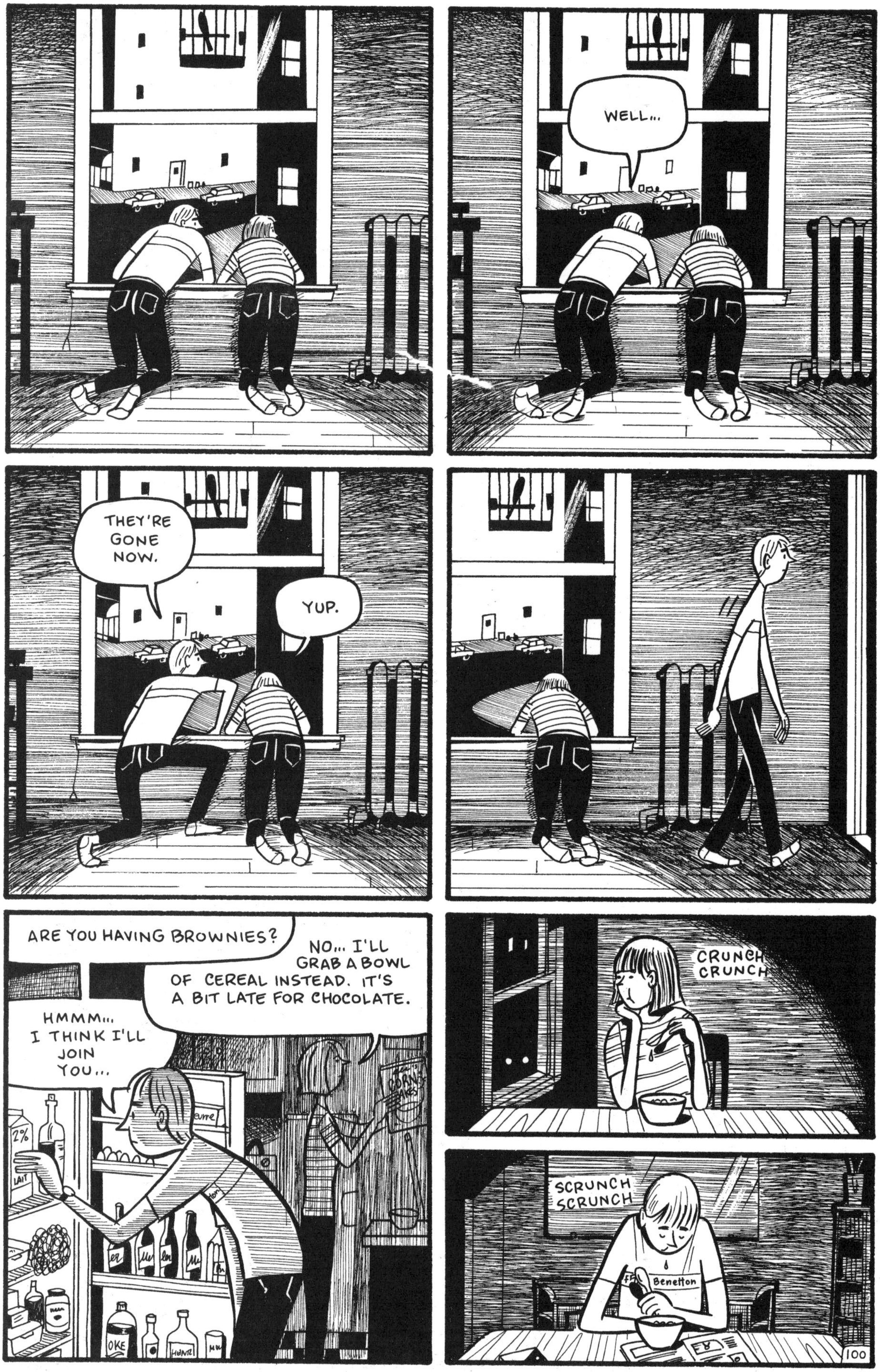
WELL...
THEY'RE GONE NOW.
YUP.
ARE YOU HAVING BROWNIES?
NO... I'LL GRAB A BOWL OF CEREAL INSTEAD. IT'S A BIT LATE FOR CHOCOLATE.
HMMM... I THINK I'LL JOIN YOU...
CRUNCH CRUNCH
SCRUNCH SCRUNCH
Benetton

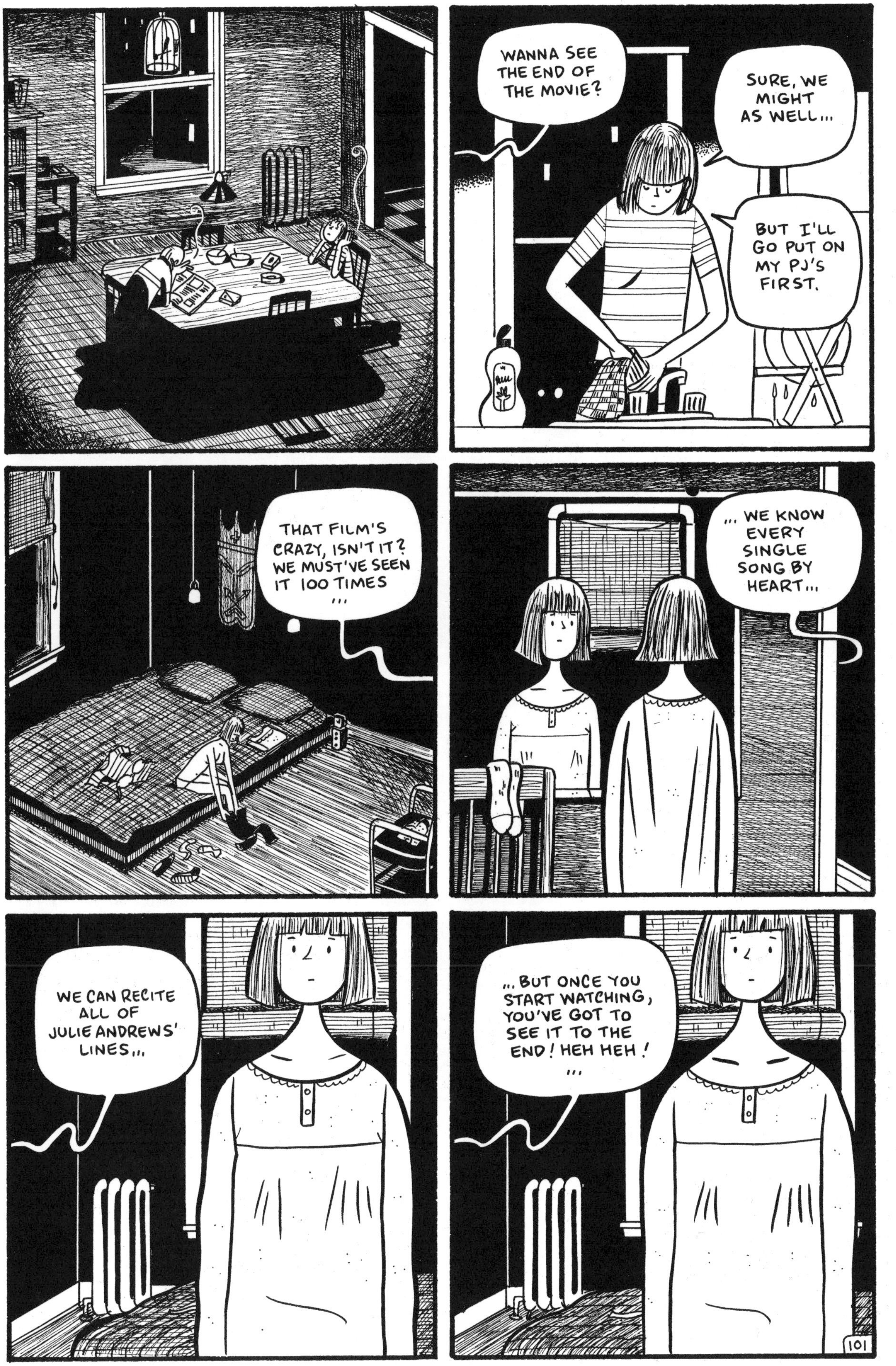
WANNA SEE THE END OF THE MOVIE?
SURE, WE MIGHT AS WELL...
BUT I'LL GO PUT ON MY PJ'S FIRST.
THAT FILM'S CRAZY, ISN'T IT? WE MUST'VE SEEN IT 100 TIMES ...
... WE KNOW EVERY SINGLE SONG BY HEART...
WE CAN RECITE ALL OF JULIE ANDREWS' LINES...
... BUT ONCE YOU START WATCHING, YOU'VE GOT TO SEE IT TO THE END! HEH HEH! ...

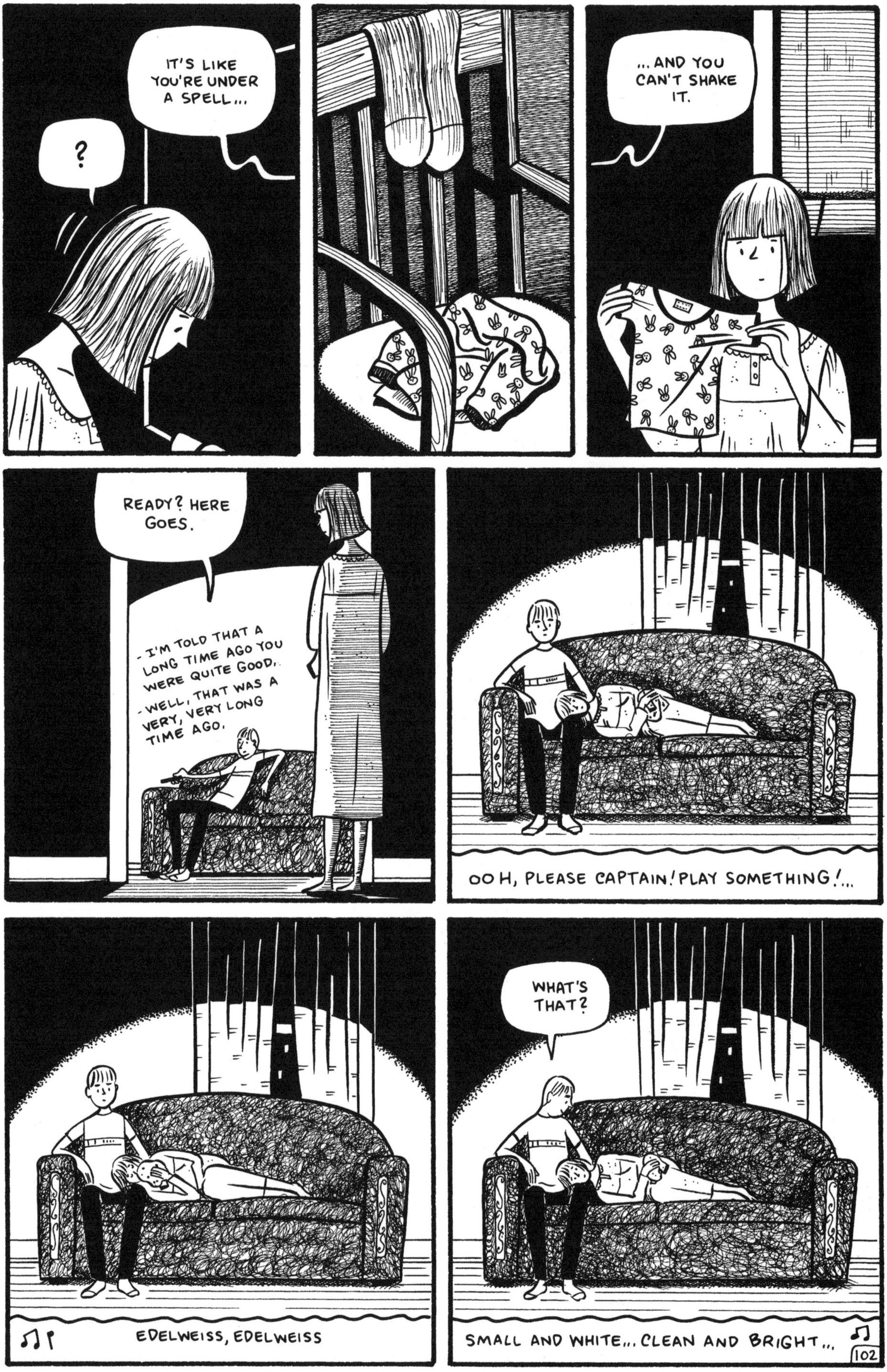
?
IT'S LIKE YOU'RE UNDER A SPELL...
...AND YOU CAN'T SHAKE IT.
READY? HERE GOES.
- I'M TOLD THAT A LONG TIME AGO YOU WERE QUITE GOOD.
- WELL, THAT WAS A VERY, VERY LONG TIME AGO.
OOH, PLEASE CAPTAIN! PLAY SOMETHING!...
EDELWEISS, EDELWEISS
WHAT'S THAT?
SMALL AND WHITE... CLEAN AND BRIGHT...

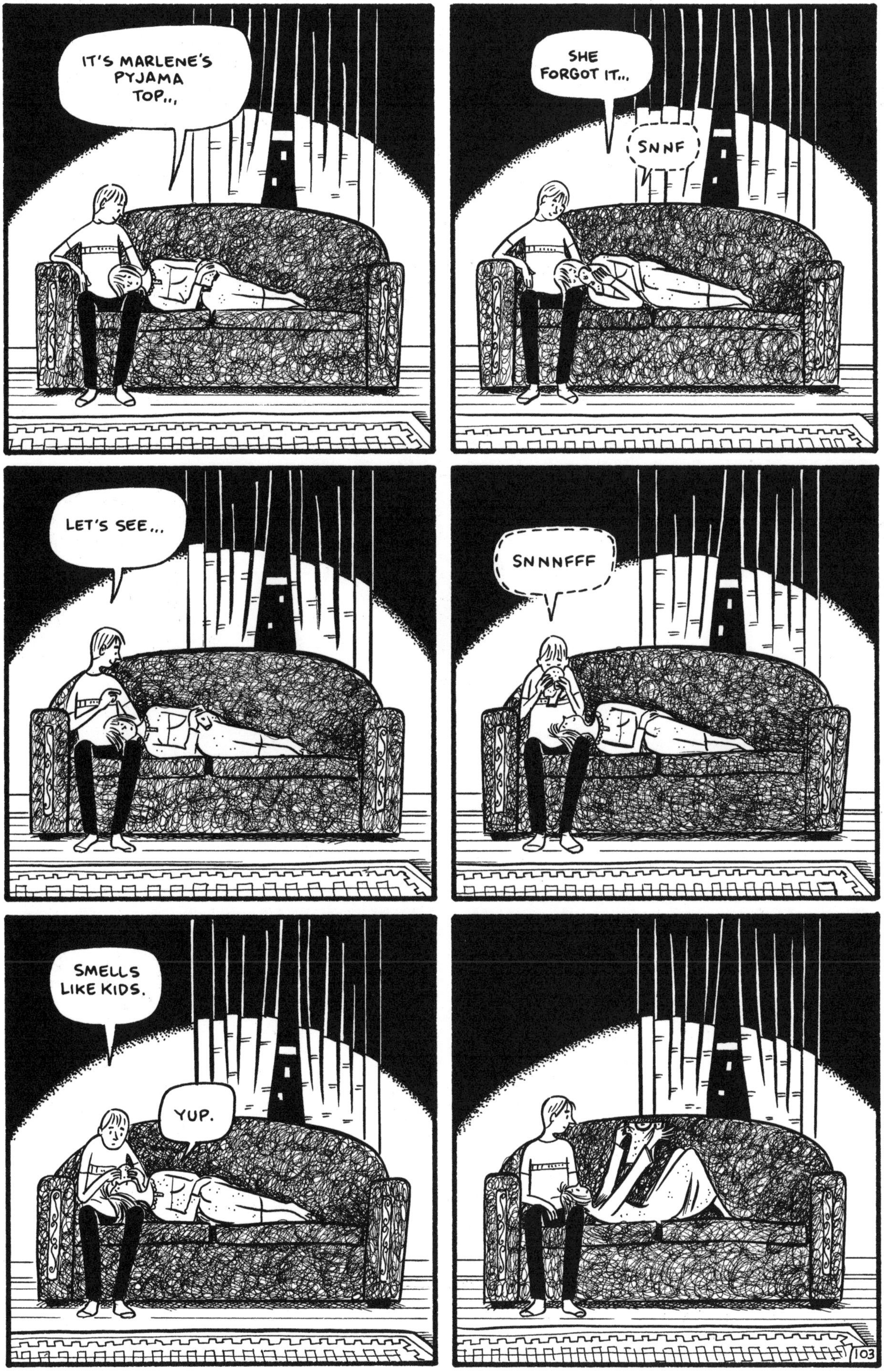
IT'S MARLENE'S PYJAMA TOP...
SHE FORGOT IT...
SNNF
LET'S SEE...
SNNNFFF
SMELLS LIKE KIDS.
YUP.

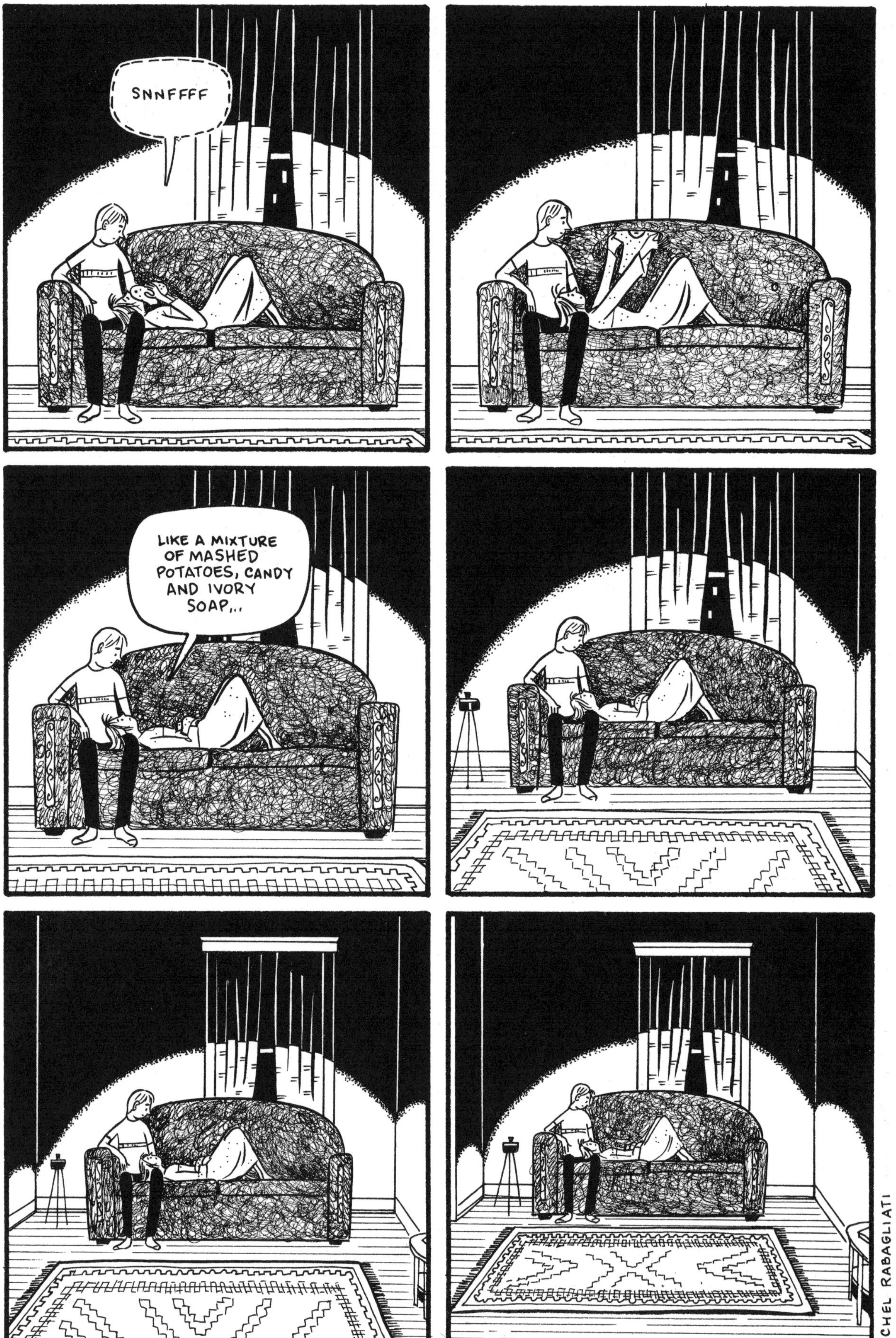
SNNFFFF
LIKE A MIXTURE OF MASHED POTATOES, CANDY AND IVORY SOAP...
FIN
MICHEL RABAGLIATI

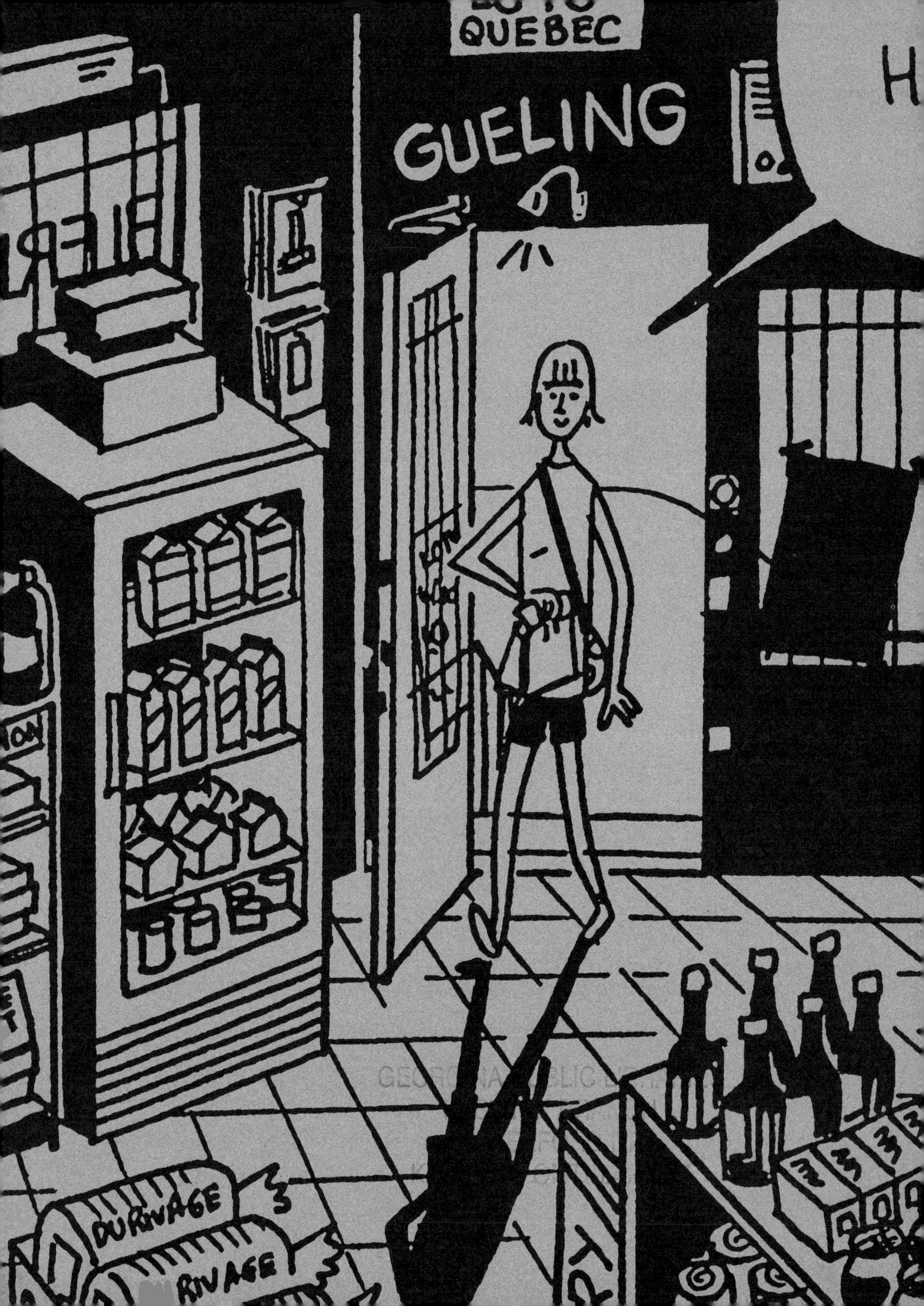
QUEBEC
GUELING